ILLUSTRATED
DICTIONARY *of*
IRISH
HISTORY

This edition first published in Ireland by
Gill & Macmillan Ltd
Hume Avenue, Park West, Dublin 12
with associated companies throughout the world
www.gillmacmillan.ie

02 04 05 03

1 3 5 7 9 10 8 6 4 2

The Foundry Creative Media Company Limited
Crabtree Hall, Crabtree Lane, Fulham, London, SW6 6TY

ISBN 0 7171 3536 5

A copy of the CIP data for this book is available from the British Library

Printed in China

SPECIAL THANKS TO EVERYONE INVOLVED WITH THIS PROJECT:
Anna Amari, Frances Banfield, Lucy Bradbury, Roger Buckley, Helen Courtney, Claire Dashwood,
Giskin Day, Karen Fitzpatrick, Vicky Garrard, Phil Hempell, George Keyes, Lesley Malkin,
Geoffrey Meadon, Sonya Newland, Colin Rudderham, Mel Shaw, Andrea Simmonds,
Graham Stride, Helen Tovey, Helen Wall, Sharon Weiss, Nick Wells.

ILLUSTRATED DICTIONARY *of* IRISH HISTORY

Guy de la Bédoyère, Michael Kerrigan, Ciarán Ó Pronntaigh, Jon Sutherland

GENERAL EDITOR - SÉAMAS MAC ANNAIDH

Gill & Macmillan

CONTENTS

THEMES

Each A–Z entry is tagged by themes which can be followed as threads throughout the book

 Culture   Politics   Royalty   War

Geography   Religion   Society

INTRODUCTION

Few countries the size of Ireland have had such a colourful and dramatic history. A small island on the periphery of Europe, Ireland had few major centres of population and little industrial infrastructure until recent times, however, its influence on British, European and world history, politics and culture has been disproportionately great.

It is a history, which despite the turbulence created by invasions and conquests, has a sense of continuity which charts the story of Ireland and her people from pre-Christian Celtic times to the present day.

In ancient times Ireland was an island on the edge of the world known to Ptolemy and Julius Caesar, even though it was beyond the sphere of Greek influence and only barely touched by the Romans. It was a place where the culture and language of the Celts, who originated in Eastern Europe (Vienna is apparently named after the Fianna), survived and continued to flourish long after they had disappeared from their earliest homelands. In the dark ages Ireland's isolation saved it from the descent into barbarism experienced across the continent and was the font to which Europe turned when it sought to revive its intellectual and cultural heart, and its spiritual soul.

Unlike most modern European countries, Ireland can clearly be identified as a politically united geographical region: as early as the eleventh century Brian Bóroimhe (Brian Boru) became High King and was able to proclaim himself emperor of the Irish. This was the culmination of a process which had been taking place for several centuries as small, local, family-based communities united and developed to become regional and provincial power-bases and administrative structures. The Viking raids of the ninth and tenth centuries may well have helped to unite the different families against a common enemy and enforce the idea of a shared identity.

We can only guess what the long-term impact of such unity might have been, not merely on the history of Ireland, but on the history of England, Europe and the world. The Irish language, for example, was the most widely spoken language in the British Isles before the English language had even developed. Yet, nowadays, Irish is spoken primarily along the Irish western seaboard, while English is one of the major languages of the world. The unity which had been so successful against the Viking enemy fragmented when internal conflict presented the Anglo-Normans with the opportunity of launching expeditions in the twelfth century. From then on, Irish unity would be constantly ruptured and thwarted by the dominance of its nearest neighbour.

The conquerors, and the uprisings against them, brought mayhem and suffering. Defeat in the Battle of Kinsale in 1601 effectively brought an end to any hope of survival for Gaelic Ireland in its traditional form, and the departure to continental Europe of the last of the Ulster chieftains in the Flight of the Earls in 1607, left the way open for the plantation of Ulster; the results of which are still felt to the present day.

Later, Ireland became the battleground where English and continental dynastic struggles were fought. The figures of Oliver Cromwell and William of Orange cast long shadows across the country. Continental Christianity, which centuries before had brought learning and literature, and later had been revitalized by the Irish, now brought division and destruction as it tore itself apart in the name of religion.

The United Irishmen of the 1790s re-invented the idea of the Irish nation and attempted to overcome religious division. The most immediate result of their idealism and the bloody events of 1798, however, was the Act of Union of 1800, which removed the Irish parliament and brought the country under direct English control once more.

The effect of decades of neglect, corruption and mismanagement was not to be reversed by a tweaking of legislation, and even though the religious freedoms won by Daniel O'Connell in 1829 were a great triumph of democracy and people-power, cataclysmic change was inevitable.

It came in the 1840s in the form of hunger; a famine of unimaginable dimensions, that brought death and disease to thousands of people across the land. The Great Famine caused a terrible haemorrhaging of humanity. Hundreds of thousands fled starvation, poverty and disease in Ireland, seeking better lives in the United States, Britain, Canada and Australia. Although most entered their adopted countries on the bottom rung of society, their cultural, religious and political influence was immense, and even nowadays continues to be felt from Washington to Glasgow, from Boston to Liverpool.

The Great Famine brought chaos and created a vacuum; it was another generation before the Irish could once more raise their heads and seek to change their miserable existence. Once again the pressure for change began to build.

Sometimes thwarted and other times abetted by international events, the revolution, when it came in 1916 was as much cultural as political or military. Irish identity as expressed through language, literature and sports, and by figures as diverse as Pearse and Yeats, Griffith and Lady Gregory, once awakened was a force not to be defeated by military might. A new Ireland emerged from the rubble, still fractured but more in control of its own destiny than it had been for many centuries. Part of that Ireland was Northern Ireland: a new construction and a different sort of problem.

History does not end some time in the past. It is a continuum of which we are all a part, but we cannot see it, except at some remove. The bloody Troubles, which marked the decline and fall of the Unionist regime in Northern Ireland, are now behind us and new perspectives influence our hopes and our fears.

This easy-to-use Encyclopedia of Irish history has been written and compiled by a team of experts who specialize in different areas of Irish history. They have been able to provide a very broad range of entries covering all the major figures and happenings; cultural, religious, ecomonic and social affairs, as well as political and military events. The entries are both factual and interpretive, and individual contributors have been free to write from their own perspectives. Entries have been classified by a number of themes and carefully cross-referenced for ease-of-use.

It is hoped that this book will become an essential reference for all those with an interest in Ireland, that it will be found in the libraries of schools and colleges, and in homes in Ireland, Britain and across the world, where the Irish diaspora is believed to be 50-million strong.

History is constantly being written in Ireland. To paraphrase two of the major players of today (Tony Blair and Gerry Adams), the hand of history is on our shoulder, it hasn't gone away, you know.

SÉAMAS MAC ANNAIDH

ABBEY THEATRE (1904)

Dublin's most famous and influential theatre, opened in 1904. The Abbey Theatre was initially directed by William Butler Yeats and Lady Augusta Gregory. It played a significant role in the literary and cultural revival experienced by Ireland at the beginning of the twentieth century and staged works by noted Irish authors such as John Millington Synge, George Bernard Shaw and Padraic Colum. Seán O'Casey's most famous plays, which were written in the immediate post-independence period, were also staged here. The original building was destroyed in a fire in 1951 and the new Abbey Theatre opened in 1966. It is still regarded as Ireland's national theatre.

))▶ *Lady Augusta Gregory, Seán O'Casey, G. B. Shaw, J. M. Synge, W. B. Yeats*

ACT OF UNION (1800)

Simultaneous acts passed in the parliaments of Dublin and London, establishing the 'United Kingdom of Great Britain and Ireland'. A constitutional response to the United Irishmen's insurrection of 1798, the Act of Union sought to settle the question of Ireland's status once and for all, affirming its belonging, now and for ever, to the British Crown. With four bishops and 28 peers in the House of Lords, and 100 MPs in the House of Commons, Ireland now had its parliamentary representation in London.

Though it would remain fiscally autonomous for some years afterwards, the exchequers not being united until 1817, the Dublin parliament had effectively disbanded itself. The Act was passed under the administration of William Pitt the Younger; the fact that it had been brought forward by Charles, 1st Marquis Cornwallis, a champion of Catholic Emancipation, did much to persuade Irish Catholics of

its benefits. That he had found the support of Viscount Castlereagh, who had dealt firmly with the recent rising, helped reassure Protestants that their interests were also being considered: which group stood to gain more by the measure is debatable now as then. The measure could, with more or less equal justice, be seen as a 'promotion', offering representation at the centre, or as the end of any pretence at autonomy for Ireland: in truth, perhaps, it was just another in a long line of pragmatic compromises. In theory, Sligo was now as much a part of Britain as Surrey; in practice, an element of quasi-colonial administration from Dublin Castle had realistically to continue.

ADAMS, GERRY (b. 1948)

Republican activist and politician. A lifelong political campaigner – and, some have said, terrorist – Gerry Adams has more recently won international acclaim as an instigator and determined promoter of the peace process. Born and educated in Belfast, Adams became involved with the civil rights movement of the late-1960s. While his internment in 1971 seems to have hardened his opinions, he never seems to have lost sight of the need to maintain the political dimension, early embracing the view that

Republicans could best hope to make progress 'with the ballot box in one hand, the armalite [automatic rifle] in the other'. Sinn Féin's president since 1983, Gerry Adams was in secret talks with the SDLP-leader John Hume long before the peace process officially began, and the IRA called its 'complete cessation of military operations' in 1994.

))▶ *Civil Rights Movement, Irish Republican Army, Sinn Féin, Social Democratic Labour Party*

ABOVE LEFT: The Abbey Theatre.
ABOVE: Gerry Adams.
RIGHT: A farmer herding cattle in County Tyrone, Northern Ireland.

AGRARIAN UNREST (19TH CENTURY)

Political movement. What we refer to as the 'nationalist tradition' really dates back only as far as the mid-nineteenth century: before that, the very idea of the 'nation' had hardly been conceived. For the Irish peasantry, moreover, the most pressing concerns were strictly local: oppressive landlords, the enclosure of 'common' land, the exacting of (Anglican) Church 'tithes' and levying of 'cess' taxes by county administrations. Resistance also took place at a local level. Groups like the 'Houghers' of Connacht and the 'Whiteboys' of Tipperary sprang up in the second half of the eighteenth century: secret societies held together by elaborate oaths, they applied pressure by means of terrible threats, backed up by acts of sabotage and violence – occasionally assassination. In the early nineteenth century myriad other organizations emerged, under such names as the 'Threshers', the 'Terry Alts' and the 'Molly Maguires'. The movement seems to have petered out after that, the Great Famine and the mass-emigration that followed having had the ironic effect of easing conditions in the countryside, while the political focus had shifted decisively from a local to a national stage.

))⯈ *Emigration, Great Famine, Ribbonism, Whiteboys*

AGRICULTURE

The land area of Ireland is 6.9 million hectares, 5 million of which are used for agriculture and forestry. Traditionally Ireland has been an agricultural island with the growing of potatoes and the cutting of peat being an essential part of rural life. Ireland's equable climate makes the growing of vegetables and other plants easy and profitable for farmers. Most of the rich farmland is used for growing hay or as pasture for the grazing animals. Having such rich grazing land and a mild climate with infrequent snow makes it possible for the stock to be kept in the pastures for most of the year, limiting the amount of animal housing required.

Most of the farms tend to be family run, their main output being livestock and livestock products, the biggest items being cattle, milk and pigs. Barley and wheat are grown, and poultry, eggs, sheep, wool, sugar beet, potatoes and other root crops are also produced. Sheep are raised predominantly on the mountains and hills of the country, whilst in the midlands and south beef cattle are raised. In the east and south-east of the island cereal growing is the main concentration. The east of the island tends to have more fertile farmlands and an expanding industrial growth.

the fishermen have to compete with other nations wishing to fish their waters. Until World War II Ireland manufactured few products for export purposes but mainly produced goods for home consumption. After the war the government set up a Programme for Economic Expansion, using tax concessions and grants to encourage Irish industry to become more competitive, to attract new manufacturing companies and to expand into new markets abroad. As a result of this programme, by the late-twentieth century more of the population was employed in the manufacturing industries than in agriculture. Since then Irish-based computer software and equipment companies and international financial service organizations have thrived, with the industrial sector contributing to the majority of Ireland's income from exports. A wide range of manufactured products are now exported to the UK, Germany, France, the Netherlands, the US and Japan. Products exported by Ireland include electrical machinery, electrical apparatus, processed foods, chemical products, clothing and textiles and beverages. Ireland is a major linen producer, manufacturing 50 per cent for exportation to the United States of America, Germany, Italy, Australasia and the Far East. Waterford, Cork and Dublin are the main centres for the Irish glass industry. The Irish developed techniques in 1676, with the help of English glassmaker George Ravenscroft, that supported the addition of lead oxide content to their glass products; this is the modern mark for 'fine lead crystal'. Ireland's main imports include machinery and transport equipment, chemicals, petroleum and petroleum products, food products and textiles.

The west, however, in areas such as West Donegal, West Mayo and West Galway has less fertile land and the population in these areas often only manage to grow enough for its own consumption. In the south-west county of Kerry some of the interior valleys are covered with peat bogs. The farmland here is very small with oats and potatoes being the main crops grown. The farmers tend to obtain their income from the sale of young cattle and sheep. In Tralee and Killarney there are several factories, including bacon curing and footwear, as well as engineering-industry and crane-manufacturing organizations. Fishing is significant in the areas of Dingle and Valencia. Brick making and corn milling are also current areas of industry where the skills and crafts have been handed down through the generations. A thriving sector of the Irish economy is the breeding of bloodstock or thoroughbred horses. Their thoroughbred horses receive worldwide acclaim. Eight per cent of Ireland's land area is given over to forests and woodlands and 80 per cent of the agricultural area is devoted to grass (silage, hay and pasture), 11 per cent to rough grazing and nine per cent to crop production. In 1988 a state agency was established to manage the commercial forestry of Ireland.

As an island surrounded by water, Ireland has the most extensive fishing grounds in the European Union, although

Ireland's income from tourism and leisure and recreation pursuits has increased enormously since the mid-twentieth century and particularly since the Irish Tourist Board (*Bord Fáilte*) was set up. Part of the Irish Tourist Board's work in promoting the island as a tourist destination has brought about the development of the country's major resorts and tourist amenities, as well as the creation of new sporting facilities and hotel construction. State-owned companies operate Ireland's rail and road transport as well as its radio and television stations, its electricity generation and distribution networks and its peat industry. On small holdings peat is still harvested manually, but in the midlands, where there are large expanses of bog, it can be mechanically cut in sufficient quantities to fire power stations. Discoveries of silver, lead, zinc and gypsum have led to the development of

ABOVE: Donkey and trap taking a churn of milk to the dairy in Tralee, 1981.

a mining industry. In the 1980s offshore natural gas wells were set up south of County Cork in the Celtic Sea. These natural gas wells dried up after a short time and now the country has pipes laid from the UK to supply its population with natural gas.

AHERN, BERTIE (b. 1951)

Fianna Fáil statesman, prime minister since 1997. Trained as an accountant and formed as a politician by the responsibilities he faced as mayor of Dublin, Ireland's youngest-ever Taoiseach is agreed to make up for in energy what he may lack in colour. Ahern's apparently unromantic background has, moreover, made him someone with whom London has felt more comfortable doing business than some of his more flamboyant predecessors, even as his (very moderate) republican leanings have helped endear him to nationalist opinion in the North.

))))▶ *Fianna Fáil*

ANCIENT ORDER OF HIBERNIANS (1838)

Friendly society. Its name largely the result of wishful thinking, this 'ancient' order was actually established as recently as 1838 by Irish immigrants newly arrived in the cities of America. Essentially it was a social club and a support-network, a sort of Catholic freemasonry (although US law enforcement came to regard the order with suspicion, as a front for Ribbonist activities). If the benefits of such an organization for new arrivals in a strange country were only too evident, their relations back home were quick to see the attractions too – especially those attempting to make their way in British-dominated Dublin and the Protestant North.

))))▶ *Ribbonism*

ANGLO-IRISH AGREEMENT (1985)

Agreement signed 15 November 1985 by British prime minister Margaret Thatcher and Irish taoiseach Garret Fitzgerald. The accord, reached between this least apparently nationalist of Irish statesmen and Britain's most hardline pro-unionist prime minister in living memory, may in hindsight be seen as having been crucial in laying the

BELOW: Dr Garett Fitzgerald and Margaret Thatcher sign the Anglo-Irish Agreement, 1985.

foundations for the peace process of the 1990s. While the IRA showed no signs of being able to overthrow British rule in the North, neither was there any sign of the strife abating: indeed the atmosphere had only been embittered by Thatcher's unsympathetic handling of the 1981 Hunger Strikes. Inaugurating a small but symbolically significant programme of intergovernmental consultation and co-operation, the agreement was designed to undermine a Sinn Féin political campaign whose success was causing nervousness in both London and Dublin. Its most profound importance, however, was arguably in drawing attention to the growing impotence of a confused and disunited Unionist community, whose angry protests failed to bring down an agreement it regarded as a clear betrayal.

))))▶ *Garret Fitzgerald, Hunger Strike*

ANGLO-IRISH TREATY (1921)

Treaty, signed in London on 6 December 1921, which brought the 'Irish Free State' into being, ending the War of Independence with Britain but provoking bitter disagreement – and ultimately civil war – in Ireland itself. By the beginning of 1921, the Anglo-Irish War seemed to be settling down into a bloody stalemate, Michael Collins's IRA failing to make any decisive impact on a British military whose ruthlessness was, however, drawing opprobrium on London from the international community. Following preliminary talks between the Sinn Féin president and leader of the Dáil, Éamon de Valera, and British prime minister David Lloyd George, an official meeting was scheduled for that December, but – perhaps suspecting that some compromise would be necessary – de Valera refused to attend in person.

ABOVE: De Valera and Lloyd George meet at Downing Street to discuss the Anglo-Irish Treaty.
ABOVE RIGHT: The limestone cliffs of the Aran Islands.

The deal brought back by Michael Collins and Arthur Griffith guaranteed self-rule for the 26 counties of western and southern Ireland, but stopped short of an all-Ireland republic. Though the Dáil ratified the treaty by a narrow margin, a group of Republicans led by de Valera remained adamantly opposed; by June 1922, civil war had broken out between 'Free Staters' and Republicans.

⟫⟫ *Irish Free State, Éamon de Valera*

ANNALS

Chronicles of historical and noteworthy events recorded on a year-by-year basis. Many sets of annals were compiled in Ireland in the 1,000-year period following the introduction of Christianity. The earliest annals were composed in monasteries, and while they recorded both secular and religious events they were initially written as attempts to validate the calendar, taking the dates of well-known events and relating lesser events to these. The entries sometimes stretch back into pre-Christian times and may include material that is of a mythological or only semi-historical nature. While the earliest references are based on oral traditions, however, later and contemporaneous entries provide extremely valuable and accurate records of events in Ireland right up to the seventeenth century. They are usually written in Latin or Irish and often run to hundreds of pages.

⟫⟫ *Annals of the Four Masters, Annals of Ulster*

ANNALS OF THE FOUR MASTERS (1632–36)

Important record of the history of Ireland from earliest times to 1616. Among the later and most important of Irish historical records, the *Annals of The Four Masters* were compiled between 1632 and 1636 by Michcál Ó Cléirigh, a lay Franciscan, and three assistants in County Donegal. The authors gathered material from a variety of earlier local and regional annals in an attempt to provide a comprehensive and learned history of the whole of Ireland. The idea for these annals came originally from the Franciscan college at Louvain and they can be viewed as an attempt to preserve the history and traditions of Gaelic Ireland when they were under great threat. Several of the other annals used in the compilation of this massive work have since been lost. The annals are particularly important since they are the main source of information from an Irish perspective in this period.

⟫⟫ *Annals, Franciscan Order, Micheál Ó Cléirigh*

ANNALS OF ULSTER (1431–1541)

Important work compiled in County Fermanagh, initially by Cathal Óg Mac Maghnusa (d. 1498) and continued for a number of years after his death by his colleagues. It is one of the most important and reliable sources for the history of Ireland, Scotland and in particular the province of Ulster, from the earliest times. The histories of the O'Neill and Maguire dynasties are well documented in this work, which has been recently republished in four volumes.

)))▶ *Annals, Maguire Dynasty, O'Neill Dynasty, Ulster*

AOIFE

Daughter of Diarmaid Mac Murchadha (Dermot MacMurrough), also known as Eva. The Anglo-Norman forces reached Bannow Bay, County Wexford, in 1169, and defeated a combined army of Irish and Viking forces. The following year they captured Waterford. The leader, Richard de Clare, Earl of Pembroke, also known as Strongbow, demanded Aoife in marriage as his prize. In 1171, Pembroke became king of Leinster on Mac Murchadha's death.

)))▶ *Richard de Clare, Diarmaid Mac Murchadha*

APPRENTICE BOYS (1814)

Protestant political grouping, formed in 1814 and named after the 13 apprentices who, erroneously fearing a massacre because of a forged letter, shut the gates of Derry against an approaching Catholic army in 1688. One of the groups involved in contentious marches in recent years, their main celebrations focus on the anniversaries of the lifting of the Siege of Derry and the shutting of the gates by the original apprentice boys.

)))▶ *Battle of the Boyne, Siege of Derry*

ARAN ISLANDS

Island group in Galway Bay. Though the merest scattering of stormlashed limestone rocks, sparsely inhabited by communities of fishermen, the Aran Islands have for a century loomed large in Irish cultural geography. From J. M. Synge's *The Aran Islands* (1907) to Andrew McNeillie's *An Aran Keening* (2001), writers have found inspiration here in one of the last outposts of traditional Irish Gaelic culture. Where the writers have come, the tourists have followed, now-obsolete economic activities finding a new lease of life as 'heritage'.

)))▶ *J. M. Synge*

ARDAGH CHALICE (8TH CENTURY)

Eighth-century ecclesiastical metalwork cup. Housed in the National Museum of Ireland, Dublin, this large, two-handled silver cup was discovered in a potato field in County Limerick in 1868. Decorated with gold, gilt bronze and enamel, it is engraved with the names of some of the Apostles in Latin on the outside.

ABOVE: The Ardagh Chalice.

ARMAGH

Small city in County Armagh, Northern Ireland. The main centre for the medieval cult of St Patrick and the site of a great monastery complex of which, however, few traces now remain, Armagh is still the ecclesiastical capital of Ireland. The *Book of Armagh*, a beautifully illuminated manuscript edition of the New Testament, is now kept at Trinity College Dublin and is a national treasure. Patrick seems to have been drawn here by the fact that Eamhain Macha was the ancient capital of Ulster, but the city's status as a secular capital would not outlast the medieval period. Lying just outside the main area of Ulster Plantation, Armagh missed the wave of economic development that went with it: its modern street-plan suggests a sleepy city centred closely on its cathedral. Yet its position at the very edge of the Plantation has left Armagh very much in the 'front line' through centuries of conflict, with predominantly Catholic settlements to the south and Protestant villages to the north.

)))➤ **Book of Armagh,** *Armagh Outrages, St Patrick, Plantation of Ulster*

ARMAGH, BOOK OF (AD 807–808)

Latin manuscript. Known also as the *Liber Armachanus*, this includes a complete text of the New Testament, copies of several biographies of St Patrick and also his *Confessio*. It was compiled in Armagh in AD 807–808 by several scribes and is now in the library of Trinity College, Dublin.

)))➤ **Confessio,** *St Patrick, Trinity College Dublin*

ARMAGH OUTRAGES (1795–96)

Series of attacks by Protestant settlers on the Catholic population of Armagh and its environs. Resolving to press their advantage after the Battle of the Diamond, Protestant rowdies launched a series of sometimes murderous attacks on Catholic households in the months that followed, taking the title of 'Peep o'Day Boys' from their custom of moving in at the crack of dawn. Up to 7,000 Catholics were dislodged from lands in and around Armagh, which accordingly came under Protestant occupation – but the dispossessed would play a key role in the uprising of the United Irishmen two years later.

)))➤ *Battle of the Diamond, Peep o'Day Boys, Plantation of Ulster, Society of United Irishmen*

ARMS CRISIS AND TRIAL (1970)

Two cabinet ministers dismissed after accusations of arms smuggling for the IRA. After a £30,000 arms find at Dublin airport, Charles Haughey and Neil Blaney were sacked by Taoiseach Jack Lynch. Both were accused of arms smuggling to Northern Ireland but both denied the accusations and the charges. They appeared in court on 28 May 1970. Blaney, the former agriculture minister, was acquitted of the charge in July 1970 and Haughey, the former finance minister, was acquitted of importing arms illegally at the High Court in October of the same year. The main defence against their charges was that the arms were part of an officially authorized intelligence operation on behalf of the Irish army. It is believed that Jack Lynch's reputation and that of his government suffered severe criticism as a result of the sackings of the ministers. He did, however, survive a vote of no-confidence in the government.

)))➤ *Jack Lynch*

ABOVE: Armagh during the nineteenth century.

ASHE, THOMAS (1884–1917)

Hunger striker. A Dingle, County Kerry, schoolteacher and enthusiastic promoter of Irish language and culture through the Gaelic League, Thomas Ashe led the battalion of volunteers who took Ashbourne, County Meath in the Easter Rising of 1916. Although he escaped execution with the Rising's ringleaders, he was held in Lewes Prison, Sussex, but made light of his captivity, dedicating his sufferings to his country. 'Let me carry your cross for Ireland, Lord!' he wrote in a famous poem, giving early expression to what would in the decades that followed become a potent rhetoric among Republicans in which Irish patriotism and Christian self-sacrifice were combined. Released and re-arrested on new charges in 1917 he died as result of force-feeding during a republican hunger-strike.

〉〉〉➤ *Easter Rising, Gaelic League*

ATHENRY, BATTLE OF (1316)

Decisive battle which effectively ended Irish resistance to the Anglo-Normans. In 1316, the Irish forces led by Feidhlimidh Ó Conchubhair (Phelim O'Connor) faced the Anglo-Norman army of Richard de Burgh and Meyler de Bermingham at Athenry. Around 8,000 men were killed. The walls of the town, begun in 1310, are said to have been built partly from the collection of booty after the battle.

〉〉〉➤ *Richard de Burgh, O'Connor Dynasty*

AUGHRIM, BATTLE OF (1691)

Disastrous decisive Irish defeat by William III's armies. In the aftermath of the Battle of the Boyne, James II's forces were in disarray. James himself had fled to France, though his supporters under Patrick Sarsfield, Earl of Lucan, and the French general St Ruth, remained in Ireland and continued the resistance. On 12 July 1691 Sarsfield was defeated at Aughrim, County Wicklow, by Godart van Ginckel, Earl of Athlone, one of William III's generals. The Irish forces had more cavalry but a lack of infantry meant they were routed, with baggage and cannon lost. English losses were about 600 against 5,000 Irish slain.

〉〉〉➤ *Battle of the Boyne, James II of England, Patrick Sarsfield, William III of England*

LEFT: Charles Haughey after his release on bail during the arms crisis and trial.
ABOVE: Thomas Ashe.

AUGUSTINIAN ORDER (12TH–13TH CENTURIES)

Religious order of monks. There were two separate Augustinian orders which founded monasteries in Ireland in the twelfth and thirteenth centuries. The Augustinian canons were promoted by St Malachy in the north of the country and by St Laurence O'Toole in Dublin. The Augustinian friars came from England and initially founded monasteries in the Pale and Anglo-Norman-held parts of Ireland. Later they spread into Connacht and their foundations continued to flourish until the sixteenth-century Reformation, with monasteries in Irish-controlled areas surviving until the reign of Elizabeth I. After this time mendicant friars continued to be active in Ireland in spite of the Penal Laws, and there were over 120 of them ministering in Ireland as late as 1750.

)))) *St Malachy, St Laurence O'Toole, The Pale, Penal Laws*

BACK LANE PARLIAMENT (1792)

Assembly of the Catholic Committee against the Penal Laws. The name of 'Back Lane Parliament' was given in derision by Irish Protestants to the assembly held in the Tailors' Hall, in Back Lane, off Dublin's High Street, by campaigners against Ireland's discriminatory Penal Laws. The gathering was organized by the young Theobald Wolfe Tone, who, though a Protestant, had lent his support as secretary to the Committee, convinced that Ireland's Protestants and Catholics shared vital interests. He would use the same premises six years later for assemblies of his United Irishmen.

)))) *Penal Laws, Theobald Wolfe Tone, United Irishmen*

ABOVE: A hermit of the Order of Saint Augustine.
RIGHT: Theobald Wolfe Tone.

BALLINAMUCK, BATTLE OF (1798)

Battle of 9 September 1798 which resulted in the total defeat of the French and Irish forces by the English. The French Revolutionary Wars of 1791–1802 saw France engaged against the armies of England, Austria and Prussia. Irish nationalism, and Ireland's strategic location, provided France with an attractive prospect.

In the aftermath of the failed rising of the United Irishmen, a small French expedition under General Joseph Humbert landed in County Mayo in September 1798; there they faced troops under the command of the viceroy and commander-in-chief of Ireland, Charles, 1st Marquis Cornwallis, at Ballinamuck, near Drumlish in County Longford.

The French, exhausted and outnumbered, rapidly disintegrated. First, the French rearguard surrendered at Kittycrevagh. The French soldiers securing the road at Ballinamuck surrendered after becoming stuck in a bog. English troops under Lieutenant-General Gerard Lake then surrounded Humbert in his position on a hill overlooking Ballinamuck, using cannon and cavalry to force a rapid surrender. Remaining resistance was rapidly overcome. Some of the rebels fled into a bog but were massacred.

)))) *Joseph Humbert, General Gerard Lake*

BALTINGLASS REBELLION (1580–81)

Rebellion that coincided with the Desmond Revolt in Munster. As a result of England's attempts to strengthen their rule there was an escalation of political and religious discontent in Ireland. The 'Old English' and the Gaelic combined, resulting in the Old English Catholic Rising. Viscount Baltinglass and Fiach MacHugh O'Byrne, a Gaelic chief, led the rebellion. They combined with a conspiracy from 'the Pale', together with small contingents from Spain and Italy. England sent in huge numbers of reinforcements from England and the Baltinglass rebels failed in their attempts, as did the Desmond Rebels. As a result Munster was devastated.

))))➤ *Desmond Revolt, Battle of Glenmalure, The Pale*

BANGOR (6TH CENTURY)

Bangor was an important monastic site on the southern shore of Belfast Lough. It was founded by St Comgall in the middle of the sixth century and became a major centre of learning and devotion. Among the monks who trained there was St Columbanus, who later set up several monasteries in continental Europe, most notably Bobbio in northern Italy. Bangor was later sacked by the Danes but several important manuscripts have survived including the *Antiphony of Bangor*, which gives an insight into the hymns used in the early Irish Church and also includes a poem on the various abbots. Bangor is frequently mentioned in the *Annals of Ulster* and it is believed that records compiled at this monastery may be the original source for much of the early material in that great work.

))))➤ **Annals of Ulster**

BANNA STRAND (1916)

Beach in County Kerry. "Twas on Good Friday morning, all in the month of May, A German ship was signalling, beyond there in the bay…'. The passenger who disembarked that day in 1916 was the famous patriot Roger Casement, his immediate capture –

BELOW: The beach at Banna Strand, County Kerry.

along with the 'twenty thousand rifles' the song records he had brought with him – represented the severest imaginable setback to Irish republican aspirations. Given that Germany and Britain were currently at war, Casement had been hoping to win more committed support for an Irish rebellion in Berlin; his main object in coming to Ireland was to have the planned rising postponed while he continued negotiations. In his absence the insurrection went ahead, doomed to failure, outnumbered and outgunned – though military defeat would of course be transmuted to mythological victory.

))))➤ **Roger Casement, Easter Rising**

BARRY, COMMODORE JOHN (1745–1803)

'Father of the American Navy'. Son of a poor Irish farmer from County Wexford, Barry rose from being cabin boy to senior commander of the US fleet. He fought several sea battles and was involved in the Battles of Trenton and Princeton, and the last naval battle of the American Revolution in 1783.

BARRY, KEVIN (1902–20)

Born in Dublin, Barry became a medical student but joined the nascent Irish Republican Army. Involved in the street ambush of an army bread lorry, Barry was captured on the spot and beaten up by police, but was rescued and sent for trial. In spite of street protests that England was executing prisoners-of-war, Barry was hanged as a response to the increasingly extreme tactics of the IRA, which had become more brutal and indiscriminate, including attacks on civilians. As Barry was so young, his execution provoked widespread outrage and led many students to join the IRA.

))))▶ *Irish Republican Army*

BEATTY, JAMES (1820–56)

Enniskillen-born railway engineer. Beatty's most outstanding achievement was the construction of a track from the port of Balaclava up to the front line to supply the troops who were besieging Sevastopol during the Crimean War. He had previously built railways in Canada and England. He died in London of injuries received in an accident on the Crimean line.

BECKETT, SAMUEL (1906–89)

Dublin-born playwright and novelist. Winner of the Nobel Prize for Literature in 1969, Beckett lived most of his life in France. He moved to Paris in 1937 and met his future wife the following year when she came to his aid after he was stabbed in the street. During World War II he was active in the French Resistance until 1942 when he was betrayed to the Gestapo. Beckett was lucky enough to escape and he moved to the south of France where he worked on a farm. He began writing before the war but it was not until he started writing in French and turned his attention to drama that his work achieved any great success. His

most famous play, *En Attendant Godot*, was staged in Paris in 1953 and was a major critical success. His own English translation *Waiting for Godot* gained a similar reception in London and New York. His work, both bleak and humorous, is often experimental and in later years it became increasingly minimalist.

BEHAN, BRENDAN (1923–64)

Dublin-born writer. Brendan Behan's best-known works are the two plays *The Hostage* (originally written in Irish as *An Giall*) and *The Quare Fellow*. He was a house-painter by trade but joined the IRA at an early age

and was arrested in Liverpool in 1939 for possession of explosives. In 1942, not long after his release, he was arrested again – this time in Dublin – and sentenced to 14 years imprisonment for attempting to kill a policeman. He was released in 1946 and, despite several further brushes with the law, began to make his living as a writer, contributing articles to Dublin newspapers. His first play, *The Quare Fellow,* was produced in Dublin in 1954 and its move to London in 1956 brought him international recognition. The great success of *The Hostage* and the autobiographical memoir *Borstal Boy*, both of which appeared in 1958, confirmed his reputation as a significant Irish writer. However, he also developed a self-destructive persona as a wild-living, quick-witted Irishman, and alcohol addiction led to his early death in 1964.

))))▶ *Irish Republican Army*

BELFAST

Ireland's pre-eminent industrial city with a current population of some 475,000 and, since 1921, the capital of Northern Ireland. Its name deriving from the Irish *Béal Feirste* ('mouth of the sandbank'), Belfast is situated at the point where the River Lagan flows into Belfast Lough, a convenient port for traffic with Scotland and England. It was as the administrative centre for the Ulster Plantation of the seventeenth century that the city first came to prominence, its identity as a strongly loyal Protestant city thus being established early on. That identity was only strengthened in the centuries that followed. Irritated by the coercive Anglicanism of English rule and inspired by the revolutionary example of the United States of America, some Belfast Presbyterians in the late-eighteenth century did find themselves drawn to the anti-British radicalism of Wolfe Tone, but they were horrified by the violent anarchy to which it eventually led in the 1798 Rebellion.

From that time on, Belfast never wavered in its Britishness, though the rise of industrialism through the nineteenth century led to an influx of Catholic labourers from the neighbouring counties. Determinedly defining themselves against these incomers, the city's tradesmen and skilled labourers made militant Protestantism and Loyalism the twin pillars of their status: membership of the Orange Order came to be seen as the badge of belonging. Sectarian violence flared repeatedly through the nineteenth century, the explosive riots of 1813, 1832, 1843, 1852, 1864, 1872, 1886 being only the gravest of innumerable outbreaks of public disorder. Though spontaneous enough in their origins, these eruptions were clear in their cumulative effect, which was to ensure *de facto* segregation between Catholic and Protestant communities when it came to housing. The two communities moved in separate spheres economically as well, Catholics being excluded from many of the most sought-after skilled jobs in the city's linen mills, as well as in the shipyards and engineering works for which Belfast was becoming celebrated worldwide.

Periodic moves towards Home Rule through the final decades of the nineteenth century emboldened a Catholic community which, until then, had been kept thoroughly cowed, but only increased the aggressive resolve of a once-ruling caste which feared marginalization and the loss of privileges in an independent Ireland. As the nineteenth century gave way to the twentieth and Catholic Ireland's wish for self-government seemed on the verge of being granted, Belfast's long-standing opposition to any such concession inevitably reached fever pitch. The economic importance of Belfast, and the Protestants' virtual monopoly of industrial muscle in the city, strengthened the hand of the Unionists immeasurably in negotiations with the British government. Hence the ultimate withholding of six counties from the self-governing entity handed over to the Irish in 1921, and the foundation there of what amounted to an 'Orange State'. The bombing of the city's docks in the Blitz of April 1941 helped cement the city's sense of Britishness (though de Valera's Free State violated its neutrality to send fire brigades from several cities).

BELOW Loyalist mural of King William of Orange, Belfast

The guarantee of the Union with Britain and the Protestant supremacy that went with it was not sufficient to allay anxieties kept sharp by the sense of impending demographic disaster. The steady growth of the Catholic population in the city's south-western districts threatened to see Ulster Protestantism overwhelmed in its own stronghold: the full gamut of sectarian violence, employment discrimination and local government gerrymandering were required to ensure that the city's Protestant rulers retained the upper hand. The introduction of direct rule from Westminster in 1972 may have wrenched the reins of power from the Unionists' grasp, but it only increased the perception Protestant Belfast had of itself as a place beleaguered. In the Protestant heartland of East Belfast, and especially in the neighbourhood of the Shankill Road, Protestants responded to the whipping away of their official institutions by creating their own – sometimes murderous – paramilitary organizations.

For their part, hardened by their experiences, Belfast's Catholics have themselves down the decades arguably become a community apart from the rest of their kind, with little in common with other northern Catholics, let alone those they would wish to have as their compatriots in the 26 counties. The capital of Northern Ireland, Belfast has also been the capital of its recent troubles, and the resentments resulting on both sides are intense and deeply ingrained. Through the years of paramilitary ceasefire and peace process since 1994, the hostilities between Protestant and Catholic communities have smouldered on. The election of Sinn Féin's Alex Maskey as Belfast's Lord Mayor in June 2002, however, is the clearest sign of the major demographic and political changes that have been taking place in the city.

)))⟩ *Catholicism, Home Rule, Protestantism, Theobald Wolfe Tone, Plantation of Ulster*

ABOVE: Travellers cower in a bus station in a Protestant/Catholic area, Belfast, 1922.

BELFAST HARP FESTIVAL (1792)

Competition held in Belfast 11–14 July 1792. This event was significant beyond its musical importance. Ten harpists, most elderly and six blind, who were among the last guardians of this ancient Irish tradition were brought together in a competition. Many of their tunes were transcribed during the event and were thus preserved. Edward Bunting, who was one of the transcribers, was so excited by what he had heard that the following year he set out on a series of journeys in search of similar material throughout rural Ireland. It was also a significant cultural moment because the riches briefly displayed inspired many of the United Irishmen and sharpened their perception of Ireland as a nation separate from England, with a rich culture of its own.

)))⟩ *Edward Bunting, United Irishmen*

BELFAST POGROMS (1920–22)

Riots, devastation and attacks on Belfast Catholics. The word 'pogrom' is derived from a Russian word for 'riot' or 'devastation' and is used to describe attacks on minority groups, often with the toleration of the authorities. This two-year period saw attacks on the Belfast Catholic community, resulting in 455 deaths and 2,000 injuries. It is reported that 23,500 Catholics were forced to leave their homes and 9,000 Catholic men were rendered unemployed.

)))⟩ *Éamon de Valera*

BENBURB, BATTLE OF (1646)

Major rebel victory against English rule during the Confederate War of 1641–53. In 1641 an Irish Roman Catholic rebellion broke out, seeking religious freedom and an Irish constitution, although remaining under the English Crown. From 1642 the northern rebels were led by Eoghan Rua Ó Néill (Owen Roe O'Neill), a highly experienced soldier who had served in Spain for 30 years. At Benburb, near Moy in County Tyrone, on 5 June 1646, Ó Néill led the rebels to victory over General Robert Munro, England's Scottish ally.

)))⟩ *Eoghan Rua Ó Néill*

BENEDICTINE ORDER (11TH CENTURY)

Religious order of monks. St Benedict's *Regula Monachorum* ('Rule of Monks') was first set down as early as AD 515: it would become the founding framework of all western monasticism. Its first appearance on Irish soil seems to have been at the end of the eleventh century, when the monks of Christ Church, Dublin, lived according to its principles. The Benedictine Order itself would go on not only to establish houses in Ireland, but also to set up missionary monasteries in continental Europe, staffed by Irish monks.

))))➤ *Monasteries*

BIRMINGHAM SIX (1974–91)

An infamous miscarriage of justice in which six Irishmen were jailed following the 1974 pub bombings in Birmingham. After 17 years in jail and two appeals, their convictions were judged to be unsafe and they were freed in 1991. Their legal team succeeded in discrediting the confessions and the forensic evidence that the West Midlands police produced at the original trial.

LEFT: A Benedictine monk offering his missal.
BELOW: The Birmingham Six outside the Old Bailey, 1991.

BLACK AND TANS (1920–21)

Auxiliary police force working in Ireland July 1920 to December 1921. Irish police resigned in large numbers after World War I, rather than face the rising Irish

nationalism led by the Irish Republican Army. The British government hired replacements, often unemployed ex-soldiers. Lack of equipment meant army jackets or trousers were utilized alongside police the black, hence the nickname derived from a hound pack in County Tipperary. Their ruthless – and often illegal – methods of retaliation against terrorists included brutal interrogation and house-burning. This made them immensely unpopular and they became a target for the Republicans. The Black and Tans were disbanded after December 1921, following the Anglo-Irish Treaty.

))))▶ *Anglo-Irish Treaty, Irish Republican Army*

BLACK DEATH (1349)

Form of the Plague that decreased the population of Britain by 50 per cent. The Black Death swept through Europe and was carried via the trade routes. Caused by rats and fleas, the disease reached Ireland in 1348, devastating the population. It killed many people and others,

ABOVE: A shop burned by the Black and Tans, 1920.
RIGHT: Blarney Castle.
FAR RIGHT: The Blasket Islands.

afraid of catching the illness, fled to England. During this period severe restrictions were placed on the population and movement from village to village was curtailed. This led to widespread labour shortages and an inability for the rural population to feed themselves or to supply the towns and cities with food. Roughly one third of the Irish population died during this period.

BLACK PIG'S DYKE

Also known as 'The Dane's Cast' and 'The Worm Ditch'. The remains of this pre-Christian defence can be seen in south Ulster counties. According to legend one man, angry that the magical schoolmaster had turned his children into piglets, turned the man into a black pig. The pig vomited and formed the embankment.

BLARNEY CASTLE (1446)

Fifteenth-century castle, semi-ruined, 10 km (6 miles) north-west of Cork. Its impressive keep and corner towers are believed to have been built in 1446. Blarney Castle remains an imposing sight over half a millennium later. The fame of the place, however, depends not upon its architectural or historical significance, but upon the mythical powers of the famous 'Blarney Stone'. Situated just below the battlements, the stone is reputed to confer the gift of eloquence on anyone who kisses it.

BLASKET ISLANDS

Island group off the coast of Kerry. Like the Aran Islands further to the north, the Blaskets have a cultural significance out of all proportion to their size, Great Blasket being perhaps the most written-about island in the world outside Manhattan. The difference is that, in the Blaskets, it has been the islanders themselves who have immortalized their home, memoirs originally written in Irish by men like Muiris Ó Suilleabháin and Tomas Ó Criomhthain and women like Peig Sayers having found an enormous international readership.

))))▶ *Aran Islands*

BLOOD, THOMAS (C. 1616–80)

Conspirator. The ferocious fame of 'Captain Blood' in Britain rests on his attempt to steal the Crown Jewels from the Tower of London in 1671, but by that time he already had an eventful career as an intriguer in Ireland behind him. 'Blood's Plot' in the Irish context unfolded in the spring and summer of 1663, when the Meath-born Blood and some fellow Protestants sought unsuccessfully to occupy Dublin Castle. By the Act of Settlement of 1662, the restored Stuart monarchy had restored lands confiscated by Cromwell to their ancestral owners, delighting them, but leaving the Protector's former beneficiaries seething. Implementation of the Act was overseen by the Earl of Ormond, whom Blood attempted to murder in 1670; that he was pardoned all these crimes serves to strengthen the suspicion that he may have been working as a government spy all along.

BLOODY SUNDAY (1920)

Day of tit-for-tat bloodletting, Sunday 21 November 1920. The name 'Bloody Sunday' was originally given to a Russian outrage of 1905, when the tsar's forces cut down a crowd of peaceful demonstrators. The phrase first entered Irish history as long ago as 1920, when IRA men put into operation a carefully planned night-long programme of assassination which left 13 suspected British agents dead,

and six others wounded. Outraged, and shocked, by the attack, British forces responded by taking the lives of two IRA leaders they were currently holding, both being killed, it was subsequently claimed, while trying to escape. Later that day, a company of Auxiliaries sent to a Gaelic Football game at Croke Park in search of wanted men opened fire on the crowd and killed 12 people.

))))➡ *Croke Park*

BLOODY SUNDAY (1972)

Name given to the killing of 14 people by British Forces on Sunday 30 January 1972. The grim events of Ireland's second 'Bloody Sunday' unfolded at a civil rights demonstration in County Derry, which had gone ahead despite the authorities' decree that it was banned. Members of the Parachute Regiment opened fire on the protestors, shooting 13 people on the spot; another of the many injured would die a few days later. The original atrocity was only compounded, as far as nationalist opinion was concerned, by the crude attempts of Lord Widgery's official enquiry to whitewash what had happened. Ill-supported claims that the paratroopers had been responding to IRA snipers, and cynical attempts to smear some of those killed as murderous nail-bombers, swayed many young Catholic men to join the ranks of the terrorists in earnest.

BLOOMSDAY

Annual celebration of James Joyce's most famous novel *Ulysses*, which is based on events in Dublin. The time-frame of the story is just one day – 16 June 1904. The festival is named after the central character of the novel, Leopold Bloom. In Dublin participants dress in

Edwardian costume and visit places mentioned in the book. The day is a focus for a celebration of the life and work of James Joyce and is now a major event on the cultural calendar in many places across the world.

))))➤ *James Joyce*

BLUESHIRTS (1932)

Ex-serviceman's association and, effectively, fascist party of the 1930s Free State. 'Any organization may adopt a special colour without infringing the law,' said General Eoin O'Duffy, leader of the 'Army Comrades' Association': his men's blue shirts were no more sinister,

he suggested, than the distinctive blazer of any sports club. In the event, Ireland's fascist party, founded in 1932, was not destined to gain the influence of its equivalents in continental Europe; nor would it ever be in a position to match their outrages. The de Valera government against which it set itself was, with all its revolutionary rhetoric, socially conservative enough to satisfy all but the most thoroughgoing reactionary, leaving Duffy and his followers no political place to stand.

))))➤ *Eoin O'Duffy*

BOOK OF INVASIONS (12TH CENTURY)

Chronicle of the legendary history of Ireland. The *Book of Invasions* has come down to us from the twelfth century, although its origins are much earlier. It tells of the different tribes and peoples who invaded Ireland in the pre-Christian period and includes both historical and mythological events and so cannot be read as pure history. It includes accounts of such groups as the Fir Bolg and the Tuatha Dé Danann as well as more reliable historical material up to the twelfth century.

))))➤ *Fir Bolg, Tuatha Dé Danann*

BOUNDARY COMMISSION (1921)

Commission appointed to establish the boundary for Northern Ireland. Set up under the terms of the 1921 Anglo-Irish Treaty to oversee the drawing up of the border between the Irish Free State and British-ruled Northern Ireland, the Boundary Commission looks in historical hindsight like a face-saving concession thrown to the Treaty's Irish signatories. While Arthur Griffith and Michael Collins were allowed, in their disappointment, to comfort themselves with the prospect of the Free State eventually acquiring Fermanagh and Tyrone as well as the City of Derry, the Treaty's wording ultimately enabled the British to keep the boundaries as first set down in 1921. Clauses stipulating that 'geographical' and 'economic' considerations were to be weighed alongside purely demographic ones permitted these predominantly Catholic territories to be retained by the Protestant state.

))))➤ *Anglo-Irish Treaty, Irish Free State*

ABOVE: The Blueshirts.
RIGHT: The flight of James II after the Battle of the Boyne.

BOYCOTT, CHARLES CUNNINGHAM (1832–97)

British estate manager in Ireland who was 'boycotted' by the Land League. After Captain Charles Boycott retired from the British army in 1873 he moved to County Mayo and worked as an estate manager for the land of the 3rd Earl of Erne. The president of the Land League, Charles Parnell, ordered him to reduce rents by 25 per cent and Boycott attempted to serve writs of eviction to tenants in September 1880. Boycott took action against the Land League by illegally employing Ulster workers to harvest his crops under the supervision of the armed forces. By the end of 1880 Boycott had left Ireland, when his own tenants and other local people refused to work for him, and the term 'boycott' entered the English language.

))))▶ *Land League, Charles Parnell*

BOYLE, RICHARD, 1ST EARL OF CORK (1566–1643)

English colonizer of Munster. Boyle went to live in Ireland in 1588 but returned to England 10 years later when he lost his land in the Munster Rebellion. In 1600 Elizabeth I of England appointed him clerk of the council of Munster. In 1602 he bought the estates of Sir Walter Raleigh in Cork, Waterford and Tipperary, founding ironworks. He was made Earl of Cork in 1620, Lord High Justice in 1629 and Lord High Treasurer in 1631 but in 1633 was fined for owning illegal titles to his estates. He had 15 children, including Richard, 1st Earl of Orrery.

))))▶ *Elizabeth I of England*

BOYNE, BATTLE OF THE (1690)

Major defeat for the deposed king of England, James II, by the new king William III on 1 July 1690 beside the River Boyne at Oldbridge near Drogheda in Ireland. The battle ended James II's chance of recovering his throne.

By the summer of 1690, the campaign in Ireland was not going well for James,

despite the defeat of the English and Dutch fleets by the French at Beachy Head on 30 June. James had not succeeded in capturing the vital towns of Londonderry and Enniskillen, and was outnumbered by William III, who also had better organized and trained forces. William's 35,000 men, made up of English, Dutch and Huguenots together with various European mercenaries, faced James's untrained and untested Irish foot soldiers, reinforced by Irish cavalry and 7,000 French infantry under the command of Richard Talbot, Earl of Tyrconnell.

A chance shot by a cannon nearly prevented the battle, when William was struck in the shoulder by a shell while reconnoitring the enemy position. When battle commenced the following day, William sent cavalry over the river on both sides of the enemy to encircle them, leading one of the wings himself. Despite difficulties crossing the river, and steady resistance from some of the French cavalry, the onslaught succeeded in routing the Irish army.

James realized the day was lost and left while the battle was still raging, fleeing to Dublin. In spite of the dramatic consequences of the battle, and the notoriety it enjoys to this day in Ireland, the casualties were small. Only around 2,000 of James's forces were killed, and William lost just 400.

Today, Orangemen commemorate the battle as a victory for the Protestant cause on 12 July (actually the date of the Battle of Aughrim).

))))➤ *Battle of Aughrim, James II of England, William III of England*

BREEN, DAN (1894–1969)

Irish Volunteer and former railway linesman. In January 1919 Dan Breen led the ambush at Soloheadbeg of two members of the Royal Irish Constabulary carrying a gelignite consignment, killing them in cold blood. With a £10,000 bounty on his head, he went on the run, fighting for the anti-Treaty IRA faction in the Civil War. From 1932–65 he sat in the Irish parliament. His auto-biography, *My Fight for Irish Freedom* (1924) was widely read.

))))➤ *Irish Republican Army*

BREHON LAWS

The Brehon Laws (*Dlithe na mBreithiúin*) were the legal system of early Gaelic Ireland and were highly complex. Their origin is pre-Christian and Celtic but over the centuries other influences are noted. Firstly the coming of Christianity had an influence and later the legal concepts and terminology employed by the Normans also became evident. In the Pale, and later in other areas under Norman control, new legal systems were introduced, but such was the influence of the Brehon Laws in Gaelic Ireland that the Statutes of Kilkenny (1366) included various articles intended to outlaw their use and to strengthen the rule of English law within the Norman communities in Ireland at that time. The Brehon Laws were largely adhered to within Gaelic Ireland until its defeat and the Flight of the Earls in 1607, and certain elements survived in popular culture long after that.

))))➤ *Flight of the Earls, Gaelic Ireland, Statutes of Kilkenny*

RIGHT: St Brendan.

BRENDAN, ST (AD 484–577)

Abbot and explorer. Born by tradition in Tralee, County Kerry, St Brendan reputedly grew up to found the great monasteries of Ardfert, Kerry and Clonfert, Galway. He is, however, chiefly famous for the ocean-going travels he made in a traditional skin-and-wicker *curragh,* as recorded in the ninth-century epic *Navigatio Sanctis Brendanis Abbatis* ('Voyage of the Abbot Saint Brendan'). While sceptical scholars say the 'Land of Promise' he reached was no further afield than the Faroes or even the Hebrides, more adventurous interpreters have found evidence in the text that he reached Iceland, New-foundland and even the Bahamas.

))))➤ *Monasteries*

BRIAN BÓROIMHE (BRIAN BORU) (AD 940–1014)

High King of Ireland (1002–14), killed while fighting the Vikings. Brian Bóroimhe of the Dalcassians was born in Munster, and emerged as a brilliant warrior and military planner. In AD 968 he recaptured Cashel from the Vikings at Sulcoit so that it became once more the seat of the kings of Munster. In AD 976 he succeeded his brother as king. Further battles, such as that at Bealach Leachta in AD 978, secured popular support for Brian and his control across southern Ireland by AD 984, followed by more fighting to wrest northern Ireland from Mael Seachnaill II of Tara. In AD 999 at Glen Mama he defeated a challenge from Mael Mordha.

In 1002 Mael Seachnaill submitted and Brian Bóroimhe was crowned Ard-Rí ('High King of Ireland'), ruling from his palace of Kincora at Killaloe, which remained capital of Ireland for another century. Ireland benefited from the stability of unification and legal reform, leading to renewed prosperity and much of the damage of war being overturned.

Churches and monasteries were rebuilt and their libraries restocked, and fortifications were renewed and installed.

In 1014, the Vikings of Dublin rebelled. Boru's forces decisively defeated Mael Mordha and the Vikings at Clontarf near Dublin on 23 April in a close-run battle which saw some of Brian's allies defecting and others abandoning the fight. Brian himself was killed by retreating Vikings; he was too old now to lead the vanguard and had remained in the rear. His son Murchadh was fatally wounded while leading the Irish army. The battle ended Viking ambitions for territorial control in Ireland, while Brian's achievement in establishing the Gaelic monarchy of Ireland secured his reputation as a national hero.

))))▶ *Battle of Clontarf, Mael Mordha, Mael Seachnaill II*

BRIGID, ST (6TH CENTURY)

Leading female saint of Ireland. St Brigid (modern Irish Bríd) is associated with the monastery of Kildare, where she was abbess in the early part of the sixth century. Although there is very little accurate historical information about her, she was a very popular saint whose fame spread to continental Europe, making her the best-known Irish saint after St Patrick. Her feast day is 1 February.

))))▶ *St Patrick*

ABOVE: Brian Bóroimhe is killed by the Vikings.
ABOVE RIGHT: Saints Brigid and Tecla.

BRONZE AGE (c. 2000–c. 500 BC)

Pottery made by the Beaker people has been found in the west of Ireland, indicating early Bronze Age settlements. Four hundred megalithic tombs in the form of wedge tombs have been found, also in the west around Counties Clare, Cork, Kerry and Tipperary. The Bronze Age settlers had a sound metal industry and would have exported bronze, copper and gold to Europe. In County Clare a substantial amount of gold was found in the 'Great Clare Gold Hoard'. In eastern Ireland examples of single, urn-burial traditions have been discovered, with examples of Beaker pottery in the form of food vessels.

BROOKE, SIR BASIL (1888–1973)

Viscount Brookeborough, prime minister of Northern Ireland (1943–63). A County Fermanagh landowner, Brooke served with distinction in World War I, but won his Unionist spurs in the 1920s commanding Fermanagh's Special Constabulary in its war with the IRA. Elected to the Northern Ireland parliament in 1929, he became prime minister in 1943: to his Protestant electorate, at least, he brought two decades of calm stability. Brooke's personal charm was disarming, and he had no difficulty in working with British governments (such as Clement Attlee's reforming Labour administration) with which he had nothing ideologically in common, but his resolve to resist southern Catholic claims on northern Protestant territory was nothing short of adamantine.

))))▶ *Boundary Commission*

BROOKE, CHARLOTTE (c. 1740–93)

Irish writer. The daughter of County Cavan writer Henry Brooke, Charlotte's literary works are now more famous than her father's. In 1789 she published *Reliques of Irish Poetry*, an influential book which brought the richness and beauty of poetry written in Irish to the attention of an English-language readership for the first time, presenting as it did the original poems along with translations and extensive notes. From a Methodist Anglo-Irish background Brooke was one of the earliest Irish-language enthusiasts and her work was a great source of inspiration to Douglas Hyde and Lady Augusta Gregory a century later.

))))▶ *Lady Augusta Gregory, Douglas Hyde*

BROWNE, NOEL (1915–97)

Minister for health (1948–51). Dr Noel Browne planned and implemented a hospital-building programme in his successful attempts to banish tuberculosis from Ireland. He brought about the introduction of many health and social welfare innovations. He served in the Opposition, as an Independent, with the National Progressive Democratic Party, the Fianna Fáil Party and the Socialist Labour Party for Dublin South East and Dublin North Central between 1948 and 1982, and was senator from 1973 to 1977. He died at University College Hospital, Galway, the hospital for which he had laid the foundation stone in the 1940s.

))))▶ *Fianna Fáil*

BRUCE, EDWARD (d. 1318)

King of Ireland (1316–18); brother of Robert I Bruce, the king of Scotland. Edward Bruce landed in Ireland in 1315 with the intention of defeating the Anglo-Norman rulers established there and founding in their place a Scots-Irish kingdom. Two years of military success against the Anglo-Norman nobles followed, aided by native chieftains and Robert Bruce himself, but no firm settlement or organization resulted. Robert Bruce's departure left Ireland in anarchy, and Edward Bruce was killed on 14 October 1318 at the Battle of Faughart, near Dundalk.

BRUGHA, CATHAL (1874–1922)

Republican soldier and statesman. Crippled as a result of wounds sustained in the Easter Rising of 1916, Cathal Brugha went on to become the first defence minister of the Dáil Éireann when it was formed in 1919. Implacably opposed to the Anglo-Irish Treaty, he was one of the first casualties when civil war broke out in 1922.

))))▶ *Anglo-Irish Treaty*

BRUTON, JOHN (b. 1947)

Fine Gael politician and prime minister (1994–97). As Taoiseach the Fine Gael leader alienated many in nationalist Ireland, who compared his well-publicized impatience with republican aspirations and his scaldingly

LEFT: Sir Basil Brooke with his wife.

RIGHT: Éamon de Valera, who presided over the Bunreacht na
Éireann Constitution.
BELOW: John Bruton.

expressed contempt for the violent excesses of republican
terrorists with his apparent eagerness to conciliate northern
Unionist opinion, however intransigent. Whatever the case it
is possible now to see that he may in this respect have been
the right Taoiseach for that particular phase of a difficult
peace process, bringing the nothern Protestants further down
the road to constitutional change than they
could ever have envisaged.

))))▶ *Fine Gael*

BUNREACHT NA hÉIREANN
CONSTITUTION (1937)

Revised Constitution of Ireland, drawn up under the
supervision of Éamon de Valera. Though based on
the Constitution of the Free State as drawn up in 1922, the
constitution de Valera brought forward to replace it differed
in significant respects. Strengthening both the office of prime
minister (now for the first time called Taoiseach) and that
of the president, the new constitution was written in close

co-operation with de Valera's friend Father John Charles
McQuaid, soon to be appointed Archbishop of Dublin, the
constitution enshrined Catholic spiritual and social doctrine
alike in Irish law, but left the door open for amendments so
that the 1937 constitution has been successfully adapted over
the years in response to the changing political and social
conditions and remains the bedrock of the Irish state.

))))▶ *Éamon de Valera, Irish Free State*

BUNTING, EDWARD (1773–1843)

Collector of Irish music. Born in Armagh, Bunting
became an apprentice organist in Belfast at the
precocious age of 11 and lived with the family of Henry Joy
McCracken. Deeply influenced by the Belfast Harp Festival
of 1792, at which he transcribed the airs he heard, he set off
on a series of journeys through Ulster and Connacht
collecting further specimens of Irish music. His *General
Collection of Irish Music* appeared in 1796. He later added to
this collection and published several more which today remain
an important early source of Irish music. These collections
were also very influential in their time, inspiring Thomas
Moore as a poet and musician and Robert Emmet as a patriot.

))))▶ *Belfast Harp Festival, Robert Emmet, Henry Joy
McCracken, Thomas Moore*

BURGH, RICHARD DE, 2ND EARL OF ULSTER (1259–1326)

Royalist supporter. Richard de Burgh upheld his beliefs by leading Royalist forces against Edward Bruce (1315). De Burgh's daughter was married to Edward's brother, Robert, and when his son-in-law joined his brother in Ireland in 1317, Richard de Burgh was imprisoned to protect him.

))))▶ *Edward Bruce*

BURKE, EDMUND (1729–97)

Dublin-born parliamentarian, first elected as a Whig MP in 1756. Noted as an orator and a political theorist, Burke helped to shape government politics, not only towards Ireland, but also in regards to India, America and France. Although sympathetic to the Catholic cause, his reformist zeal lessened considerably after the shocking events of the French Revolution in 1789.

BURNTOLLET BRIDGE AMBUSH (1969)

In January 1969 a Civil Rights March, organised by students at Queens University set off to walk from Belfast to Derry. Constantly harrassed by loyalists along the way and often impeded by the police, the marchers were viciously assaulted by a large crowd at Burntollet bridge a few miles from their destination. Many of the attackers were later identified as police reservists and Orangemen. The event clearly showed that the Unionist authorities would not tolerate any opposition and were prepared to use violence to quash it.

))))▶ *Terence O'Neill*

BUTLER, 'BLACK' THOMAS, EARL OF ORMOND (1532–1614)

One of the most politically astute of the Butlers, he had been raised as a Protestant at the English court and was a favourite of Elizabeth I. He acted as her commander in Munster at the time of the second Desmond rebellion, and as her lieutentant general from 1957 during the Nine Years' War. At the same time, he was safeguarding his own ancestral territories, which remained secure until after Elizabeth's death. Late in life he became a Catholic.

BUTLER, RED PIERS (1467–1539)

Piers (also Pierce) Butler, 8th Earl of Ormond, 'the Red Earl', who fought against rebel Irish lords. In 1515 the 7th Earl of Ormond died without issue. Piers, his cousin, assumed the title of 8th Earl and in 1522 was made lord-lieutenant of Ireland. In 1528 he was obliged to relinquish the title to his cousin, Thomas Boleyn, and was created Earl of Ossory as compensation. Boleyn died without male issue in 1537 and Piers was restored to the earldom of Ormond in 1538.

))))▶ *Earls of Kildare*

LEFT: Edmund Burke.
ABOVE RIGHT: A cartoon of Isaac Butt from an 1937 edition of Vanity Fair.
BELOW RIGHT: Carrickfergus Castle.

BUTT, ISAAC (1813–79)

Home Rule campaigner. Born into a Protestant Donegal family, as a young lawyer Butt spoke out against Daniel O'Connell; over time, though, he came to favour a limited form of Home Rule. Never forsaking his primary Protestant allegiances, or his respect for Britain and its Empire, he argued for what today might be described as 'devolution', an arrangement by which an Irish parliament would take charge of the island's domestic affairs, leaving London to handle foreign policy.

))))▶ *Home Rule, Daniel O'Connell*

BYRNE, MILES (1780–1862)

United Irishman and a leader of the 1798 Rebellion. Byrne subsequently worked in an Irish timber-yard for four years but he became involved in a rebellion planned by Robert Emmet in 1803, visiting Napoleon to solicit support. He served in Napoleon's Irish forces throughout the Napoleonic Wars and retired to Paris.

))))▶ *Robert Emmet, Napoleonic Wars*

CALLAN, BATTLE OF (1261)

Decisive battle in the Irish Gaelic resistance to Anglo-Norman expansion. During most of the thirteenth century, Anglo-Norman success was based on military superiority in technology, but not numbers. The Irish chieftains improved their military equipment and hired gallowglass mercenaries. In 1261 the MacCarthys, confined to south-west Ireland, decided to stand firm against the Anglo-Normans under Lord FitzThomas at Callan in County Kilkenny. The victory was decisive and ended Anglo-Norman expansion from northern Kerry. A further battle in the north at Áth an Kip (1270) held the Anglo-Normans back in Ulster. As a result Anglo-Norman control of three-quarters of Ireland shrank to one-third over the next century.

))))▶ *Conquest of Ireland*

CAREW, SIR GEORGE (1555–1629)

Soldier and statesman. In 1574 George Carew travelled to Ireland to serve as a soldier against Irish rebels. Earning distinction at the defence of Leighlin Castle, County Carlow, in 1577, he was marked out for promotion and enjoyed favour from the English queen Elizabeth I. In 1586 he was knighted and served as Master of Ordnance in Ireland from 1588–92. Between 1600–03 Carew acted as president of Munster, ruthlessly suppressing a rebellion led by Aodh Ó Néill (Hugh O'Neill), Earl of Tyrone. In 1626 he was created Earl of Totnes. Carew accumulated a substantial and important collection of manuscripts and books recording Irish history and genealogy.

))))▶ *Elizabeth I of England, Aodh Ó Néill*

CARRICKFERGUS CASTLE (1180)

Strategic Norman castle with a 27-m (89-ft) high keep, built in 1180. Carrickfergus has played a major role in Irish military history. From the Irish *Carraig Fhearghais*, 'Fergus's Rock', the name refers to the spur overlooking the harbour at Carrickfergus on Belfast Lough, and the ancient King Fergus, is said to have been shipwrecked there in the early AD 300s. In 1316 Edward Bruce seized the castle. Two years later it fell to Edward I's forces and remained an English stronghold thereafter. The deposed King James II held it in 1689 but lost it to William III's forces the same year. The castle is one of the best-preserved in Ireland and retains its portcullis.

))))▶ *James II of England, William III of England*

CARSON, EDWARD (1854–1935)

Lord Carson of Duncairn; Unionist politician.
Edward Carson has a footnote in Irish literary history
as the barrister who savaged Oscar Wilde to such devastating
effect in court in 1895, yet his real fame came later, in the
realm of politics. In the Home Rule Crisis of 1912–14, he
joined another hardline Unionist, James Craig, in calling for
armed resistance in the face of any 'betrayal' by London.
'Ulster will fight, and Ulster will be right!' was the slogan
under which Carson marched; to back up his threat, he
founded the Ulster Volunteer Force (UVF). A Solemn
League and Covenant signed by almost half a million
Ulstermen and women, along with a Declaration that they
would defend the Union to the death, presented London
with a moral – and a military – force to be reckoned with.
The willingness of Carson, a Dubliner, to accept leadership
of the Ulster Unionists did not stem from any enthusiasm
for the notion of partition. On the contrary, he hoped the
exemption of Ulster from Home Rule
would render the whole project
unworkable: for him the 'victory'
of 1921 was a bittersweet moment.

▶ *James Craig, Ulster*
Volunteer Force,
Oscar Wilde

ABOVE: Sir Edward Carson speaking at Drumbeg.
ABOVE RIGHT: Sir Roger Casement.
RIGHT: The Rock of Cashel.

CASEMENT, SIR ROGER (1864–1916)

British diplomat and Irish patriot. Born in Dublin
into an Anglo-Irish family, Casement grew up to enter
the diplomatic corps, but was appalled by what he saw of
colonialism in action in Africa and South America. Though
knighted by the Crown in 1911, he had been becoming
increasingly disenchanted with British rule. Retiring, he
enlisted in the Irish Volunteers. Arrested while attempting
to import arms on the eve of the Easter Rising, he was
condemned to death; the British authorities doing their best
to blacken his character in the eyes of his Irish supporters by
the release of his 'Black Diaries'. With their frank accounts
of the hero's homosexual activities, these were long (but
perhaps wrongly) dismissed as British forgeries. Hanged at
Wandsworth Prison, London, in 1916, his remains were
disinterred in 1965 and brought back to Dublin for an
official state funeral.

▶ *Banna Strand, Easter Rising*

CASHEL, ROCK OF

Limestone formation of 60 m (200 ft) in the middle
of the Tipperary Plain. The site of this mystic citadel,
which would be home to generations of Eoganacht kings of

Munster, is said to have been revealed to the dynasty's founder, Corc mac Luigthig, in a dream, when he saw a yew bush growing on top of a stone. Another visionary, St Patrick, is also said to have resided there for a time: it was there, chroniclers claim, that he introduced the idea of the

shamrock as a religious symbol. Such mythical associations apart, the rock has appealed to more down-to-earth generals: Brian Bóroimhe and his successors occupied the rock from AD 978 onwards. With the Synod of Cashel in 1101 began the rock's history as an important centre for the Irish Church: an impressive 'ecclesiastical fortress' flourished there until the eighteenth century.

))))➤ *Brian Bóroimhe, Synod of Cashel, Shamrock*

CASHEL, SYNOD OF (1101)

Meeting of leading figures in Irish Church in 1101. Called in response to persistent papal complaints of abuse, the reforming Synod of Cashel set out to settle what seems to have been a degree of ecclesiastical anarchy, with bishops and abbots at local level dividing up the territory – and the tithes – as best suited them. Dividing the island into two, tightly defined archdioceses run from Cashel and Armagh respectively, the reforms also toughened up Ireland's notoriously lax rules on divorce and marriage laws which had permitted matches well within the normally forbidden degrees of kinship.

))))➤ *Armagh, Rock of Cashel*

CASTLEREAGH, LORD (1769–1822)

Robert Stewart, Viscount Castlereagh; statesman. Born in Dublin to a County Down family, Stewart was elected to the Irish parliament in 1790; as Chief Secretary (1798–1801) he helped steer the Act of Union through parliament. Keeping a cool head through the tumult of 1798, he advocated the big stick during but the carrot after, supporting Lord Cornwallis's call for moves towards Catholic Emancipation in the years that followed. Appointed foreign secretary in 1812, he won renown as a skilled diplomatic operator on the European stage. Apparently fearing that his homosexuality was about to be revealed, he committed suicide in 1822.

))))➤ *Catholic Emancipation*

CASTLETOWN HOUSE (1722)

Grand Palladian house, situated beside the River Liffey in Celbridge, County Kildare. Castletown House was built by William Connolly, Speaker of the Irish House of Commons and Commissioner of the Revenue. The architect who designed the house was Alessandro Galilei (1691–1737) from Florence. The house stayed with the Connolly family until the death of Lord Carew's mother in 1965, when it was put up for auction. In 1967 Desmond Guinness bought Castletown and made it the headquarters of the Irish Georgian Society. In 1990 The Office of Public Works acquired the house and it is currently undergoing refurbishment.

CATHACH

Probably the oldest surviving manuscript in Ireland. The *Cathach* is a Latin psalter which is attributed to St Colm Cille and is now preserved in the library of the Royal Irish Academy in Dublin. Its name derives from the Irish word *cath*, meaning 'battle', and it was carried into battle by the O'Donnells of Donegal for good luck. It is also believed by some to be the actual copy of the psalms made without permission by Colm Cille which led to his exile in Scotland.

))))➤ *St Colm Cille*

CATHOLIC ASSOCIATION (1824)

Mass-movement for Catholic Emancipation, established in 1824. To begin with the Catholic Association was just the latest in a line of movements set up by middle-class Catholics attempting to lobby for political representation, but this society was transformed by the introduction of the 'Catholic Rent'. Raising a charge of a penny per person per month on members drawn from every section of Catholic society, the Association harnessed huge popular support – and, over time, huge sums of money. Closed down in 1825 to avoid prosecution by the authorities, the Association was re-formed the following year, its constitution, in theory at least, committing it to avoid 'political' action.

))))➤ *Catholic Emancipation, Daniel O'Connell*

CATHOLIC COMMITTEE (1760–1811)

Eighteenth-century broad-based body set up to represent Catholic interests and to work towards Catholic Emancipation. Although established in 1760 it was not until 1791 that the movement became most active. United Irishman Theobald Wolfe Tone became secretary in 1792. A representative Catholic Convention was organized for December 1792 to work towards the repeal of the remaining Penal Laws. While predominantly middle class, the convention was important in the process of Catholic politicization and helped pave the way for Daniel O'Connell in the nineteenth century. The Catholic Relief Act of 1793 granted some of the demands and was followed by disbandment of the organization.

))))➤ *Catholic Relief Acts, Penal Laws, Theobald Wolfe Tone, United Irishmen*

CATHOLIC EMANCIPATION

The granting of political rights to Catholics, since the 1690s severely restricted by Penal Laws. Although universal adult suffrage would not be achieved in the United Kingdom until women won the vote in 1928, the property-holding qualification meant that the majority of men were also disenfranchised until well into the nineteenth century. What was by any standards an injustice seemed a national affront to Catholic Ireland, forbidden to participate in the political process at any level. Prohibitions on Catholics occupying minor official positions had been progressively

relaxed since the late-eighteenth century, but still in the 1820s no Catholic was allowed to become a judge, a king's counsel, an MP or a member of the Privy Council. The small-scale lobby of a Catholic elite took off when Daniel O'Connell turned the campaign for emancipation into a mass-movement, yoking the demand for representation together with a number of other grievances of the Irish poor. Despite parliamentary support at Westminster, proposed legislation fell foul of the House of Lords and George IV, but victory was finally won with the Catholic Relief Act of 1829.

))))➤ *Daniel O'Connell, Penal Laws*

CATHOLIC RELIEF ACTS (1774–93)

Acts relaxing Penal Laws. The last quarter of the eighteenth century saw a relaxation of the Penal Laws brought in to curtail Catholic participation in civil society. The most important of these, the Relief Act of 1778, granted certain hereditary land rights

ABOVE: The statue of Daniel O'Connell in Dublin, commemorating his role in Catholic Emancipation.
BELOW LEFT: St Kevin's Church, Glendalough.

to Catholics. Other Acts allowed Catholics to buy land and to organize education. Measures against Catholic clergy were also relaxed. The 1793 Act, following pressure from the Catholic Convention, permitted Catholics to have the right to vote and to hold some government jobs. Most of the remaining restrictions were lifted with Catholic Emancipation in 1829.

)))➡ *Catholic Association, Catholic Committee*

CATHOLICISM

Christian Church. The 'one holy, Catholic and apostolic Church' as it calls itself, traces its ecclesiastical ancestry – and hence its spiritual authority – back to Christ Himself. Its priests are, it claims, the direct successors to Jesus's hand-picked apostles, its presiding popes the heirs of St Peter – with all the powers that implies. 'Thou art Peter,' said the Saviour (Matthew, 16:18), 'and upon this rock I will build my church. And the gates of hell shall not prevail against it. And I will give to thee the keys of the kingdom of heaven. And whatsoever thou shalt bind upon earth, it shall be bound also in heaven: and whatsoever thou shalt loose on earth, it shall be loosed also in heaven.' Yet the history of Christendom can be seen as a series of setbacks for the Church and challenges to its universal authority, from its rejection by the Eastern Orthodox Church in the Middle Ages to the Reformation of the sixteenth century. Henry VIII's break with Rome in 1534 was a matter of more political than theological significance, but increasingly through the decades that followed England was coming to define itself as a militantly Protestant power to rival the Catholic superpowers of France and Spain. Catholicism has tended to be regarded in this context not so much as a church, but as an ideological empire, bent on enforcing and extending the repressive rule of 'popery'.

The Roman Catholic Church in Ireland accordingly found itself in the unaccustomed position of being an institution marginalized, even driven underground, as the authorities set about hunting down those aristocratic 'recusants' who, though nominally loyal to the English Church were believed to be guilty of backsliding into Roman ways. Yet while the persecutions of the sixteenth and seventeenth centuries were severe, even the fanatical Cromwell stopped short of his original plan to extirpate Catholicism completely in Ireland, thus ensuring the faith's survival, if only among a despised and disregarded peasantry.

BELOW: The banishment and exile of Irish Catholic youths, 1655.

Its adherents kept down by state-sanctioned discrimination well into the nineteenth century, and by unofficial Protestant prejudice long after, the Irish Catholic Church took on a peculiarly schizophrenic character. An instinctively conservative institution, time and again it found itself forced into the radical camp, its hierarchy often badly at odds with its rank-and-file members in the rural parishes. While the Church's day seemed at last to have come with the explicitly Catholic administration of Éamon de Valera, time was arguably running out for Catholicism's unique authority in Ireland. Not only did the Church's close relationship with the Free State government clearly stand in the way of nationalist aspirations for a united Ireland, to include northern Protestants, but its rules on moral issues, such as contraception and divorce, were becoming increasingly irksome to a people beginning to covet the personal freedoms on offer in other countries touched by what churchmen scathingly called 'the permissive society'.

)))⟩ *Bunreacht na hÉireann, Catholic Emancipation*

CATTLE RAID OF COOLEY (*TÁIN BÓ CUAILGNE*)

One of the great tales of early European literature. First written down in the eighth century – but belonging to a much older vernacular tradition and containing a mixture of legendary and semi-historical material – it tells of how Méadhbha (Queen Maeve of Connacht) goes to Ulster to get the Brown Bull of Cooley, the only bull in Ireland comparable with the white one owned by her husband. When the Ulstermen refuse to give her the bull she sends in her army but because of a magic spell only Cú Chualainn is left to stand against them. The story has many episodes but eventually the Ulstermen triumph and the brown bull kills the white one and carries it off on its horns across the country. The epic reflects the political tensions between provincial rulers in early Ireland.

)))⟩ *Connacht, Cú Chualainn, Méadhbha*

CEANNT, EAMON (1881–1916)

Republican leader. Born in Galway, a policeman's son, Ceannt went on to serve the administration as a Dublin Corporation clerk but was from early on discontented with British rule. A member of the Gaelic League from 1900, he joined the secret Irish Republican Brotherhood in 1913, becoming a founder-member of

the Irish Volunteers. One of the leaders of the 1916 Rising, he was among those executed in its aftermath.

)))⟩ *Gaelic League, Irish Republican Brotherhood, Pádraig Pearse, Joseph Plunkett.*

CÉIDE FIELDS

Early Neolithic farm. The Céide Fields, on the north coast of County Mayo, consists of a large set of early field systems, hut sites and court cairns (burial mounds). These are all believed to date from early Neolithic times. The walls of the fields are said to be part of the prehistoric landscape that has been protected and preserved over the years by the growth of the bogland in the area. Modern farmers and archeologists have discovered the fields and have mapped the wall systems. A visitor centre was established at the Céide Fields in 1994.

)))⟩ *Neolithic People*

CÉILE DÉ

The Céile Dé, or 'companion of God', sometimes known in English as the Culdee, was a member of a strict religious movement within the early Irish monastic Church. Their ascetic beliefs and practices differentiated them from other monks who lived under less severe regimes. They believed in fasting, abstention from alcohol and many

ABOVE : The aftermath of the Easter Rising, after which Eamon Ceannt was executed.
ABOVE RIGHT: The monastery at Clonmacnoise, where members of the Céile Dé lived.

of them lived as hermits, devoting their lives to prayer and meditation. However, they were sometimes associated with major monastic establishments such as Tallaght and Clonmacnoise, where they appear to have lived as part of the community.

>>> *Clonmacnoise*

aspects. At its most obvious, straightforward level this can be seen in the swirling abstracts of the great works of Christian calligraphic art, the monks' illuminations recognizably kin to the weapons and jewellery of older generations of pagan craftsmen in Celtic Europe. Yet the influence can be traced topographically too: Christianity's evolution as

CÉITINN, SEATHRÚN (C. 1580–C. 1644)

Irish writer. Céitinn (Geoffrey Keating) is the author of *Foras Feasa ar Éirinn*, a major history of Ireland, written at the same time as the *Annals of the Four Masters* but quite different in approach and content. A native of County Tipperary, he trained and was ordained as a Catholic priest in Ireland before going to France for further study. His family was of Norman origin and in his work he tried to draw together the different strands of Catholic tradition in Ireland (including the Gaels, the Normans and Old English) against the new English enemy. He also wished to contradict the negative picture of Ireland and the Irish given by Elizabethan commentators such as Edmund Spenser.

>>> **Annals of the Four Masters**

CELTIC CHRISTIANITY

Christianity as distinctively defined and reimagined in its early-Irish context. A new spiritual and social overlayering applied to a pre-existing pagan, Celtic culture, Irish Christianity inevitably reflected that fact in many of its

a popular creed in Ireland seems to have involved a large degree of what is known as 'syncretism' with existing pagan beliefs. The revered St Brigid, for example, is now assumed by scholars to have been a Christianized version of the Celtic fire-and-fertility goddess Brigit, while Ireland's many holy wells will almost certainly have had previous pagan significance as sacred springs. It is unlikely to have been a complete coincidence, moreover, that the nation's Christian centre at Armagh should have corresponded more or less exactly with the site of Ulster's legendary capital of Eamhain Macha.

>>> *St Brigid, Celts*

RIGHT: Saint Brigid, believed to be the christianized version of the Celtic fire-and-fertility goddess Brigit.

CELTIC LANGUAGES

Irish, Scots Gaelic and Manx are three mutually intelligible languages belonging to the same branch of the Celtic language. They are known as Q-Celtic languages, while Welsh, Cornish and Breton – to which they are more distantly related – are known as P-Celtic languages. The speakers of the Q-Celtic languages were unable to pronounce 'p' and either dropped it completely – *pater* in Latin, meaning 'father' is *athair* in modern Irish – or replaced it with a 'c' or 'q' sound, so the modern Irish for 'purple' is *corcora*.

CELTS (C. 300 BC)

Iron Age settlers in Ireland. The Celts, believed to have arrived in Ireland around 300 BC, were Indo-European in origin and had gradually swept across central Europe, establishing their Iron Age cultures, known as Hallstatt and La Tène. These descriptions relate to the types of metalwork and stone sculpture left as evidence of their settlement. For many, the Celts are accepted as the dominant ancestors of the modern-day Irish. Their mythology and sagas remain an integral part of Irish pagan mythology.

The Celts organized themselves by clans, or Tuatha, which operated independently, only joining together when their elected king required it. By the beginning of the Christian era in the tenth century, five Tuatha existed, the Ulaidh (Ulster), the Midhe (Meath), the Laighin (Leinster), the Mumhain (Munster) and the Connacht (Connacht). Wealth was measured in terms of cattle rather than land and the Celts, although essentially farmers, had specialists such as lawyers and writers. With no major settlements the Celtic farmers sowed wheat, barley, oats and flax, and harvested hay. Pigs were their preferred meat source, as were fish and wild animals, although they also had sheep they bred for wool. Their buildings were made using a post-and-waffle system and they tended to congregate within hill forts or other sites known as ring forts. Wherever possible settlements would be situated in easy defendable positions.

Celts were adept at milling, dairy work, malting, dyeing, spinning and weaving. The preferred clothing was a long, linen tunic, belted at the waist. Most men and women wore a woollen cloak called a 'brat'. Richer Celts also wore shoes. The Celts were renowned for their metalwork, evidenced by the eighth-century Tara Brooch. Musicians tended to play the harp. Most Celtic oral history is confused and it was not until the seventh century that written sources began to tell how the five Tuatha operated and interacted. In the beginning the Celts were not a coherent race or nation. They were, however, united with a similar dialect. As their population increased the Celtic influence spread across Ireland and the rest of the British Isles. The Celtic colonization of Ireland began when they moved westward from the mainland of Britain. Essentially they replaced the older Mesolithic people who had inhabited the land until then. Although

ABOVE: Celtic bronze disc from Ireland.
CENTRE: Reconstruction of Celtic village, near Quin, Ireland.
RIGHT: A traditional High Cross, in County Clare.

several Celtic dialects were spoken in the British Isles, it is the 'Q' dialect that was spoken in Ireland and in Scotland as opposed to the more common 'P' dialect that was spoken in England, Wales and Brittany. Although hill forts had been constructed in prehistoric Ireland, the ones that have been questionably identified as Celtic dominate this aspect of the Irish landscape. The most famous hill fort in County Meath, called Tara, incorporates graves, farmsteads and the remains of a palace. More recent excavations at Navan, near Armagh, have uncovered a large bank within which a circular wooden structure, believed to be a palace, had been built. In the south-west of Ireland about 50 hill forts show the Celts' fear of a sea-borne invasion from Spain. Unreliable dating of finds and the forts themselves make it difficult to pinpoint their origin or purpose.

Much of what is known about the social system of the Celts derives from Roman writing or from other classical authors of the period. It appears that Julius Caesar considered them to be closely connected to the Gauls. They had a king, a warrior aristocracy, which Caesar called *Eques*, or 'warriors', and freeman farmers, which in Roman is translated into *plebs*, or 'commoners'. Outside these groups were the Druids or 'men of learning and religion'. They came from the warrior class. The Celts were patriarchal, valued art and music and had a vibrant literary culture in the form of orally delivered sagas and stories.

Gradually, over the centuries, the five Tuatha vied for dominance of the island. Initially it appears that the Ulaidh were dominant but by the fifth century the Midhe were in ascendancy due to their close connections with the Connachts. By the sixth century the descendants of Niall of the Nine Hostages ruled most of the Laighin from Tara, in addition to claiming kingship of the Ulaidh, the Connacht and the Midhe, although in effect their rule was very loose. Between AD 734 and 1002 two branches of Niall's descendants, the Cenel Neogain (the northern) Uí Néill and the Clan Cholmain (southern Uí Néill) took it in turns to be kings of Ireland. Eventually, having gradually gathered all their strength, the Mumhain contested this deal and took part of Connacht, later to become County Clare, in battle. The Mumhain, based at Cashel, did not manage to follow up this success with a greater claim to the Irish throne until Brian Bóroimhe became the king of the Mumhain in the eleventh century. Soon, however, the Normans would lay claim to their kingdoms and by 1155, Henry II of England – a Norman – was given over lordship of Ireland by Pope Adrian IV. In time this would seal the Celts' fate and make a Norman invasion inevitable. The Normans did land in 1167.

))))▶ *Celtic Languages, Halstatt Civilization, Niall of the Nine Hostages, Tara Brooch, Tuatha*

CHICHESTER, SIR ARTHUR (1563–1625)

English soldier and colonial official. Sent to Ireland by Elizabeth I in 1597 to put down Aodh Mór Ó Néill's (Hugh O'Neill's) rebellion, he proved well-equipped for the task, his scorched-earth policy in Tyrone and his transportation of communities from the Ulster marches proving brutally effective – though they left a bitter aftertaste for generations. As lord deputy of Ireland from 1604, Chichester showed himself to be a softer touch where religion was concerned, being prepared to tolerate Catholic observance where it posed no threat to public order. Criticized for this liberalism, he was demoted from his position in 1614, although he was granted the title of lord treasurer of Ireland.

))))▶ *Elizabeth I of England*

CHILDERS, ERSKINE (1870–1922)

Writer and Republican. Born of Anglo-Irish stock, Erskine Childers fought for Britain in the Boer War of 1899–1902, winning fame the following year as author of the classic espionage adventure *The Riddle of the Sands*. He seems to have taken a leaf out of that book in his attempt to run German guns to the Irish Volunteers in 1914, yet he remained committed enough to Britain to serve in the Royal Navy in World War I. A fully-fledged Sinn Féiner by 1921, he opposed the Anglo-Irish Treaty; captured by the Free State government in the ensuing civil war, he was executed by firing squad.

))))▶ *Anglo-Irish Treaty, Volunteers*

CHILDERS, ERSKINE (JR) (1905–74)

Fianna Fáil politician and president. Son of Erskine Childers, the famous arms smuggler. A well-respected and loyal Fianna Fáil member, he served in a number of posts in Fianna Fáil governments, particularly in the foreign office, and became the second Protestant president of the republic on the death of Éamon de Valera 1973. However he died of a heart attack the following year.

))))▶ *Éamon de Valera*

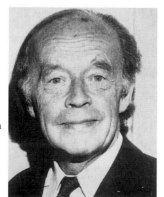

CHILDREN OF LIR

Famous legend known as one of the 'Three Sorrows of Storytelling', the other two being 'The Fate of the Children of Tuireann' and the 'Death of the Sons of Uisneach'. The latter was the basis of J. M. Synge's last play, *Deirdre of the Sorrows*. The story of the Children of Lir tells of how they were changed into swans by their stepmother, who was jealous of their father's attachment to them, and they were forced to spend 900 years on a lake in Westmeath, on the Atlantic and on the sea between Ireland and Scotland. When the spell was eventually lifted, they were so terribly old that they only lived long enough to be baptised by one of the early Christian saints.

))))▶ *J. M. Synge*

CHOLERA (1832–66)

Disease which killed up to 100,000 people in Ireland. First seen in Ireland in the second quarter of the nineteenth century, it was caused mainly by poor sanitation. The first outbreak (1832–33) was mainly an urban affair because of inadequate sewerage facilities, causing approximately 25,000 deaths. The Famine of 1847–49 weakened the population and about 35,000 died in the 1848–50 outbreak. Emigrants who left Ireland at this time contributed to the spread of the disease to Britain and the US. There were further outbreaks in 1853 and 1866, but advances in sanitation and medical science meant that the threat from the disease was virtually eliminated by end of the century.

))))▶ *Great Famine*

CHRIST CHURCH CATHEDRAL, DUBLIN (1038)

Church of Ireland Cathedral, Winetavern Street, Dublin. A cathedral church has stood on this site since around 1038, when Dublin's Norse ruler King Sitric constructed it in collaboration with the city's Bishop Dunan. That building having been destroyed in the Anglo-Norman invasion of 1169–70, however, the victorious Norman Richard de Clare – known as 'Strongbow' – had a new cathedral built on the same site. This is, in its, essentials the church that we see today, though it was expanded in the fourteenth century and extensively rebuilt in 1871 in the then-prevailing Gothic revivalist style.

))))▶ *Richard de Clare, Vikings*

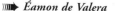

CHRISTIAN BROTHERS (1802)

Catholic teaching order; founded by Edmund Rice (1762–1844) in Waterford in 1802, to enable poor Catholic boys to receive education. Emphasis was placed on primary education but it also developed at a secondary level. Disagreement over the National Board led to a withdrawal from the state system in 1836. It played a central role in Irish education throughout the nineteenth and twentieth centuries, teaching history and Irish, and incul-cating a sense of national identity as opposed to the state system, which sought to produce compliant pro-British citizens. Many Irish revolutionaries and leaders, including Pádraig Pearse and Éamon de Valera, were past pupils.

)))➤ *Éamon de Valera, Pádraig Pearse*

CHURCH DISESTABLISHMENT (1869)

Ending of the privileged position of the (Anglican) Church of Ireland. Until the early nineteenth century the Church of Ireland was entitled to a 'tithe' or tax on the production of every Irish farmer – despite the fact that comparatively few of Ireland's people were members of

LEFT: Erskine Childers Jr, President of Ireland 1973–74
BELOW: Christ Church Cathedral, Dublin.
BELOW RIGHT: William Gladstone, who disestablished the Church of Ireland in 1869.

the Anglican Church. What seemed an outrageous imposition to the Catholic majority was regarded no less impatiently by the Presbyterians who had nothing but suspicion for the established Church. The more incongruous the prohibitions against Catholics came to seem, the less justification there could be for the favouring of the Church of Ireland: it was finally disestablished by Gladstone in 1869.

)))➤ *William Gladstone*

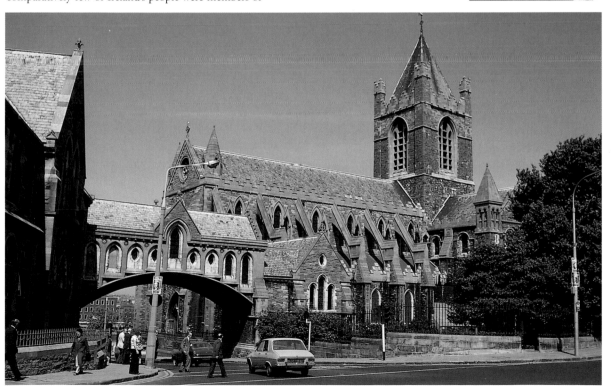

CHURCH OF IRELAND

 Name for the fully autonomous Anglican Church in Ireland. Though its doctrines are more or less identical with those of England's Anglican Church, and its members may worship at will in Anglican churches, the Church of Ireland is not subject to the authority of Canter-bury, and takes its independence – and its Irishness – extremely seriously. Tracing the ministry of its clergy back in a continuous succession to St Patrick, it shares many of its saints

with the Catholic Church. Though nominally 'Protestant', the churches of the Anglican communion do not in general depart so much as might be expected from Catholicism in terms of beliefs and values: the rupture with Rome that brought Anglicanism into being was, of course, more immediately political than theological. Though rejecting the ultimate authority of the pope, the Anglican Churches did not dispense with the whole idea of hierarchy; nor did they replace respect for institutional structures with an invididual-istic concern for personal piety.

Yet thanks to the special conditions prevailing in Ireland, the need to define itself against a peasant-Catholic 'Other', the Church of Ireland has generally proved more actively 'Protestant' than the average arm of Anglicanism. With its jealously-guarded autonomy, moreover, the Church could offer a home to many whose Protestant zeal the English Anglican Church had felt unable to accommodate. By Irish Protestant standards, however, the Church of Ireland remained doctrinally very easy-going. As in England, where the Anglican Church was known as the 'Tory Party at

ABOVE: Cross of the sculptures, at Clonmacnoise monastery, founded by St Ciarán.
RIGHT: Cistercian monk.
FAR RIGHT: Seán MacBride, founder of Clann na Poblachta.

prayer', the Church of Ireland became closely associated with the Anglo-Irish ruling caste or 'ascendancy'. The Church's own ascendancy in Ireland was resented equally by Catholics and dissenting Protestants – neither of which group was exempt when it came to paying tithes or taxes to the Church of Ireland clergy. This glaring injustice was eased in 1831 but the anomalies were not finally done away with until 1871, when William Gladstone's Disestablishment Act of 1869 was put into practice.

))))➤ *Catholicism, Church Disestablishment, Protestantism*

CIARÁN, ST (d. c. AD 556)

 Saint and scholar. Founder of the famous monastery at Clonmacnoise on the banks of the Shannon, County Offaly, St Ciarán was author of what is traditionally known as the *Lebor na hUidhre* ('Book of the Dun Cow'), since it was supposedly written on parchment made from the hide of his favourite cow. On it, legend has it, he wrote, to the dictation of the hero Fergus mac Roich, that great epic which has come down to us as the *Táin Bó Cuailgne* – 'The Cattle Raid at Cooley'.

))))➤ **Cattle Raid of Cooley,** *Clonmacnoise, Monasteries*

CISTERCIAN ORDER (1142)

Order of monks, founded in Cîteaux, France, 1098. A breakaway branch of the Benedictine Order formed to get back to the austere basics of the founder's Rule, the Cistercians were seen by the Church as an important weapon against complacency and corruption in the monasteries. They were brought to Ireland in 1142 by St Malachy specifically to assist in the process of reform of a monastic system which was deemed to have gone too much its own way: by the end of the twelfth century they had 27 establishments the length and breadth of Ireland. Yet, while introduced to impose order on monastic chaos, the order in Ireland was soon showing signs of 'going native' itself: the Irish houses had to be placed under the direct control of Cistercian monasteries in England, Wales and France.

))))➤ *Benedictine Order, Early Christian Ireland, St Malachy, Monasteries*

CIVIL RIGHTS MOVEMENT (1967)

Popular protest movement of the late 1960s and early 70s. Inspired by the US Civil Rights Movement and its efforts on behalf of Black Americans, the Northern Ireland Civil Rights Association (NICRA) was created in 1967 by Catholic activists. Their main demand was for electoral reform, an end to gerrymandered constituency boundaries that artificially promoted Protestant power as well as to property qualifications which were discriminatory in their effect. But the activists also pointed to a long list of other injustices, calling for the disbandment of the B Specials (a force of belligerently Protestant police reservists), and measures to prevent anti-Catholic bias in housing allocation and employment.

))))➤ *Bloody Sunday*

CLAN NA GAEL (19TH CENTURY)

Irish-American Revolutionary movement. With the failure of the Fenian rising of 1867, American sympathizers saw a need to rebuild the revolutionary effort from the ground up. Led by journalist Jerome J. Collins, Doctor William Carroll and John Devoy, within 10 years it had a list of 10,000 members. Allying itself with the Irish Republican Brotherhood, it supported the constitutional campaign of Charles Stewart Parnell. His disgrace appeared to leave no way to independence except a return to the path of violent struggle. From around 1900 it dedicated itself to funding – and arming – Republicans in Ireland.

))))➤ *John Devoy, Irish Republican Brotherhood, Charles Stewart Parnell*

CLANN NA POBLACHTA (1946)

Irish political party of the late-1940s and 50s. Founded in 1946 by ex-IRA chief of staff Seán MacBride to recover the radical idealism of the Republican cause, Clann na Poblachta brought together a motley group of malcontents, including die-hard anti-partitionists and socialists, and others disillusioned with de Valera's government. Yet despite his background as the son of John MacBride, the 1916 martyr, his own revolutionary past and his future role as a leading figure in Amnesty International, Seán MacBride was himself profoundly conservative in his outlook. Surpassing de Valera himself in his exhibitionistic Catholic piety, he joined Dublin's reactionary Archbishop MacQuaid in a crusade against godless communism while his party's fortunes foundered.

CLARE, RICHARD DE, 'STRONGBOW' (d. 1176)

Norman warrior and adventurer in Ireland. He succeeded as 2nd Earl of Pembroke in 1148. In 1153 he signed the Treaty of Westminster, which guaranteed the succession of Henry II of England. In 1168 he was persuaded by the deposed king of Leinster, Diarmaid Mac Murchadha (Dermot MacMurrough), to intervene on his behalf. By 1170 he had taken Waterford and married Diarmaid's daughter, Aoife, as his reward. By the end of the year he had added Dublin and Meath to his lands.

On Diarmaid's death in 1171 Strongbow became king of Leinster, an event which led to a rising by Ruairí Ó Conchubhair (Rory O'Connor) and Murchadh Ó Briain (Murrough O'Brien), who both died at Strongbow's hands. His conquests provoked Henry II's jealousy, however and when, in 1171, Henry arrived in Ireland, Strongbow offered his lands to the king as appeasement. In 1173 Strongbow helped Henry in Normandy and the following year Henry restored to Strongbow Wexford, Waterford and Dublin. He continued to meet resistance from Irish chieftains until his death.

⫸ *Diarmaid Mac Murchadha, Murchadh O'Briain*

CLARKE, THOMAS (1857–1916)

Irish Republican Brotherhood revolutionary; member of the Supreme Council of the IRB which organized the Easter Rising in 1916. Clarke was involved in the Fenian bombing campaign in England and was sentenced to life with penal servitude in 1883. He endured a brutal regime and went to the US when he was released after 15 years to work with John Devoy. He returned to Ireland in 1907 and helped reorganize the IRB, becoming a member of the Supreme Council. In 1915 he  persuaded its executive to set up a military council, which he joined in September. One of the seven signatories to the Proclamation of Independence which was read out at the Easter Rising in 1916, Clarke was in the GPO headquarters during the rising and was executed on 3 May 1916.

⫸ *John Devoy, Easter Rising, Fenian Movement, Irish Republican Brotherhood*

CLONMACNOISE (AD 545)

Early monastery, now a ruin, in County Offaly. Founded in AD 545 by St Ciarán, Clonmacnoise was destined to become pre-eminent as a centre not only of Christianity but of Celtic culture. Ciarán himself is said to have contributed to some of the illuminated manuscripts created here; the monks were also famous for the quality of their metalwork. So sumptuous a prize inevitably proved irresistible to raiders, both native tribesmen and seaborne Vikings: between the ninth and twelfth centuries the complex was sacked no fewer than 36 times. Yet the complex would endure, not finally closing down until 1552 when the English garrison from Athlone came down to put an end to its popish practices once and for all. Today, though in ruins, Clonmacnoise remains an impressive site, with several high crosses, two round towers and eight abandoned chapels.

⫸ *St Ciarán, High Crosses, Monasteries*

CLONTARF, BATTLE OF (CATH CHLUAIN TAIRBH) (1014)

Decisive battle ending Viking ambitions in Ireland. On the night of 22–23 April 1014 the Vikings of Dublin, under their leader Brodir of Man, rebelled against the High King of Ireland, Brian Bóroimhe, who had made Gaelic power supreme in Ireland. The Viking army was made up of local Viking troops, Vikings from Denmark and allies from Irish clans who hoped to seize territory from Brian. On 22 April Irish forces set up camp near Dublin. The Vikings planned to trick Brian's army into believing they had fled and Viking boats sailed off into the darkness, planning a surprise attack for the following morning. The Irish army suffered an initial setback when the Meath forces under Mael Seachnaill refused to fight. Brian himself, now an old man, remained in the rear in a tent, praying for victory. Brian's son Murchadh rallied the Irish forces but the battle was hard-fought until the loss of Viking leaders led to their disarray. Murchadh, however, was mortally wounded and Brian was killed in his tent by retreating Vikings.

))⟫ *Brian Bóroimhe*

COLLINS, MICHAEL (1890–1922)

IRA commander, chairman of the provisional government (January–June 1922). Collins cut his revolutionary teeth as a participant in the Easter Rising of 1916, but it was only in the years that followed that he found his true métier. As the IRA's director of Intelligence, he managed to penetrate the innermost reaches of British officialdom in Ireland. A consummate man of action, Collins was uncomfortable in his role as negotiator at the Anglo-Irish conference in October–December 1921 (Éamon de Valera chose him, it has been suggested, precisely to 'take the fall'). Despite mixed feelings of his own, Collins accepted his place in the provisional government and the led the pro-Treaty forces in the civil war that followed. Although he repeatedly sought reconciliation with the Republicans – and indeed embarked upon a peace-making mission in his final moment – he was killed in an ambush in West Cork on 22 August 1922.

He had said at the time that in signing the treaty he was effectively signing his own death warrant. It has also been suggested that he should not have underestimated the envy of de Valera.

))⟫ *Anglo-Irish Treaty, Easter Rising, Irish Republican Army*

NEAR LEFT: Modern statue of thirteenth century pilgrim at Clonmacnoise monastery.
RIGHT: General Michael Collins at Portobello barracks.

COLM CILLE, ST (AD 521–597)

Early Irish Christian saint. The most influential figure in the early Irish Church after St Patrick, Colm Cille (the 'dove of the church') was born in Gartan in County Donegal into the ruling Uí Néill dynasty. He founded a

number of important monasteries, including those at Durrow, Derry (the Irish name for Derry is *Doire Cholm Cille*, 'St Colm Cille's Oakgrove') and Iona, from where Christianity spread across Scotland. There he is more usually known by the Latin form of his name, St Columba. In truth he was anything but dove-like, for he had a great energy and strong personality which naturally drew people to him wherever he went. He got into trouble for making a copy of a psalter in the possession of St Finnian of Moville without permission, and this led to what is sometimes refered to as the world's first copyright ruling – 'to every cow belongs its calf, and to every book its copy'. It is possible that the *Cathach,* a manuscript now preserved in the Royal Irish Academy in Dublin may actually be the book in question.

ABOVE: St Colm Cille arrives in Inverness to convert the Picts.
RIGHT: O'Brien's Castle in Galway, which was destroyed by Cromwell's troops during the Confederate War.

He played an important diplomatic role at the Convention of Druim Ceat, and although often regarded as a self-imposed exile from Ireland, neither he nor his followers severed their links with their native land. Thus, long after his death, when Iona became subject to Viking attack, a new Columban centre was set up at Kells in County Meath.

))))▶ **Cathach, *Convention of Druim Ceat***

COLUMBANUS, ST (C. AD 543–615)

Sixth-century christian saint. Originally a monk who trained at Bangor Abbey in County Down, Columbanus played a major role in revitalizing Christianity in continental Europe, setting up monasteries in Gaul and Italy. A number of his letters to various popes and his sermons written in a scholarly Latin have survived, and these show him to be a strict disciplinarian and a committed churchman. Among his most important foundations are Luxeuil and Bobbio. Shortly after his death a monk from the Bobbio community, Jonas of Susa, wrote a life of Columbanus which gives an insight into his life and personality.

CONFEDERATE WAR (1641–53)

War against English control in Ireland. In 1641, parliament brought a bill of attainder against Thomas Wentworth, Earl of Strafford and lord-lieutenant of Ireland, which led to his execution. Released from Strafford's oppressive rule in Ireland, and frustrated at decades of English and Scottish settlement across the country, a Catholic rebellion broke out, combining the interests of Catholic peasantry and the old Anglo-Irish aristocracy, leading to the massacre of many Protestants in Ulster. Panic in England soon exaggerated the figures and this fuelled fears that Charles I and his Catholic queen, Henrietta Maria, were behind the rebellion; this fear was exacerbated by the fact that rebel leaders swore allegiance to the Crown and the rebellion spread across Ireland. In England terror of

Catholicism reached fever pitch, and eventually led to the English Civil War. Ormond defeated the Catholics in 1641, and again at Ross in 1643.

Despite this, the Catholic Confederation controlled most of Ireland. Charles I made a peace – known as the Cessation – to release some of his troops to England. This settled suspicions that were already rife in parliament of Charles's papist sympathies and made Ireland a royalist threat after the Civil War; this was confirmed by further peace deals negotiated by Ormond on the king's behalf in 1646 and 1649.

In 1649, Cromwell entered Ireland to destroy Irish resistance, initiating the massacres at Drogheda and Wexford; the problems did not die out, however, until 1653.

))))▶ *Oliver Cromwell, Rebellion of 1641*

CONFESSIO (5TH CENTURY)

The *Confessio* is said to be the work of the patron saint and national apostle of Ireland. This spiritual autobiography tells of a dream St Patrick had in Britain when Victoricus gave him a letter entitled 'The Voice of the Irish', and as he received it he heard the Irish population pleading with him to return to his native land. Despite the fact that he felt unable to fulfil the needs of the Irish people, he did return and toured the country baptizing and confirming his followers. His feast day is celebrated on 17 March.

))))▶ *St Patrick*

CONN CÉADCHATHACH (FL. AD 200)

King of central Ireland, Conn of the Hundred Battles was also ancestor of Niall Naoi nGiallach (Niall of the Nine Hostages). Around AD 200 Conn Céadchathach created a kingdom in the central part of Ireland. His enemy, Eoghan Mór, created the kingdom of Munster. They arranged a division of Ireland into 'Conn's Half' (the north) and 'Mogh's Half' (the south). Brian Bóroimhe was the first High King to overcome the division.

))))▶ *Brian Bóroimhe, Niall of the Nine Hostages*

CONNACHT

Province of Ireland; also known as Connaught. Battered from the west by the waves of the Atlantic, bordered to the east by the waters of the Upper Shannon, the present-day province of Connacht comprises the counties of Galway, Mayo, Sligo, Leitrim and Roscommon. Like the other Irish provinces, its territories correspond very roughly with those of one of the island's old Celtic kingdoms, this one largely under the control of the Ó Briain dynasty and its vassal families. The kingdom had its capital at Cruachain (now Rathcroghan, near Tulsk, Roscommon) where extensive earthworks still remain: it was from here, according to legend, that Méadhbha (Queen Maeve) and King Ailill sallied forth to do battle with the heroes of Ulster, the *Connachta* or Connachtmen's traditional rivals.

Relatively inhospitable, rugged and wet, and remote from the main areas of Anglo-Norman and later English settlement, Connacht remained outside the economic and political swim for several centuries. Galway apart, the province has few towns of any size. This lack of development has stood it in good stead in the era of heritage, and in an

BELOW: Lough Inagh, Connacht.

independent Ireland concerned to rediscover its 'Celtic' roots: what was once dismissed as 'backwardness' is now prized as cultural authenticity. Coastal and central Connacht now boast some of the most important remaining areas of Gaeltacht (literally 'Gaeldom'), districts in which Irish is still spoken on a daily basis. The long, slow decline of the Irish language was massively accelerated by the disruption that came with the Famine. As long ago as the mid-nineteenth century, the patriot Thomas Davis argued that 'A people without a language is only half a nation': today it can seem that the rest of Ireland look to the men and women of the Gaeltacht as their better half. To a considerable degree they have become keepers of the national identity as a whole: the tradition-bound nation, unsullied by Englishness, the Irish wish they were but know they have not been for a very long time.

))))▶ *Gaeltacht, Méadhbha*

CONNOLLY, JAMES (1868–1916)

Revolutionary, one of the leaders of the 1916 Easter Rising. Born in Edinburgh of Irish parents, Connolly joined the British Army at the age of 14, deserting seven years later to throw himself wholeheartedly into revolutionary activities. Having founded a number of socialist groups, he came to the fore during the Dublin lockout of 1913, taking up the baton when the workers' leader Jim Larkin was arrested by the authorities. As leader of the Irish Citizen Army, Connolly was one of the instigators of the Easter Rising of 1916, its military commander and the keeper of its socialist conscience. Seriously wounded in the fighting, he had to face the firing squad propped up in a chair: one of the most poignantly iconic images of the whole iconic episode.

)))▶ *Easter Rising, Irish Citizen Army*

CONQUEST OF IRELAND (12TH CENTURY)

Anglo-Norman control over Ireland from the late-twelfth century onwards. Anglo-Norman military activity was well-established in Ireland by the 1100s, principally by Richard de Clare ('Strongbow'), who became king of Leinster. This posed a threat to Henry II of England, who recognized the possibility of a rival Norman kingdom across the Irish Sea. In 1171, Henry crossed to Ireland to establish his authority over Strongbow, demand allegiance from the Irish kings and force the Irish Church to accept him as their overlord.

Henry's power remained conditional. In 1175 the High King Ó Conchubhair payed homage to Henry and acknowledged him as his overlord, but he was forced to abdicate under pressure from the other Irish kings, who resented the authority Henry had granted him in return for this homage. Irish kings in the north-west continued to resist the English king and initially he found there was little he could do about men such as John de Courcy, who conquered large parts of Ulster and set up his own lordships.

Under King John (1199–1216), Anglo-Norman power became more systematic and effective. In 1200 an Irish

ABOVE RIGHT: Henry II.
RIGHT: The Grand Parade, Cork.

exchequer was created, and in 1210 John by-passed the lords and set up a civil government, based on a series of new counties, created to act as administrative districts. He planned to reduce the feudal powers of the lords by instituting the rule of English law.

Nevertheless, despite increasing representation in the Irish parliament, the system was really only devised in the interests of the Anglo-Norman settlers, not the indigenous Irish. This contributed to the uprising in support of Edward Bruce. In the aftermath of his defeat in 1318, Anglo-Norman control was increased by the creation of new earldoms: Desmond, Kildare and Ormond. However, intermarriage and a shared

resistance to English royal power led the Anglo-Normans to become increasingly merged with the Irish. In the event, the earls of Kildare became effective rulers of Ireland until the 1500s. Following the Reformation, Ireland's Catholicism and England's Protestantism began a different agenda.

)))▶ *Earls of Kildare, Henry II of England*

COOKE, HENRY (1788–1865)

Protestant preacher and politician. As a speaker at the Synod of Ulster, the main forum of Presbyterian opinion, in 1829, Henry Cooke succeeded in driving the unitarians from the assembly for their denial of the divinity of Christ. The pious celebrity that achievement brought him prompted him to launch a more ambitious crusade, to publish what he called the 'banns' for a marriage between Presbyterianism and the Church of Ireland. This project polarized opinion more, many resenting what they saw as his presumption in appointing himself the protector of Protestantism.

CORK

Port city on south coast of Ireland. Situated at the marshy mouth of the River Lee (the Irish name *Corcaigh* means 'boggy'), the Irish Republic's second-largest city can probably claim to be the island's oldest. A settlement seems to have grown up here around St Finbar's monastery as early as the sixth century, and by the ninth century Vikings had established a port for trade with the interior. The Anglo-Normans came in their turn, and in 1189 the town was granted a royal charter by Henry II: a peaceful and prosperous future seemed to beckon. The reality was quite otherwise; the Anglo-Norman lords never managed to take a firm hold and for several centuries rival Gaelic warlords fought for advantage all around the city. Not until the late-sixteenth century did the English ascendancy colonize the city and its hinterland in earnest: when they did so, however, they came to stay; the presence of a significant Protestant population would markedly exacerbate tensions here through the years of Home Rule Crisis and Anglo-Irish War.

CORMAC MAC AIRT (d. AD 260)

King of Ireland from AD 218 after having his rivals Lugaidh Mac Con and Fergus Dubhdéadach murdered. Also known as Cormac Ua Cuinn and Cormac Ulfada. His rule was characterized by constant fighting with chieftains, and he was briefly exiled to Scotland. He is said to have brought water-mill technology into Ireland. In AD 254 Cormac abdicated and thereafter drafted laws. His activities and those of his grandfather, Conn Céadchathach (Conn of the Hundred Battles), are recorded in the Fenian cycle of Irish literature, which concentrated on the mythical band of warriors, the Fianna, led by Fionn mac Cumhaill, active in the reign.

))) ➤ *Fionn mac Cumhaill*

CORN LAWS (1815)

Laws prohibiting unlicensed grain exports; originally applied in England to ensure sufficient supplies of grain for the population there. After the Act of Union (1800), and with a changing economic situation, the purpose of the laws changed with the levies they imposed on imported grain, supporting the price, and thus benefiting farmers in both England and Ireland. By repealing these laws in 1846, Robert Peel made grain more affordable for the consumer, while farmers had to accept lower prices. The liberalization of the trade also meant that grain exports from Ireland actually increased during the Famine years when people were starving.

VOTE FOR COSGRAVE, A FELON OF OUR LAND.

COSGRAVE, WILLIAM THOMAS (1880–1965)

Fine Gael leader (1935–44). An Irish Volunteer from 1913 and a veteran of the Easter Rising of 1916, William T. Cosgrave was one of the most influential voices to be heard in favour of the Anglo-Irish Treaty. He was President of the Executive Council of the Irish Free State (1922–1932). First as founder of Cumann na nGaedheal and then afterwards as vice-president, then leader of Fine Gael, he argued tirelessly against what he saw as the idle irredentist fantasies of Éamon de Valera and Fianna Fáil. His son Liam Cosgrave was Taoiseach (1973–77).

➤ **Anglo-Irish Treaty, Cumann na nGaedheal, Easter Rising, Fine Gael**

COSTELLO, JOHN A. (1891–1976)

Irish prime minister (1948–51 and 1954–57). Attorney-general for the Irish Free State between 1926 and 1932, John Aloysius Costello joined the Dáil in 1933 as a Fine Gael member. Elevated to Taoiseach on the formation of the first inter-party government, or coalition, in 1948, he sprang an immediate surprise by announcing his intention to introduce the Republic of Ireland Act. After that, his tenure was anticlimactic: he had to mediate between the different demands of partners representing Labour, National Labour, the small farmers of Clann na Talmhan ('Party of the Land') and the purist Catholic republicans of the Clann na Poblachta. His second government, again a coalition, ended when Clann na Poblachta jumped ship in 1957, unwilling to condemn the border campaign the IRA had mounted the previous year.

➤ **Clann na Poblachta, Fine Gael**

COUNTER-REFORMATION (16TH CENTURY)

Religious and cultural movement which, although part of a European response within the Catholic Church to the Reformation, had a particular significance in Ireland, where a predominantly Catholic people found themselves under Protestant rule. Here, it was not merely a revision and revitalization of the practices and teachings of the Catholic Church, but also an attempt to put new structures in place in an atmosphere that was becoming increasingly hostile. The Penal Laws, including the Bishops' Banishment Act of 1697, which ordered all Catholic bishops and regular clergy to leave the country, and the destruction of the monasteries, meant that the Church could not function as before and new forms of ministry and instruction were urgently required. Catholics were neither permitted to teach or organize schools within the country, nor to go abroad to be educated. As part of the Counter-Reformation, however, a network of Irish seminaries was established across continental Europe, which not only trained priests, but also provided the impetus for significant cultural programmes such as the compilation of the *Annals of the Four Masters*.

➤ **Annals of the Four Masters, *Penal Laws***

LEFT: Election poster showing Cosgrave in prison uniform, 1919.

COURCY, JOHN DE (d. 1219)

Anglo-Norman conqueror of Ulster. De Courcy arrived in Ireland in 1176 as one of Henry II's entourage. In 1177 he seized the county of Downpatrick, adding Down and Antrim by 1182. His rule as an Anglo-Norman lord was ruthless, and he instituted merciless revenge when his brother was killed by an Irishman. De Courcy's success was a threat to the English Crown. In 1200 he was outlawed and his English estates seized. In 1204 he was captured by Hugh de Lacy, but won his freedom and his English lands back by providing hostages. De Lacy was awarded the lands that had previously belonged to de Courcy in Ireland, so the latter rebelled and operated a fleet to attack the Antrim coast. He was finally defeated in 1207.

)))➤ *Dundrum Castle, Henry II of England, Hugh de Lacy*

CRAIG, JAMES (1871–1940)

Unionist statesman and first prime minister of Northern Ireland. Born into the Belfast bourgeoisie, James Craig served with distinction in the Boer War of 1899–1902 and became a Unionist MP for East Down in 1906, campaigning with Carson in opposition to Home Rule. Interrupting his parliamentary career to go to the front in World War I, he became leader of the Ulster Unionist Party in 1921. As such he found himself the first prime minister of the new polity of Northern Ireland: he would hold the position for the rest of his life. In 1927 he was ennobled as Viscount Craigavon.

)))➤ *Sir Edward Carson, Home Rule*

CROAGH PATRICK

Mountain and place of pilgrimage on the coast of County Mayo. What scholars suspect may well have been a sacred site in pagan times has been hallowed in Irish Christian tradition since its association with St Patrick in the fifth century. The Saint is said to have climbed this conical mountain to fast and pray during Lent in AD 441, calling on God to preserve His faith in the land of Ireland. At the end of his fast, reassured by divine visions, Patrick blessed the Irish people and announced that, in token of God's grace, snakes would thenceforth be banished from the entire island. Penitential pilgrims in their tens of thousands – often barefoot – process to the summit each year on the last Sunday in July, known as 'Reek Sunday'.

)))➤ *St Patrick*

ABOVE: A statue of St Patrick, with the sacred mountain of Croagh Patrick in the background.

CROKE PARK (1913)

National headquarters of the Gaelic Athletic Association since 1913. Croke Park is the stadium at which the most important games and finals are played in Ireland. Named after an archbishop who was an early patron of the organization, it was also the scene of the first Bloody Sunday massacre, when Auxiliary police opened fire during a football match in November 1921, killing 12 people, including one of the players.

)))➡ *Bloody Sunday, Gaelic Athletic Association*

CROMWELL, OLIVER (1599–1658)

Parliamentary soldier and Lord Protector of the Commonwealth from 1653. By 1649 Cromwell was commander-in-chief and lord lieutenant of Ireland. He faced the consequences of the Catholic Confederate Rising in Ireland which, since 1641, had allied itself with the forces of the now-executed Charles I. Ireland was now viewed as a major threat, a potential power-base for a Royalist revival.

In 1649 Cromwell arrived in Ireland and attacked rebel strongholds at Drogheda and Wexford, massacring the defenders – most of whom were English Royalists – as well as many civilians. Cromwell saw these ruthless victories as a just revenge, authorized by God, for the massacre of Protest-ants in 1641. In 1650 he seized Cahir, Cashel, Kilkenny and Clonmel, and outlawed Catholic worship. Cromwell ordered that all Catholic lands east of the River Shannon should be seized and distributed amongst his troops. Former land-owners were expelled to Connacht. Only 22 per cent of Ireland was left in Catholic ownership. Thus, Cromwell laid the foundations for Irish support of James II in 1689.

)))➡ *Confederate War, English Civil War*

CROMWELLIAN PLANTATIONS (1652)

Protestant takeover of Gaelic-Irish land. Following the English Civil War and the beheading of England's Charles I in 1649, Oliver Cromwell took his army to Ireland, massacring thousands at Wexford and forcing the town of Drogheda into surrender. He instigated the Cromwellian Plantations, which reduced the Catholic ownership of land by 37 per cent amongst the native Irish. Cromwell took the land mainly from 'Old English' Catholics and gave it to new immigrants from Scotland and England, and to his men in lieu of their wages, as well as to investors of the Civil War effort. This meant that the landlords of the estates were often not present but simply reaped the benefits of the work of the poorly paid tenants, who had once owned the land. This situation led to serious levels of class warfare with the rich Protestant landlords against the poorer Catholic tenants, and ultimately Cromwell's actions resulted in the Land Wars.

)))➡ *Oliver Cromwell, English Civil War, Land Wars*

CROSS OF CONG (1123)

One of Ireland's greatest treasures. Abbot Maol Íosa Ó Conchubhair bestowed the Cross of Cong on the monastery at Roscommon. It had been brought from Rome and presented to him in 1123. It is housed in the Royal Irish Academy in Dublin and is regarded as a masterpiece of design and workmanship.

ABOVE: Oliver Cromwell.
NEAR RIGHT: A Druid warns Méadhbha about Cú Chulainn.
FAR RIGHT: William Cosgrave, founder of Cumann na nGaedheal.

CÚ CHULAINN

One of the great figures of Irish mythology. Cú Chulainn is central to the Ulster cycle of myths and is the hero of the *Táin Bó Cuailgne*, where he single-handedly defends Ulster against Méadhbha (Queen Maeve of Connacht) and her army. His father was the god Lugh and his mother a princess of Ulster. Originally his name was Sétanta but one night, after arriving late for a feast at the house of a smith called Culann and killing the guard dog to gain entrance, he promises to act as his host's protector ever more, and thus took the name Cú Chulainn, 'Culann's Hound'. Numerous stories of his wondrous deeds and heroic exploits are found in both the manuscript and oral traditions.

))))➤ *Méadhbha*

CUMANN NA mBAN (1914)

Women's revolutionary movement. The Cumann na mBan was a radical organization established in 1914 and which played a supportive role in the 1916 Easter Rising. In the period after the Rising its members were active in promoting the ideals of the protagonists. The movement took an anti-Treaty stance during the Civil War which followed the War of Independence and as late as the 1930s was actively involved in a 'Buy Irish' Campaign.

))))➤ *Irish Civil War, Easter Rising, Irish Republican Army*

CUMANN NA nGAEDHEAL (1923)

Political party. Established by William Thomas Cosgrave in 1923 to give political voice to the pro-Treaty side which had prevailed in the civil war, Cumann na nGaedheal was able to form the first peacetime Free State government – helped in no small measure by Fianna Fáil's policy of abstentionism. Though a force for some years after, the party would find it much harder to advance as time went on and Fianna Fáil gathered strength; Cumann na nGaedheal never really recovered from Fianna Fáil's shock victory in the 1932 elections.

))))➤ *William Thomas Cosgrave, Fianna Fáil, Fine Gael*

CURRAGH MUTINY (1914)

Mutiny of British officers stationed at the Curragh, County Kildare in 1914. With feelings running high about Home Rule, and Carson's Ulster Volunteer Force arming to resist, many in the British Army feared that they might be deployed to put down their fellow Unionists. Ordered north from their base at the Curragh (though in fact only to reinforce key depots and keep the peace), one group of officers became convinced that they were being sent against the UVF: 57 of them refused to go. In itself, perhaps, insignificant, the 'Curragh Mutiny' took on immense symbolic resonance – especially when the war secretary in London undertook never to use British forces to 'coerce' Ulster into accepting Home Rule.

))))➤ *Home Rule*

CUSACK, MICHAEL (1847–1906)

Founder of the Gaelic Athletic Association (GAA). An Irish-speaker and teacher from County Clare, Cusack founded the GAA on 1 November 1884 in Thurles, Tipperary, to promote native sports and as a bulwark against the growth of foreign sports such as cricket, which he saw as sapping Irish national spirit. He was known to have Fenian sympathies and some members of the movement were present at this meeting. He helped begin the revival of national feeling in Ireland, particularly in the countryside.

))▶ *Gaelic Athletic Association, Fenian Movement*

CUSTOM HOUSE

'Architecturally the most important building in Dublin'. The original Custom House was built in 1707 by Thomas Burgh but was considered unsafe. The current building, begun in 1781, is situated on the riverfront and was the first major public building. It cost £200,000 and has four different, though consistent, façades linked by corner pavilions.

))▶ *James Gandon*

ABOVE: The Custom House in Dublin.

DÁIL ÉIREANN (1919)

Republic of Ireland's parliament. Elected representatives, Teachtaí Dála (TDs) elect the government. The first Dáil (January 1919–May 1921) comprised the 73 MPs chosen in the 1918 election who refused to go to Westminster and who formed a separatist government. In April 1919 the Dáil elected Éamon de Valera as its president. With partition and the Anglo-Irish Treaty the Dáil had jurisdiction over the 26 counties of the Free State. The 1937 Constitution lays down the machinery for the running of government at present, with elections being called at least every five years. There is also an upper chamber, Seanad Éireann, whose members are mostly appointed by TDs and local councillors. Graduates of the National University of Ireland and Trinity College also elect six members.

))▶ *Anglo-Irish Treaty, Éamon de Valera, Government of Ireland Act*

DÁL CAIS

Dominant Munster dynasty from the tenth to the twelfth centuries. The Dál Cais under the kingship of Brian Bóroimhe demonstrated their power against the Vikings, before being drawn into a 17-year conflict with Mael Seachnaill, who was alarmed by their rise. The north, which was controlled by the Uí Néill and the Dalcasian-controlled south, eventually came under the united kingship of Brian Bóroimhe in 1002. The influence of the Dál Cais declined after the death of Brian, who was slain at the Battle of Clontarf in 1014.

))▶ *Brian Bóroimhe, Battle of Clontarf*

DÁL RIADA

Ancient Celtic kingdom including parts of northern Ireland and western Scotland. Named for its mythical progenitor, Eochu Riada, the Dál Riada dynasty first emerged in the Glens of Antrim. By the third century, they and their vassals had started colonizing in western Scotland, in the upland regions to the north of the River Clyde.

DAVIS, THOMAS (1814–45)

Radical thinker and writer. Davis was one of the leaders of the Young Ireland Movement, which split from the ageing and mellowing Daniel O'Connell in the 1840s. In 1842 he was co-founder – with Charles Gavan

Duffy and John Blake Dillon – of *The Nation*, a periodical which vigorously promoted Irish cultural and political nationalism. He wrote many ballads in an effort to get his message across to the ordinary people and the influence of his writings – as well as songs such as 'A Nation Once Again' – lived on long after his premature death from a fever in 1845.

)))**▶** *John Blake Dillon, Charles Gavan,* **The Nation,** *Nationalism, Daniel O'Connell, Young Ireland*

DAVITT, MICHAEL (1846–1906)

Nationalist campaigner and founder of the Land League. Born in County Mayo, but brought up in Lancashire where his family had emigrated after eviction from their home, Davitt would, throughout his life, feel called upon to strive for the rights of tenants. Having lost his arm in a mill-accident at the age of 11, he joined the Fenians a few years later in 1865, and was imprisoned for gun-running in 1870. On his release he founded the Land League to agitate for agrarian reform, much-influenced by the views of the radical American economist Henry George, but ultimately felt his grassroots campaign had been hijacked to serve the interests of larger farmers.

)))**▶** *Fenian Movement, Land League*

DE VALERA, ÉAMON (1882–1975)

Statesman; president of executive council of the Irish Free State (1932–37); Taoiseach (1937–48, 1951–54, 1957–59); president (1959–73). Born in Brooklyn, of Spanish-Irish parentage, de Valera was brought up by relatives in County Limerick and, completing his education at University College in Dublin, became a maths teacher. A member of the Gaelic League from 1908 and a Volunteer from 1913, he was the last republican commander to surrender after the 1916 rising. Sentenced to death, he was

reprieved on the intervention of the US consul. Released from gaol in 1917 he was rearrested the following year, accused of plotting with Germany, but was sprung from prison and became president of the first Dáil Éireann between 1919–20. Having, some said, manoeuvred Michael Collins and Arthur Griffith into signing the Anglo-Irish Treaty, de Valera indignantly rejected its terms, leading an opposition that would finally flare up into civil war. When the pro-Treaty faction won, de Valera was imprisoned for a time with other Republican leaders. He emerged to re-enter constitutional politics, resigning his leadership of the abstentionist Sinn Féin to found a new party, Fianna Fáil, in 1926. Prime minister from 1932 (his Constitution of 1937 changed the title to 'Taoiseach'), he would dominate politics in the Free State for the next 40 years.

)))**▶** *Bunreacht na hÉireann, Easter Rising, Fianna Fáil*

ABOVE: Michael Davitt.
RIGHT: Éamon de Valera.

DECLAN, ST

 Early Irish saint. One of Ireland's oldest saints, perhaps pre-dating Patrick himself, Declan is famed as the founder of the Monastery at Ardmore, Waterford. Though venerated throughout Ireland, Declan was especially associated with south-eastern Munster and its early inhabitants, the Déisi.

DECLARATION OF 1460

Proclamation of Ireland's legislative independence. The Irish parliament in Drogheda declared that it had the right to be sole legislator for all of Ireland 'free of the burthen of any special law of the realm of England'. Poynings' Law of 1494 overturned much of the basis for this declaration.

))))➤ *Poynings' Laws*

DEFENDERS (1795)

This Catholic grouping formed after Protestant aggression against Catholics in the 1790s, particularly in County Armagh. In time, they too became aggressors and were organized as a secret society, active particularly in rural districts. In some areas they were closely connected with the United Irishmen and many were involved in the 1798 Rebellion. After the rebellion they went into decline, only to re-emerge later in the nineteenth century as Ribbonmen.

))))➤ *Ribbonism, United Irishmen*

DEMOCRATIC UNIONIST PARTY (1971)

Northern Irish political party. Founded in 1971 by the charismatic preacher-politician Reverend Ian Paisley, the DUP represents a more uncompromising – some would say a more intransigent – strand in Protestant opinion than the Ulster Unionist Party from which it originally seceded. Drawn largely from the urban working class, the DUP's culture is also 'more Protestant' than that of 'Official' Unionism, whose upper echelons especially include many Church of Ireland members. Though small in number, the DUP has proved influential in blocking moves towards power-sharing or cross-border co-operation: it has from the first been opposed to the peace process introduced by the Downing Street Declaration.

))))➤ *Ian Paisley, Ulster Unionist Party*

DERRY

Northern Ireland's second city. Situated at the mouth of the River Foyle, Derry has been settled at least since the sixth century, but it received its charter as a trading post for the London Companies who set up shop here at the time of the Ulster Plantation, hence the name 'Londonderry', which is still the official title of the city, although in 1978 the newly nationalist council suc-

ceeded in dropping the hated prefix for the name of the local authority. Always a flashpoint for conflict, the city came under attack from James II's Catholic forces in 1689, but the Protestant Apprentice Boys closed the gates in their faces and a 105-day siege ensued in which thousands died. Derry has ever since retained its status as a sort of loyalist Leningrad, despite the fact that, demographically speaking, it has always been a Catholic city. Just a stone's throw from the border laid down in 1921, Derry was one of those places expected to be returned to the Republic by the Boundary Commission. Although it was retained by the northern state, desperate measures would be required to

justify continuing Unionist domination: some of the most outrageous gerrymandering of electoral boundaries took place here. Derry was, as a result, the main centre for Northern Ireland's Civil Rights Movement; the Bloody Sunday shootings of 1971 took place here.

))))➤ *Apprentice Boys, Boundary Commission, Civil Rights Movement, Siege of Derry, Plantation of Ulster*

DERRY, SIEGE OF (1689)

Siege during the War of the English Succession between James II and William III; also known as the Siege of Londonderry. In 1613, James I had granted Derry

to a group of Londoners who laid out a new city and erected huge fortifications around it.

On 7 December 1688, hearing rumours that Irish Catholics were starting to murder Protestants, Derry apprentice boys locked out a new Catholic garrison sent by the deposed English king, James II. James began his campaign to recapture his Crown, using Ireland as his power-base. Recognizing the possibility of a Catholic revival, around 30,000 Ulster Presbyterians fled to Londonderry for protection. In April James laid siege to the city. Its fortifications made it a vital stronghold, and its seizure was essential to his campaign's success. However, a lack of training, large cannon and equipment meant James could not press home his advantage, despite the privations within the walls. On 28 July 1689, William III's ships came up the River Foyle and broke the siege.

))))➤ *Battle of the Boyne, James II of England, William III of England*

DERRY'S WALLS (1618)

Seventeenth-century walls symbolizing unionist control. The stone walls which encircle the old city of Derry were the last to be built in western Europe. Completed in 1618, the walls' symbolic importance arises from the fact that they held out for 105 days against James II's forces during the war against William III. The Protestant defenders shut the gates and defied James's Catholic forces. This act is often recalled in Orange song, with the refrain 'To guard old Derry's Walls' being a rallying call not to give up the Unionist cause, or not to surrender, as advocated by Robert Lundy during the siege.

))))➤ *Apprentice Boys, Robert Lundy, Siege of Derry*

DERRYVEAGH EVICTIONS (1861)

Eviction of tenants from an estate in north-west Donegal. In the period 1846–87 there was an estimated one million people affected by eviction, as landlords had virtual free rein to evict tenants whenever they liked. This could be done merely by serving notice to quit and informing the RIC, the body which carried out the operation. Houses were usually rendered uninhabitable so that tenants could not return. In the notorious case of Derryveagh the evictions took place to 'improve the view'. The landlord in Derryveagh, John Adair, had his agent killed and this was used as a pretext to clear 244 tenants from the land in 1861.

))))➤ *Land Act*

DESMOND, EARLS OF (1329–1601)

Ancestors of Maurice Fitzgerald de Windsor, known as 'The Invader of Ireland'. This family of feudal lords were independent rulers who had enormous power and immense wealth, which caused concern to the English rulers. They occupied the district of 'Deasmhumhain' (Desmond) or southern Munster from 1329 to 1601. During Elizabethan and Cromwellian times in particular, the earls of Desmond underwent varying degrees of military suppression. Elizabeth, in an attempt to strengthen England's control of Ireland, confiscated land from the Earl of Desmond and divided it into estates (plantations) which were given to the Englishmen Sir Walter Raleigh and Edmund Spenser. The death of the last earl, Gerald Fitzgerald, known as the 'Rebel Earl', during the rebellion he led against English rule under Queen Elizabeth I brought an end to the Desmond line, and the earldom, combined with that of Denbigh, was granted to the English Fielding family in 1675.

➠ *Gerald Fitgerald, Thomas Fitzgerald*

DESMOND REVOLT (1569–73, 1579–83)

Series of rebellions against English rule in Munster. Arguably as much about political economy as religion, the unrest that seethed in the Desmond earldom of Munster in the late-sixteenth century was prompted by the demands of the Tudor government in London for modernization. Under the comparatively easy-going control of the Fitzgerald family since the Anglo-Norman Conquest, large areas of Limerick, Kerry and other counties had been allowed to continue in their Gaelic traditions of culture, language and above all land-use. By the second half of the sixteenth century, London was calling for more efficient landholding practices, but the earls felt unable to oblige: as the Tudors prepared to enforce change, their vassals and tenants prepared for resistance. The first rising was brutally put down in 1573 and the ringleader, James Fitzmaurice Fitzgerald, went into exile in Spain; six years later he returned with a tiny force, for what he was now describing as a Catholic 'holy war'. From unpromising beginnings, this revolt grew, and was finally only quelled in 1583, at the cost of great devastation and loss of life.

DESPARD PLOT (1800–03)

Irish-based conspiracy against George III of England. Colonel Edward Marcus Despard (1751–1803), a British army officer and colonial administrator, former governor of Roatan Island was imprisoned on charges of involvement in the Irish Rebellion. After his release, Despard organized a conspiracy against the British king and government, who had refused to employ him. He hoped to combine an army mutiny with a rising in London. His aim was to capture both the Tower of London and the Bank of England. He also plotted to assassinate the king, George III. His plot was discovered and Despard was convicted of high treason. He was executed in 1803.

D'ESTERRE DUEL (1815)

Duel between John D'Esterre and Daniel O'Connell in which D'Esterre was killed. John D'Esterre, a member of the Guild of Merchants, took exception to O'Connell's phrase 'beggarly' with regard to the Dublin Corporation, and when failing to get O'Connell to withdraw his statement challenged him to a duel. Bonfires were lit throughout Dublin when news of O'Connell's triumph was heard. It was O'Connell's last duel.

➠ *Daniel O'Connell*

LEFT: The death of Gerald Fitzgerald, Earl of Desmond.

DEVENISH ISLAND (AD 570)

 Island on Lower Lough Erne, several miles below Enniskillen. Devenish Island was an important early monastic site associated with St Molaise, who died in AD 570. During the Viking period the monastery was attacked several times and the church was burned by them in AD 836. Although the Plantations and the Protestant Reformation saw the end of Devenish as an active monastic site the graveyard continued to be used for several centuries, until 1825 when 19 people were drowned when a boat bearing a coffin overturned in a wintery squall. Now a popular visitor attraction, Devenish island has one of the best-preserved round towers in the country and the remains of the Augustinian St Mary's Abbey.

)))➤ *Vikings*

DEVLIN, BERNADETTE (MCALISKEY) (b. 1947)

Republican socialist activist and politician. Born 23 April 1947, Devlin played a prominent role in the Civil Rights Movement to gain equal rights for Catholics, particularly in the Battle of the Bogside (August 1969). Despite her age she was elected MP for Mid-Ulster in April 1969 and was renowned for hitting the home secretary in the Commons. Bernadette and her husband survived a loyalist assassination attempt in which they were both badly wounded.

)))➤ *Civil Rights Movement*

DEVLIN, JOE (1871–1934)

Nationalist Party leader in Ulster. With working-class origins in Belfast he won the West Belfast seat for Nationalists in 1906. He persuaded Nationalist party supporters in Ulster to accept temporary exclusion of six counties from the Irish Free State. Devlin grudgingly accepted partition and eventually led Nationalist MPs into Stormont in 1925.

)))➤ *Nationalist Party, Partition*

DEVOY, JOHN (1842–1928)

Member of the Fenian Movement, prominent in agitation in the US. The Fenian revolutionary was jailed in 1866–71 and exiled to the US, where he campaigned effectively for the nationalist cause. This American support was channelled through the Clan na nGael, which he established, and was formally linked to the Irish Republican Brotherhood. Devoy was also linked to the Land League and had input into the planning of the 1916 Easter Rising.

)))➤ *Clan na nGael, Easter Rising, Fenian Movement, Irish Republican Brotherhood, Land League*

ABOVE: *The round tower and abbey on Devenish Island.*
BELOW: *Bernadette Devlin.*

DIAMOND, BATTLE OF THE (1795)

Battle outside Loughgall, County Armagh, in 1795. By some accounts more of a brawl than a battle, the Diamond was one of a number of violent sectarian encounters that were flaring up sporadically all along the edges of the Ulster Plantation by the 1790s. Named after the crossroads by which it took place on 21 September, the battle resulted in a decisive victory for the outnumbered Protestant force. Emboldened, they and their supporters embarked on what amounted to an anti-Catholic pogrom in the area.

))))▶ *Armagh Outrages, Defenders, Peep o'Day Boys*

DIASPORA (1780)

Derived from the Greek, meaning 'dispersion'. The Irish Diaspora, or scattering of the population into other countries, came about for a number of reasons. Both during the Great Famine and after the introduction of the Penal Laws, large numbers of Irish people left Ireland to form new lives in English-speaking countries like the US, the UK, Canada, Australia and New Zealand, as well as to Argentina, which has the largest non-English speaking Irish community in the world. The negative version of the Diaspora began with the transportation of Irish convicts to Australia in 1780. During the Famine it is said that some Irish feigned guilt of a crime in order to receive free transportation to Australia. By 1861 the Irish community made up 20 per cent of the Australian population. In 1822 the British parliament financed an emigration plan to Canada in order to increase the number of settlers available to defend Canada against the USA.

))))▶ *Great Famine, Penal Laws*

DILLON, JOHN (1851–1927)

Nationalist statesman, son of John Blake Dillon. Despite their early friendship, John Dillon became Charles Stewart Parnell's chief critic on the nationalist side, believing him to have settled for far too little in the way of land reform in the campaign of the 1880s. After Parnell's disgrace and exile, constitutional nationalism was left effectively leaderless: Dillon stepped into the vacuum, with John Edward Redmond, the two pushing for Home Rule which they hoped would be won peacefully, in friendly co-operation with British radicals.

))))▶ *Land League, Charles Stewart Parnell, John Redmond*

DILLON, JOHN BLAKE (1816–66)

Nationalist politician. A founder, with Thomas Davis and Charles Gavan Duffy, of the Young Ireland movement, set up in 1842 to campaign for an independent country in which Catholics and Protestants would live happily side by side. Initially supportive of O'Connell's campaign for repeal of the Union, the Young Irelanders became increasingly impatient not only with his apparent readiness to accept a federalist compromise, but also with his willingness to side with the Catholic bishops in their denunciation of the new non-sectarian universities, or 'Queen's Colleges', set up by British prime minister Robert Peel. In this, O'Connell was arguably only recognizing the political realities of his day: while respecting his integrity, historians have tended to be severe on Dillon's romantic idealism.

))))▶ *Thomas Davies, Charles Gavan Duffy, Daniel O'Connell, Young Ireland*

DINNSEANCHAS

An important literary form in Irish, *dinnseanchas* can be defined as the lore of places. It consists of stories connected to specific locations, often to explain how they

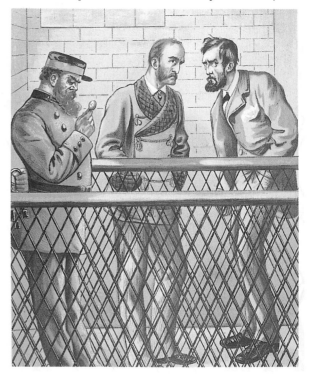

got their names. These stories range from little local episodes from the recent past to episodes from the great epic tales such as the *Cattle Raid of Cooley*. For instance, the townland of Stranadarriff (*Sraith na dTarbh* – 'the Bulls' Strip') near Ederney in County Fermanagh is so-called because this is the place, according to legend, that a confrontation between the Brown and the White bulls took place according to the legend.

)))➤ **Cattle Raid of Cooley**

DOLLY'S BRAE (1849)

Sectarian flare-up of 1849. The tensions and tumults of Ulster's summer 'Marching Season' have a long pedigree: the Orange Order has been marching more or less continuously since the 1790s. When a 12 July parade was fired on by Catholic Ribbonmen at Dolly's Brae, County Down, in 1849, the Orangemen reacted with an orgy of violence. Thirty Catholics were killed, although there were no casualties on the Protestant side; the Catholic village of Magheramayo was left a smouldering ruin. In large part a response to this episode, parliament passed the Party Processions Act of 1850, the first of a long series of legislative attempts to reconcile the often very different demands of civil liberties, 'identity' and public order.

)))➤ *Drumcree*

DOLMEN

Dolmens are some of the most striking monuments from early Celtic times which still grace the Irish countryside. Generally consisting of three large upright stones with a huge capstone on top, in fact they are all that remains of ancient grave chambers, which would have originally been completely covered in earth. These monuments are also to be found in Brittany and parts of Celtic Britain. Other types of Neolithic graves include cairns and passage graves, where the bodies were buried deep within artificial mounds such as at Knowth and Newgrange.

)))➤ *Celts, Neolithic People, Newgrange*

FAR LEFT: John Dillon in jail with Charles Parnell.
BELOW LEFT: A dolmen on The Burren, County Clare.
BELOW: Dominican friars.

DOMINICAN ORDER (1224)

Roman Catholic religious order, founded by St Dominic in 1216. Not a community of working, praying monks but of preaching friars, the Dominicans opened their first Irish house in Dublin in 1224. The 'Black Friars', as they were known for the black mantle they wore over their white robes when preaching, played an important evangelizing role for the Church at a time when it was feared that monastic corruption had created a climate of widespread cynicism.

)))➤ *Early Christian Ireland, Monasteries*

DOWNING STREET DECLARATION (1993)

Joint declaration on Northern Ireland by the British and Irish governments, 15 December 1993. Issued outside the British prime minister's official London residence at 10 Downing Street by Conservative prime minister John Major and Fianna Fáil Taoiseach Albert Reynolds, the Downing Street Declaration effectively ratified what had been agreed over months of backroom negotiation. No sooner had it been issued than both sides started disputing the interpretative details of its convoluted text. Put simply,

though, by setting it on record that the United Kingdom had no 'selfish strategic or economic interest in Northern Ireland', the Declaration opened the door to Sinn Féin participation in peaceful politics, while assuring Ulster's Unionists that their consent would be required for any constitutional change. Critics pointed with some justice to the ambiguity of a document which appeared to offer incompatible terms to implacably opposing factions, yet – in concert with lasting ceasefires from the paramilitaries of both sides – the Declaration helped create a climate in which real political progress in Ulster could at last be made.

))))➤ *Fianna Fáil*

DOWNPATRICK

Small cathedral city in County Down, Northern Ireland. Situated on the south-west shore of Strangford Lough, Downpatrick is believed to have been where Ireland's patron saint made landing at the start of his Irish mission in AD 432. But Patrick is only one of three saints said to lie buried outside the city's eighteenth-century cathedral: the relics of St Brigid and St Colm Cille have both been interred alongside him. Down, or 'Dún' (the name means 'fort') was the capital of the ancient kingdom of Ulaid dynasty, eventually subsumed into the over-kingdom of Dál Riada.

))))➤ *St Brigid, St Colm Cille, St Patrick*

DROGHEDA

City in the south of County Louth, at the mouth of the River Boyne. To begin with a Viking fortress, Drogheda grew and prospered under Anglo-Norman rule, and became the second economic and administrative centre of the English Pale. Its notoriety in Irish history, however, stems from the events that unfolded here in the autumn of 1649, when the parliamentary forces of Oliver Cromwell laid siege to the Stuart-sympathizing city. Determined to prevent a potentially dangerous link-up between the Royalist garrison and the Catholic forces of Eoghan Rua Ó Néill, Cromwell adopted a carrot-and-stick policy, pounding the city walls with his artillery, but also offering quarter to defenders prepared to surrender. When, seeing the hopelessness of their situation, the garrison agreed to come to terms, Cromwell had the whole city slain, including up to 1,000 civilians.

))))➤ *Oliver Cromwell, Eoghan Rua Ó Néill, The Pale*

DROGHEDA, SIEGE OF (1649)

Notorious siege conducted by Oliver Cromwell. In 1649 Drogheda was defended by English Royalist soldiers under the command of Sir Arthur Aston. Cromwell arrived to suppress the Catholic Confederate Rebellion. On

ABOVE LEFT: John Major and Albert Reynolds during talks leading up to the 1993 Downing Street Declaration.

12 September 1649, the walls were breached but soldiers sent through the gap were initially forced back with severe losses. Cromwell ordered the outright massacre of defenders. Around 2,000 were killed and many more were sent to the West Indies to undertake forced labour as a punishment. Cromwell justified his actions as God's work, and revenge for the massacre of Protestants in the 1641 Rebellion. Despite the English garrison, the episode has entered Irish tradition as the ultimate expression of English brutality.

))))➤ *Oliver Cromwell, Rebellion of 1641*

DRUIDS

Celtic priests. The earliest records of Celtic druids come from classical writers such as Caesar and Strabo and although they are frequently mentioned in early Irish tales as adversaries of saints such as Patrick and Colm Cille, little is known about their function in society, as their influence seems to have declined soon after the introduction of Christianity. It is possible that the filí, or poets, were their true successors.

))))➤ *Celts, Filí*

DRUIM CEAT, CONVENTION OF (C. AD 575)

Major political conference held in around AD 575 at Mullagh near Limavady in County Derry. At the convention an agreement was reached between the leader of the Ó Néills (O'Neills), the northern dynasty, and the king of Dál Riada, the Celtic kingdom of north-east Ulster and western Scotland, which maintained the peace and the

balance of power. Also present was St Colm Cille, who intervened on behalf of the filí, or poets, who had become so numerous and demanding that they were in danger of being banished from the country by their erstwhile patrons. New regulations regarding their conduct were agreed and they were allowed to stay.

))))➤ *St Colm Cille, Dál Riada, Filí, O'Neill Dynasty*

DRUMCREE (1807)

Sectarian flashpoint in the south of County Down. Every year since 1807, the Orange Order's Portadown Lodge has paraded down the Garvaghy Road to Drumcree and to the little hilltop Church of the Ascension where they hold a service. Much has changed in that time, however, in particular the siting of a housing estate alongside what was once a country lane: since 1995 its largely Catholic residents have protested against what they see as at best a nuisance and at worst a dangerous provocation. Moves by the authorities to prevent the march have had the effect of making it a Protestant *cause célèbre*, with crowds of supporters far out-numbering the actual marchers. Regarding the Garvaghy Residents' Committee as no more than a cynical Sinn Féin front, Unionists remain resolute in their determination to express their identity by parading along the same route they have followed for generations.

))))➤ *Dolly's Brae*

BELOW: Orange march, Portadown.

DUALTACH MAC FIRBHISIGH (c. 1600–71)

Important scribe and historian. He was born in County Sligo into a family known for their scholarship. His family lost its lands following the 1641 Rebellion and he moved to Galway where he compiled a major genealogical work on Irish families. He made copies of several annals, and of other works which would otherwise now be lost. He died after being stabbed in an inn in County Sligo in 1671, while travelling on foot to Dublin.

))))➤ *Annals, Rebellion of 1641*

DUBHGALL

Irish word meaning 'black foreigners'. Dubhgall is the term used by the Irish during Viking times to refer to the Danes. Ragnald 'the grandson of Ivarr', was a Danish chieftain and was known as Ragnald, King of the Dubhgall. He seized the lands of Ealdred of Bamburgh in AD 913.

))))➤ *Vikings*

DUBLIN

Capital of the Republic of Ireland, and the island's largest city, with 953,000 inhabitants – a quarter of the Republic's population and almost a fifth of the total for the whole of Ireland. The Irish name *dubh-linn* ('dark pool') masks the Viking origins of a settlement founded as comparatively recently as AD 841, and not firmly established as a town until the end of the tenth century.

From the first the invader's city, Dublin became a capital for the conquering Anglo-Normans in 1204, after which it served as the administrative centre for the English Pale. The

very existence of the Pale suggests a certain fear of what lay beyond, and indeed by the mid-fifteenth century Dublin's English rulers were passing laws to exclude those of 'Irish blood' from the city's trades. Though a tragedy for Catholic Ireland, the dissolution of the monasteries which followed Henry VIII's historic break with Rome was to the inestimable advantage of Dublin's great English merchant families, who were in a position to exploit the resulting economic vacuum. Though considerably grown in size, its population reaching nearly 10,000, the seventeenth-century city still had the haphazard, provisional air of an obscure trading post. While its leading citizens had grown rich, the mass of the people had lived in squalor, their city battered by fire, plague, famine and just about every other adversity.

The poverty of the average Dubliner would persist, but the city would at least be given a serious civic facelift when, under the reigns of the first four Hanoverian kings (1714–1830), it was reinvented as the British Empire's Second City and extensively redesigned. From this

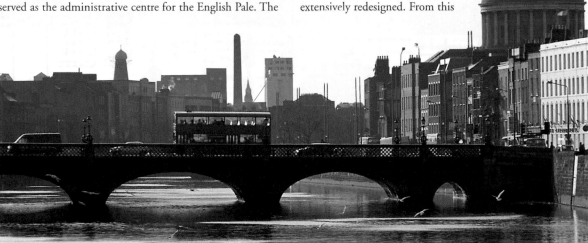

period date the sweeping crescents and elegant squares for which Dublin is now celebrated, and the graceful public buildings erected by an ascendancy which, while not interested in independence, still felt some pride. Though founded as early as 1592, Trinity College was given fine new premises at this time, nicely complementing such shapely piles as the domed Four Courts, the City Hall, the Old Parliament House, the Custom House, and many more in Dublin's perhaps unrivalled collection of Georgian buildings. It was in this 'Athens of the West' that, for instance, Handel's *Messiah* was first performed in 1742: Dublin's self-image was now that of one of the great European capitals.

Although the Act of Union of 1800 officially ended Dublin's significance as a political centre, in doing so it ushered in a whole new era of distinctively 'Irish' politics. Dublin's Catholic middle classes began to see their disenfranchisement not just in religious but in national terms, while the city's poor came to feel there was an external enemy to blame for their many miseries. Though not directly affected by the Famine, Dublin could not escape the indirect effects of the crisis in the countryside: refugees streamed into the city to swell the population of its already teeming slums. As professional families moved out to new suburbs outside the city, the poor made tenement-dwellings of their old homes, once-stately townhouses turned into unspeakably filthy and overcrowded rookeries. In 1849, 49 per cent of Dublin families lived in single-room accommodation; by 1914 things had eased, but the figure still stood at an appalling 25 per cent. Some 16,000 families lived below the official poverty line, but those hoping to harness discontent politically had to contend with the powerlessness of the poor in an employment culture characterized by low-paid, casual work, with a relatively small sector of skilled industrial workers.

This was the context in which the Dublin Lockout of 1913 took place – a doomed undertaking, despite the determination of the workers. Equally ill-fated, the 1916 Easter Rising was beheld with more horror than sympathy by most Dubliners. The longer-term impact of the Rising is of course disputed – some suggest that it was triumphantly vindicated

ABOVE LEFT: Sackville Street, Dublin.
LEFT: The River Liffey and the green-domed Four Courts.
ABOVE RIGHT: The Campanile, Trinity College.

in time: its immediate legacy, however, was a more or less flattened city centre. This at least gave the infant Free State the opportunity to embark upon a popular construction programme, building a prestigious main boulevard in the new O'Connell Street and beginning the task of creating much-needed public housing on peripheral estates. Like other such ventures throughout the developed world, these schemes have fallen short of expectations, replacing problems of insanitary conditions and material deprivation with those of social alienation. Dublin is now as famous for its drug problem as it is for its Georgian architecture, and there is as yet little sign of the success of Ireland's 'Celtic Tiger' economy trickling down to society's most impoverished levels. That problem is hardly unique to Dublin, however, a city whose more optimistic citizens may point to their country's continuing economic buoyancy and to encouraging news from the North and claim that their city really is at last joining the ranks of the major European capitals.

))))▶ *Act of Union, Dublin Lockout, Easter Rising, Republic of Ireland*

DUBLIN, BATTLE OF (AD 919)

Failed attempt to recover Dublin from Viking control. In AD 919 the Viking Sitric captured Dublin and its surrounding territory; he then set sail for England to assist his brother Ragnald in his claim to the kingdom of Mercia. Niall Glúndubh, styled 'King of Ireland', took the opportunity to attack Dublin. At Coill Moramocc, about 10 km (6 miles) from Dublin, Sitric's sons met him with an army. The Irish suffered a catastrophic defeat. Glúndubh was killed, along with his stepson and heir Conchobhar, and many of the other chieftains.

)))⟩ *Niall Glúndubh*

DUBLIN CASTLE (13TH CENTURY)

Formerly 'Dubh linn' (Black Pool) Castle. Standing on a ridge at the junction of the River Liffey and the Poddle, Dublin Castle is situated in the centre of Dublin itself. The original fortification may have been a Gaelic ring fort, later a Viking fortress. The record tower is believed to be part of the original thirteenth-century Norman castle and the chapel royal part of the nineteenth-century Gothic one. The great courtyard contains buildings of the post-medieval castle. The south of the castle houses the state apartments, built as the residential quarters of the Vicarage court.

)))⟩ *Dublin*

DUBLIN LOCKOUT (1913)

Labour dispute and public-order crisis. The refusal of William Martin Murphy's Dublin United Tramways Company to take on members of the Irish Transport and General Workers' Union (ITGWU) brought to a head two years of increasingly tetchy industrial relations in the city. As other employers locked out union members – and workers in other companies came out on strike – the economic life of Dublin came to a virtual standstill, the violent intervention of the police simply increasing the bitterness. Yet as both sides settled down to weeks of attrition, the fundamental weakness of the workers became clear: without the resources to go on fighting, they had nowhere to go but back to work. For some, this episode is one of the great 'might have been's of modern Irish history, a narrative in which national and sectarian passions have always tended to crowd out those of class. The Dublin Lockout of 1913 represents the great exception to this rule: not only did it place Protestant and Catholic workers side by side on the picket lines, but it set both against Dublin's leading capitalist – who turns out to have been a Catholic Home Rule MP.

ABOVE: The Wedgewood room in the state apartments at Dublin Castle.
RIGHT: Dundrum Castle.
FAR RIGHT: The Book of Durrow.

DÚN AENGUS

The remains of a pre-Christian stone fort on Inis Mór in the Aran Islands. The most notable of many pre-Christian remains in and around the island has four semi-circular thick defence walls and limestone slabs. The land approach is guarded by angular boulders protruding from the earth to break up attacks. It is situated on the edge of a 61-m (200-ft) cliff top overlooking County Kerry and County Galway. It is unknown how old the stone fort is, although it is estimated that it dates from 3,000 to 6,000 years ago. Due to coastal erosion about one-third of the fort has been lost.

))))➤ *Rock of Cashel*

DUN COW, BOOK OF (*LEABHAR NA HUIDHRE*) (11TH CENTURY)

Important Irish manuscript anthology, written on vellum made from the skin of a cow which St Ciarán took with him to Clonmacnoise. It dates from the eleventh century and contains an early version of the *Cattle Raid of Cooley* and several other well-known stories. Missing for many years, it was located by a Dublin bookseller in 1837 and bought by the Royal Irish Academy in 1844.

))))➤ *Cattle Raid of Cooley, St Ciarán, Clonmacnoise*

DUNDRUM CASTLE (1177)

Thirteenth-century castle situated in County Down. The walls of the castle surround a circular keep. It was begun by John de Courcy in 1177 to guard the land

from Drogheda to Downpatrick. The castle has been variously held by the Earls of Ulster and by Magennises of Mourne, captured by the Earl of Kildare in 1517 and lord deputy Grey in 1538, and surrendered to the Crown in 1601 by Phelim Magennis. The castle stands on a high hill overlooking the sea and coastline.

))))➤ *John de Courcy, Earls of Kildare*

DURROW, BOOK OF (C. AD 650)

Early illuminated manuscript of the gospels, dating from around AD 650. The Book of Durrow was associated with the Columban monastery of Durrow in County Offaly. Its style of decoration is not as ornate as that of the later Book of Kells. It is now in the library of Trinity College Dublin.

))))➤ *Book of Kells, Trinity College Dublin*

DWYER, MICHAEL (1771–1826)

Irish rebel. Dwyer joined the United Irishmen in 1797 and took part in the rebellions of 1798 and 1803. After 1798 Dwyer remained at large, continuing to attack English soldiers. He chose to surrender rather than risk more lives in 1803 after the collapse of Robert Emmet's rising in Dublin, and was sentenced for transportation to Australia.

))))➤ *Robert Emmet, Society of United Irishmen*

DYSERT O'DEA, BATTLE OF (1318)

Dysert O'Dea, now in County Clare, lies in the ancient kingdom of Thomond or North Munster, once the territory of the Ó Briain (O'Brien) clan. Brian Rua (king from 1268–76) was captured in battle at Moygressan and killed during his campaign against the Normans. The Ó Briains fought back and in 1318 defeated Richard de Clare (a descendant of Strongbow) at Dysert O'Dea, ending Anglo-Norman power in Thomond.

))))➤ *Richard de Clare*

EAMHAIN MACHA (c. 700 bc–ad 400)

Ancient capital of Ulster in pre-Christian Ireland. Eamhain Macha was situated near the present-day city of Armagh, at a site known in English as Navan Fort where a large earthen mound remains. Recent archeological investigations seem to confirm descriptions of the site found in legends and pseudo-historical material. At the centre was a great hall and various round houses stood close by. It is the location for much of the action in many of the stories in the Ulster cycle of myths and is also mentioned in the *Táin Bó Cuailgne*. The skull of a barbary ape is among the more unusual archeological finds from this site.

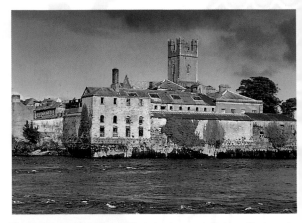

EARLY CHRISTIAN IRELAND

The Church in Ireland prior to Norman settlement and the reforms of the twelfth century. Thanks to its trade with Roman Britain, the south-eastern corner of Ireland appears to have been Christianized quite early. There were already flourishing establishments of British monks in Leinster when St Patrick took his mission to the northern part of Ireland in the late-fifth century: the saint's uniqueness seems to have lain in his willingness to proselytize among the common Irish people. The distinction has to be drawn between settlement by Christians and Christianization, since Christians came to Ireland for space long before they came to spread the Gospel.

If some have always seen Christianity as a religion of energetic evangelism, for others it has been a more contemplative creed entirely: the tension between the two can be traced all the way back to Jesus's own ministry. Yet there were sufficient preachers like Patrick to go on spreading the Word by slow degrees: by the end of the seventh century, Christianity seems to have been accepted throughout most of Ireland.

For all their apparent introversion, however, the contemplatives were touching the lives of the people too, Ireland's increasing number of monasteries assuming more and more importance in their local economies. According to the Benedictine Rule, spiritual contemplation did not merely involve meditation: the monks offered up their work to God, from consummate calligraphy to hard labour in the fields and creative time in workshops. The typical medieval monastery – not just in Ireland but elsewhere – was as much an economic complex as a place of prayer. As consumers of foodstuffs and raw materials, and as producers of luxury goods (mead and beer, metalwork, etc.), the monasteries became crucial to the development of extensive hinterlands. As educators and employers, too, they had their impact on a way of life which had previously gone unchanged for centuries. The view that, since this far-flung corner of the European continent had never been subjected to Roman rule, the monks were moving into a complete administrative vacuum is no longer taken as seriously as it once was by historians. According to the old orthodoxy, the abbots effectively ran Ireland, while the warlords stole one another's cattle and the bishops prated impotently in their pulpits. The more we discover, not only about the sophistication of political life in Celtic Ireland, but also about the organization of the early Church, the more absurd a travesty this appears to be of how things really were. It does seem to have been the case, however, that monasteries had more economic and administrative importance here than they did elsewhere in medieval Europe, and that their abbots accordingly had a great deal more in the way of personal authority.

Yet this monastic autonomy had to be exercised within the restrictions imposed by the Church's bishops: the confusion condemned by the hierarchy in Britain, and even in Rome, was much exaggerated. Evolving as it did *ad hoc*, responding to traditions on the ground at the most local level, Celtic Christianity inevitably took on a certain anarchic, wayward quality. The Irish Church was nothing like so remote from the centre as it might seem, however; nor would it have felt anything like as isolated as we might imagine from the institutional structures of the wider Church. Europe was a much smaller place, in some ways, before the days of the nation state, when Latin was the *lingua franca* and Christianity a truly catholic, common currency. Irish monks were proud to be citizens of Christendom, and were indeed famous for their love of travel, the tradition of spiritual exile, or *peregrinatio*, being vital to the vocations of many monks. St Columbanus was born in Leinster and trained as a monk at Bangor, on the northern coast of Ulster, but he went on to found monasteries in France, Switzerland and Italy. The work of Columbanus, Killian and Donatus, and of hundreds of other less-celebrated compatriots, helped ensure that, however geographically remote, Ireland remained in the very mainstream of European Christianity.

If reports of the Irish Church's effective implosion are now believed to have been exaggerated, so too is the assumption that it was all but destroyed by the Viking raids. The alarm of the monkish chroniclers is of course understandable, but with the luxury of hindsight it can be said that the effects of the attacks on Irish Christianity as a whole were not so significant. After the first few raids, from AD 795 onwards, the Vikings came increasingly as settlers, and over the next two centuries they established major towns at Dublin, Wexford, Waterford, Cork and Limerick. Converted to the faith themselves, the sometime plunderers became a force for order in Irish Christianity, their kinship with fellow-Northmen across the Irish Sea promoting links with the English Church.

BELOW LEFT: Donation of bread to the Benedictine monks.
LEFT: Limerick Cathedral.
BELOW: St Patrick opening his 'Purgatory'.

For all that, Early Irish Christianity did to a certain extent end up going its own way. Policies on marriage-law, for instance, arguably owed more to Celtic tradition than papal teaching. Men and women were permitted to marry well within what other countries regarded as the forbidden degrees of kinship, while a blind eye seems to have been turned to divorce, freely available to men and women in the Gaelic tradition. It was easy, then, for critics abroad to berate the Irish Church for presiding over a stew of moral turpitude, and to make a connection between monastic autonomy and institutional corruption. How far this was really true must now be a matter for interpretation: what is clear is that by the twelfth century, the wider Church felt a need to assert its own authority in Ireland.

⫸ *Benedictine Order, Synod of Cashel, Celtic Christianity, Saint Patrick, Vikings*

EASTER RISING (1916)

Rebellion against British rule. The long-established tensions between the constitutionalist and revolutionary wings of Irish nationalism were tested to breaking-point by the outbreak of World War I. To the former, any differences with Britain had to be shelved for the duration of the conflict. That view seems to have been shared by the vast majority of ordinary Irishmen, who answered Kitchener's call to enlistment in their thousands, fighting and dying alongside British comrades on the Western Front. A very different attitude was taken by the more militant core of Republican activists, for whom any such truce seemed sentimental, a tacit admission that Ireland's enmity to England was not really serious. They argued that Britain's quarrel with Germany was not their quarrel – that, indeed, as the Fenians had said, 'England's difficulty is Ireland's opportunity'.

So it was that, in 1915, plans began to be made for an armed insurrection, to be centred on Dublin but to involve other outbreaks too – ultimately, a general rising of the Irish people. How far such an outcome was really expected, and how far the organizers were really thinking in terms of military success can only be a matter for speculation now. The event was planned for the following Easter, the festival that recorded Christ the Saviour's rising from the dead – in a Catholic country like Ireland no one could possibly miss the symbolism. The idea was first conceived by members of the Irish Republican Brotherhood, including Pádraig Pearse, Tom Clarke, Seán Mac Diarmada, Éamon Ceannt, Joseph Plunkett and Thomas MacDonagh, but they were soon joined by the socialists James Connolly and Constance Markievicz. Eoin MacNeill, founder and leader of the Irish Volunteers, had taken a middle way in his thinking on the war, urging his supporters not to enlist on Britain's behalf, but not to make trouble in Ireland either. He could obviously not be brought into the conspiracy, therefore, but he nevertheless played an important part, the schemers hoping to use his forces – who were due to hold manoeuvres at the crucial time – as a diversion and cover for their own endeavour.

The Rising began to unravel as a going military concern when, on Good Friday, Roger Casement was arrested on the coast of County Kerry; the guns he had brought with him were impounded by the authorities. He had also brought news that no further help would be forthcoming from the German government – how seriously the organizers had been hoping for this is again a matter for speculation. Things went from bad to worse in the course of the weekend as, realizing that he was being taken for a fool, Eoin MacNeill commanded his Irish Volunteers to stand down. His order was taken by many in the country to mean the cancellation of the Rising itself: having been too clever for their own good, the organizers were forced to put the insurrection off a day. Whether or not it had been expected to succeed in

operational terms to begin with, by the time Easter Monday came the Rising had surely modulated from realistic military action to heroic gesture. Undaunted, though, 1,000 Volunteers, along with 200 members of James Conolly's Citizens Army, occupied the General Post Office and other public buildings. Pádraig Pearse read out the proclamation of the Irish Republic from the Post Office steps: it was a moment pregnant with symbolism – history in the making.

There was nothing symbolic about the British response, however: the government was plainly rattled by this course

of events, and cracked down with a force and brutality that did untold political damage in the long term, their artillery razing much of central Dublin as the fighting went on, their soldiers carrying out summary executions and indiscriminate arrests in the streets. This tough reaction to an insurrection which demonstrably had very little public support reflects British alarm at having been caught so badly unawares. They had in fact known of the planned Rising for quite some time, but had allowed themselves to relax in the days immediately before, believing it to have been prevented by the interception of Casement with his German guns. The execution of 15 leaders in the aftermath compounded what was already a public-relations disaster for the authorities,

LEFT: Government barricade during the Easter Rising.
ABOVE: Dublin General Post Office where the Easter Rising was launched.
RIGHT: Edward IV of England.

crowning with the dignity of martyrdom what had been a military fiasco for the Republicans. From their quicklime graves at Kilmainham Barracks would spring, not a living nation perhaps just yet, but a world of trouble and unpopularity for the British in Ireland. Yeats' poem 'Easter 1916' gives the classic summation of what those ill-judged executions would ultimately achieve: from grim death, it says, 'A terrible beauty is born'.

))))▶ *Roger Casement, James Connolly, Irish Volunteers, Irish Citizen Army; Seán Mac Diarmada, Thomas MacDonagh, Constance Markiewicz, Pádraig Pearce*

ECONOMIC WAR (1932–38)

Trade dispute between the Irish Free State and the United Kingdom. Money lent by the London government to Irish tenants who wished to buy out their smallholdings under the terms of the Land Acts of 1891–1901 had to be paid back through small annuities over time. Often the repayment period continued long after the end of British rule: in such cases the Free State government had agreed to collect the payments on Britain's behalf. In 1932, Éamon de Valera went back on this agreement, dismissing it as a hangover of colonial rule which need not be observed. The UK responded with economic sanctions which caused great problems for Irish agriculture and industry through the next few years, until the dispute was resolved diplomatically in 1938.

))))▶ *Land Act*

EDWARD IV OF ENGLAND (1441–83)

King of England (1461–83). In Ireland, Edward faced the powerful earls of Desmond, Kildare and Ormond. In 1468 he executed Desmond for treason but failed to bring Kildare under his control. In 1471 he made Thomas Fitzgerald, 7th Earl of Kildare, lord deputy in Ireland, a title the family retained into the 1500s.

))))▶ *Sir John Butler, Thomas Fitzgerald, Earls of Kildare*

ELIZABETH I OF ENGLAND (1533–1603)

Queen of England (1558–1603). Resentment of settlement and support from the Counter-Reformation led to three rebellions in Ireland during Elizabeth's reign: those of Shane O'Neill, Desmond and O'Neill-O'Donnell.

After the murder of Shane O'Neill in 1567, further English colonization was allowed in the provinces of Munster, Leinster and Ulster following a series of land confiscation. Resistance from the Butler (Ormond) and Fitzgerald (Desmond) families led Elizabeth to order a withdrawal from colonization and diplomatic pardons to be offered to the opponents.

In 1579 the Fitzgeralds led a papal-sponsored Catholic rebellion, provoked in part by a scorched-earth policy of expelling the Catholic Irish in Munster. The Desmond rebellion was wholly defeated in 1580, leading to further land confiscation and restrictions on Catholics. These and the arbitrary rule provided Aodh Ó Néill, Earl of Tyrone,

ABOVE: Elizabeth I of England.
ABOVE RIGHT: Emigrants on the quayside at Cork.
RIGHT: Cromwell at the head of his troops after The Battle of Marston Moor, 1644.

with much support for his 1594 rebellion. Despite having the initiative, Aodh Ó Néill lacked enough Spanish support to avoid defeat in 1601.

))))➤ *Aodh Ó Néill, The Pale*

EMIGRATION (19TH CENTURY)

The flight of many people from Ireland during the nineteenth century. Emigration peaked as a result of the Great Famine. The population of Ireland had risen to 8.5 million by the year 1845. By the outbreak of World War I in 1914 it had declined to only 4.4 million. Much of this decline can be attributed to the Great Famine (1845). Many of the population migrated to growing urban industrial

centres, particularly to Merseyside, Clydeside and London. Outside the UK, America was the main destination for migration. Other popular destinations for migration included Canada, Australia, New Zealand and Argentina.

))))➤ *Great Famine*

EMMET, ROBERT (1778–1803)

Irish nationalist hero. Robert Emmet was born in Dublin. He was the youngest son of Dr Robert Emmet, a state physician. Robert entered Trinity College in 1793 and became one of the leaders of the United Irishmen within the college. In 1802, whilst on the continent with his brother Thomas, the two men discussed Irish independence with Napoleon and Talleyrand. Emmet returned to Ireland in 1802 and began organizing a rising that he hoped would coincide with Napoleon's invasion of England in August, and established a depot of arms in Dublin. He hid at his father's house in Milltown until July 1803, when he called for the rising to begin following an explosion in one of the depots. The event ended in disaster. The assistance he was expecting from outside Dublin never materialized, the men were ineffective and the leaders were arguing among themselves. In the evening Emmet marched to attack Dublin Castle, murdering Arthur Wolfe, Lord Kilwarden, the Lord Chief Justice whilst on his way to the castle. Emmet and his

fiancée, Sarah Curran, had planned to escape to America after the rising, but Emmet was arrested by Major Henry Sirr and tried for treason. He was found guilty and was hanged and beheaded in Dublin on 20 September 1803. A commemorative statue was erected close to Emmet's place of birth in Dublin.

))▶ *Trinity College Dublin, United Irishmen*

ENGLISH CIVIL WAR (1642–51)

War between Royalists and Parliamentarians in England. The Civil War's origins lay in constitutional differences over powers enjoyed by the Crown or parliament. In the increasingly volatile religious climate, events in Ireland proved significant.

Since the reign of Elizabeth I, England's commitments in Ireland had steadily increased. Under Charles I, Thomas Wentworth, Earl of Strafford, operated a ruthless government in Ireland until his execution in 1641. This triggered the Confederate War in which Catholics combined against the Protestants, who were then synonymous with power and land ownership. Swearing allegiance to the Crown, the Catholic rebels linked Charles to their cause and ensured that parliament would seek to suppress them in order to prevent Ireland acting as a royalist base.

))▶ *Confederate War, Oliver Cromwell*

ENNISKILLEN

County town of Fermanagh; known in Irish as Inis Ceithleann, meaning 'Ceithle's Island'. Enniskillen is situated originally on an island between upper and lower Lough Erne. It first came to prominence in the late Middle Ages as a stronghold of the ruling Maguire dynasty. Later it was captured by the English and became a garrison town. It had a major strategic importance, being located close to the Ulster–Connacht boundary and controlling an important crossing over Lough Erne. After the expulsion of Catholic residents it became a significant Protestant outpost during the war between James II and William of Orange. Nowadays it is a busy market town, and important education and tourism centre where, despite a number of tragic events during the Troubles, Protestants and Catholics live together quite happily.

))▶ *James II of England, Maguire Dynasty, the Troubles, William III of England*

ERIUGENA, JOHANNES SCOTTUS
(C. AD 820–80)

Irish-born philosopher and theologian. Eriugena spent most of his adult life in continental Europe. He was master of the palace school at the court of the west-Frankish king Charles II (the Bald), and played a leading role in several significant philosophical and theological debates of his time. He was reportedly stabbed to death in Oxford by students with their pens.

)))➤ *Johannes Duns Scottus*

ESSEX, EARLS OF (16TH CENTURY)

Family of English nobles who exerted control in Ireland in the sixteenth century. In 1576 Walter Devereux, 1st Earl of Essex (*c.* 1541–76) was sent to Ireland to conquer the rebellious O'Neills of Ulster and to expel the Scots. He operated a campaign of ruthless massacre of ordinary people – including Scottish women and children – and captured and executed the leaders of the O'Neill rebellion.

After his withdrawal he was awarded estates and made earl-marshal of Ireland. His son, Robert Devereux, 2nd Earl of Essex (1566–1601), was a favourite of Elizabeth I, despite his constant intrigues and insolence. In 1599 Elizabeth made him governor-general of Ireland and sent him to suppress Aodh Ó Néill and his rebellion. He was defeated at Arklow the same year and made a truce with Ó Néill which was to be renewed every six months. On his arrival back in England he was charged with making a dishonourable and dangerous treaty and imprisoned, but was freed in 1600. In 1601 he was tried for treason on other charges and executed.

)))➤ *Elizabeth I of England, Battle of Kinsale, Aodh O'Néill*

EUCHARISTIC CONGRESS (1932)

Catholic convention held in Dublin in 1932. Although in Church terms this was just another in a series of international gatherings held to promote devotion to the Blessed Sacrament (Holy Communion), the Eucharistic Congress represented a crucial point in the life of the Irish Free State, healing many of the wounds of the civil war by bringing the whole country together under the banner of Catholicism. A week of meetings, masses and festivities culminated in an open-air service in Phoenix Park to which over a million worshippers came, and heard the famous tenor John MacCormack singing the Latin hymn *Panis Angelicus* ('Bread of Angels').

)))➤ *John MacCormack*

EUROPEAN UNION (1973)

Economic and, increasingly, political partnership between a growing community of European countries. Neither the Irish Republic nor Northern Ireland, as part of the UK, belonged to the European Economic Community inaugurated in 1958 by the Treaty of Rome. Having applied unsuccessfully in 1962, Ireland was admitted at the same time as Britain, in 1973. In some ways an ignominious moment – Ireland was effectively drawn into the Community in Britain's wake – the long-term consequences

LEFT: Walter Devereux, Earl of Essex.
NEAR RIGHT: Brian Faulkner.
FAR RIGHT: Banner of the Fenian Brotherhood.

of membership have been economically liberating, freeing the country from its disabling dependence on the UK trade.

The Irish have for the most part been far more enthusiastic Europeans than the British, voting by a majority of five to one in favour of joining in the referendum of 1972 – they have seen an enlargement of their economic horizons, where the British have tended to see a reduction in political sovereignty. Ideas of a federalist Europe, far from frightening the horses as they have in Britain, have been seized on as suggesting imaginative solutions to the problems of partition.

FAULKNER, BRIAN (1921–77)

Unionist statesman, last prime minister of Northern Ireland. As prime minister from 1971, Brian Faulker presided over the introduction of Internment and some of the most serious civil-rights violations of Stormont rule. He was pragmatic enough, however, to sign the Sunningdale Agreement of 1973 and to take his place as chief executive of the resulting power-sharing assembly in 1974, although this was scarcely formed before it was brought down by a strike of Protestant workers.

))))➤ *Sunningdale Agreements, Unionists*

FÉIRITÉAR, PIARAS (c. 1600–53)

Chieftain and poet from County Kerry. Féiritéar surprised the Anglo-Irish establishment (who thought him trustworthy because of his family's Norman origins) at the onset of the 1641 Rebellion by leading a successful attack on Tralee Castle. He maintained his defiant stance until 1653. Although promised safe conduct after his surrender he was seized and publicly hanged in Killarney. He was also a significant Irish-language poet whose work survives to the present day not only in contemporary manuscript copies but also in the oral tradition in the Kerry Gaeltacht, where he is regarded as a folk-hero.

))))➤ *Gaeltacht, Rebellion of 1641*

FENIAN BROTHERHOOD (1858)

Revolutionary organization. Founded on St Patrick's Day in 1858 by veterans of the abortive 1848 Rising in both Dublin and New York, the Fenian Brotherhood set out to establish an independent, non-sectarian Ireland by means of the armed struggle. Its leading figures, James Stephens in Ireland and John O'Mahony and Michael Doheny in America, had despaired at what they saw as the derisory progress made for the national cause by the constitutionalist Repeal and Young Ireland movements. The name O'Mahony chose for his brotherhood harked back to the *Fianna*, the legendary warrior-band of Fionn mac Cumhail: this was self-consciously not just a militant but a military organization.

))))➤ *Irish Republican Brotherhood*

FENIAN MOVEMENT

Wider political movement that grew up around activities of Fenians. Despite its fiery rhetoric, the Fenian Brotherhood's first major coup was impeccably peaceable, the organization of a major publicity coup involving the repatriation for burial of the remains of Terence Bellew McManus, an 1848 veteran who had died in exile. Brought across America by train and then on to Dublin by ship, the late revolutionary was acclaimed by cheering crowds at every stage. James Stephens' attempts to raise funds by founding a newspaper, the *Irish People* was a most incautious move on the part of one running a supposedly 'secret' organization – and did indeed lead to his own arrest in 1867 – but it reflects the extent to which, despite its creation as a revolutionary clique, 'Fenianism' was by degrees becoming a mass political movement, its actions arguably more symbolic than seriously military.

)))➤ *Fenian Rising*

FENIAN RISING (1867)

Political rebellion. The conclusion of the American Civil War in 1865, with the resulting demobilization of large numbers of Irish-American soldiers, trained and battle-seasoned, represented an obvious opportunity for

Fenianism in the Old Country. So obvious an opportunity, unfortunately, that the authorities were on the highest state of alert and promptly swooped to round up such leading figures as James Stephens, T.C. Luby, John O'Leary and O'Donovan Rossa. Although Stephens escaped to America, the group's organizational core had been smashed, but a militant faction among those left at liberty was determined that, come what may, there must be a rising. After a failed effort in February 1867 the Fenians tried again the following month, though as so often in the annals of Irish rebellion it was the subsequent clampdown by the British that did most to advance the rising's cause.

)))➤ *Fenian Movement, Manchester Martyrs*

FIANNA FÁIL (1926)

Political party. Founded by Éamon de Valera in 1926, Fianna Fáil ('Soldiers of Destiny') was dedicated to attaining an independent, Irish-speaking united Ireland by peaceful means. That such an aspiration came close to being oxymoronic, given the diehard opposition of northern Protestants and the British state, did not prevent its resonating strongly with a good many Irish voters who, while accepting that the all-Irish Republic would have to wait, did not feel ready to renounce it completely. The party's first achievement was, as anticipated, to marginalize Sinn Féin, whose members were still boycotting the Dáil; much less expected was the progress made in Irish politics in general. Since its surprise victory in the elections of 1932, Fianna Fáil has been in government more often than not, its popularity outlasting the career of its founding father de Valera.

)))➤ *Éamon de Valera*

FIELD, JOHN (1782–1837)

Dublin-born pianist and composer. Field settled in Russia in 1803 and enjoyed considerable success as a performer and teacher. His development of a new musical form, the nocturne, was an important influence on later musicians most notably Frédéric Chopin. His compositions include about 20 nocturnes, many of which remain popular with pianists.

LEFT: Fenian prisoners at Dublin are brought out of the lower castle-yard on their way to Mounjoy Prison.

FILÍ

Irish word, meaning 'poets'. In Gaelic Ireland, from the earliest times until the destruction of the Gaelic social order following the Flight of the Earls, poets enjoyed considerable status at the courts of the chieftains, having the same social standing as a bishop. Their praise poems and satires exerted great influence on those to whom they were addressed and their work can often be found in the family poem-book, or *duanaire*, of the leading Gaelic families.

))⃗ *Flight of the Earls*

FINE GAEL (1933)

Political party. Formed in 1933 in response to Fianna Fáil's shock election triumph the previous year, Fine Gael ('Irish Kin') brought together three parties in hopes of mounting a coherent opposition. The parliamentary voice of the civil war's victors, Cumann na nGaedhea had come to regard itself as the 'natural' party of government: its desperate results of 1932 suggested that desperate remedies were needed. Hence, perhaps, the inclusion in the new party of Eoin O'Duffy's Blueshirts, along with the conservative farmer's grouping, the National Centre Party. The new organization seems to have shaken down over time, however, offering an increasingly credible conservative voice against Fianna Fáil, but it has apparently been fated to serve by and large as an opposition party.

))⃗ *Blueshirts, Cumann na nGaedheal*

FIONN MAC CUMHAIL (FINN MCCOOL)

Fionn mac Cumhail appears in many guises both in folklore and in early Irish literature. He was the leader of the Fianna – a band of warriors loyal to Cormac mac Airt – and is the hero of the Fionn cycle of tales. There

are two great story cycles belonging to the early Irish: one is the Fionn cycle and the other is the Ulster cycle, which features Cú Chulainn. In these stories and in present-day folklore Fionn mac Cumhail is described as having great physical, mental and magical powers. Often portrayed as a giant, he is credited in the *dinnseanchas*, with building the Giant's Causeway in County Antrim, and with creating both Lough Neagh and the Isle of Man, when he scooped up a sod of earth and threw it at his rival in Scotland.

))⃗ *Cormac mac Airt, Cú Chulainn,* **Dinnseanchas,** *Giant's Causeway*

LEFT: Fine Gael leader John Bruton on the eve of the Irish elections, 1997.
ABOVE: Fionn mac Cumhail and Princess Tasha.

FIR BOLG

According to the semi-mythological histories of Ireland, such as the *Book of Invasions* the Fir Bolg were one of the earliest peoples to invade and live in Ireland. Their name implies that they carried large bags or had big stomachs, but it is possible that they were actually the Belgiae, a continental tribe who have given their name to modern-day Belgium. Archeological evidence of their presence in Ireland is lacking, however.

))))▶ **Book of Invasions**

FITZGERALD, LORD EDWARD (1763–98)

Radical leader of the United Irishmen. Son of the Duke of Leinster, he served in the British Army in America. Fitzgerald was republican in outlook and greatly admired the principles of the French Revolution. He joined the Society of United Irishmen in 1796 and advocated armed insurrection and was involved in plans to bring this about. He was strongly opposed to Grattan's cautious approach in parliament. Fitzgerald died from a wound inflicted during his arrest in May 1798. His loss was critical for the United Irishmen and he was fondly remembered by those involved. Wolfe Tone described him as the only real representative of the powerless people of Ireland in parliament.

))))▶ *Rebellion of 1798, United Irishmen, Theobald Wolfe Tone*

FITZGERALD, GARRET (b. 1926)

Fine Gael statesman; Taoiseach (1981–82, 1983–87). Apparently one of modern Ireland's less colourful statesman, with little time for the usual patriotic pieties, Garret Fitzgerald may well be revealed by history as a crucial influence on nationalist history. Challenging the

ABOVE LEFT: The arrest of Lord Edward Fitzgerald for high treason.
ABOVE RIGHT: Garret Fitzgerald.
FAR RIGHT: Gerald Fitzgerald flees to Brittany.

Nationalist–Catholic conflation of Éamon de Valera's Fianna Fáil, invoking the memory of such distinguished Protestant republicans as Theobald Wolfe Tone and the Repealer Thomas Osborne Davis, Fitzgerald did everything he could to ease the anxieties of the Protestant North. An Irishman even the uncompromising Mrs Thatcher felt she could do business with, it was he who signed the Anglo-Irish Agreement of 1985.

))))▶ *Anglo-Irish Agreement, Fine Gael*

FITZGERALD, GERALD, EIGHTH EARL OF KILDARE (1456–1513)

Governor of Ireland (1478, 1479–92, 1496–1513). One of the most successful lord deputies, Kildare served under five successive English kings. This alone, given the treacherous court politics of the time, would have made him remarkable, but he proved just as sure-footed on the ground in Ireland; his 'carrot-and-stick' policy towards the native clans enabled him to establish a powerful English presence in the Pale and beyond. Allying his family with those of the Irish chieftains both by marriage and diplomatic ties, Kildare cultivated certain Gaelic airs when it suited him, but came down hard on native chiefs who showed signs of resistance to English rule.

))))➧ *Conquest of Ireland, Earls of Kildare*

FITZGERALD, GERALD, 9TH EARL OF KILDARE (1487–1534)

Garret Óg or 'Gerald the Younger'. Gerald acceded in 1513 on the death of his father, Gearóid Mór, and was appointed lord deputy in 1513 by his cousin, Henry VIII. Following allegations of conspiracy by the English in 1526 he was summoned to Cardinal Wolsey and denounced

as a traitor. He had appointed his son 'Silken Thomas' as vice deputy and whilst away in London, the young Thomas started the rebellion that led to his execution. Gerald died in the Tower of London. In 1537 an Act decreed that all the Fitzgerald counties be forfeited to the English Crown.

))))➧ *Thomas Fitzgerald, Earls of Kildare*

FITZGERALD, THOMAS, 8TH EARL OF DESMOND (1426–68)

Governor of Ireland (1463–67). The tensions between the earls of Munster and the English Crown would finally flare up in the Desmond Revolt of the late sixteenth century, but they were a problematic presence in Irish governance long before this. The appointment of Thomas Fitzgerald to the lord lieutenancy after his assistance in defeating the Earl of Ormond's forces at Pilltown seemed the perfect way not only to reward service, but also to cement the loyalty of this most remote and wayward of Irish earldoms. As things turned out, however, the Crown came to feel that Fitzgerald was only making Munster's problems more general: his Gaelicizing ways alarmed the lords of the English Pale. He was accordingly deposed from the deputyship in 1467 and executed for treason the following year.

))))➧ *Earls of Desmond, Edward IV of England*

FITZGERALD, WILLIAM VESEY (1783–1843)

As MP for County Clare from 1818, Fitzgerald had to stand for re-election in 1828, having been appointed a government minister by the Duke of Wellington. Daniel O'Connell decided to contest the seat to demonstrate the extent of his support – despite the acknowledged popularity of Fitzgerald, himself a known supporter of Catholic Emancipation. O'Connell's victory over such a well-regarded candidate, despite his own inability, as a Catholic, to take his seat, seems to have persuaded both Wellington and Peel of the need to accept Emancipation.

))))➧ *Catholic Emancipation, Daniel O'Connell*

FITZWILLIAM EPISODE (1795)

On 21 February William Wentworth, the lord lieutenant of Ireland was recalled, having been accused of trying to reconstruct the Irish administration. Earl Fitzwilliam's appointment was part of a deal with elements in the English Whig Party to entice them into government. There were also rumours that he was too close to Catholic reformers' demands and indeed he had asked to be able to support Grattan's Catholic Relief Bill. It has been claimed that he did not sufficiently realize what was expected of him as lord lieutenant. His replacement Earl Camden was in charge at a time of repression which helped lead to the 1798 Rising.

FLANN SINNA (d. AD 916)

King of Ireland from AD 876; also known as Flann Siona O'Neill. In AD 908 he defeated and killed his son-in-law Cormac MacCullenan, king-bishop of the Eóganacht of Munster at Ballaghmoon, destroying their hold on the southern half of Ireland. In AD 909 he built the 19-m (62-ft) long cathedral at Clonmacnoise, Ccounty Offaly, and endowed it with decoration including a cross of the scriptures. He was buried here, and was succeeded as king of Ireland by Niall Glundubh.

)))▶ *Battle of Ballaghmoon, Niall Glundubh*

FLIGHT OF THE EARLS (1607)

After his defeat at Kinsale, and following his surrender at Mellifont in 1603, O'Neill had been forced to relinquish his title 'O'Neill' and took that of the Earl of Tyrone. Rory O'Donnell, under similar circumstances, had become the Earl of Tyrconnell and the two met with James I of England to sign the Treaty of Mellifont. After returning to Ireland, rumours were spread that the two were planning a rebellion and they were summoned back to London. Finding English rule unacceptable, they boarded a French ship from Rathmullen, together with their family and followers, and set off for Spain. Fierce storms forced the ship into France and they decided to travel instead to Rome. The government declared their flight treasonous and confiscated their lands.

)))▶ *Treaty of Mellifont*

FLIGHT OF THE WILD GEESE (1690)

Exile of Ireland's Catholic gentry in the aftermath of the Williamite wars. Long before its lower orders were taking ship for America, Ireland's young Catholic aristocrats were going abroad to serve as mercenaries in the armies of the Catholic powers. But in the wake of William's victory at the Boyne in 1690, the number of exiles suddenly swelled. William himself was not in a magnanimous mood, but some of his foreign generals were more pragmatic: a defeated enemy allowed freely to go into exile would have no interest

in staying on in Ireland to wage a guerrilla war. The irony, of course, was that they would still come back to haunt Britain in the end. One general allowed an army of 12,000 to leave with its women and children: they promptly enlisted in the service of France. Throughout the eighteenth century young Irish Catholics would seek the advancement abroad they could not expect to find at home, enlisting in the armies not only of France and Spain but of Sweden, Austria and Russia too. The Wild Geese's finest hour, perhaps, came at the Battle of Fontenoy in 1745, when an Irish brigade swung what seemed a doomed encounter with the Duke of Cumberland's army in France's favour.

)))▶ *Battle of the Boyne, William III of England*

FOUR COURTS (1786–1802)

Seat of the High Court of Justice in Dublin. The Four Courts was built by James Gandon on the former thirteenth-century Dominican monastery between 1786 and 1802. The building was completely destroyed by shells, leading to the outbreak of Civil War (1922–23), and irreplaceable records were destroyed. In 1932 the Four Courts was completely restored.

)))▶ *James Gandon*

FRANCISCAN ORDER (1230)

Religious order. Founded *c.* 1210 by St Francis of Assisi, the Franciscans were recorded in Ireland as early as 1230. An order of mendicant friars, dependent on the charity of others, they had a particular commitment to the welfare of the very poor. Although they were no more immune from institutional corruption than any other order – and indeed at times riven by internal faction-fighting along ethnic lines – the Franciscans survived to stand by the Gaelic peasantry in their resistance to Tudor colonization, and to work underground with them through much of the

ABOVE: The Four Courts, Dublin.
ABOVE RIGHT: The Franciscan Abbey, Askeaton, County Limerick.
RIGHT: The Reverend Ian Paisley, founder of the Free Presbyterian Church.

grown to about 13,000 members in Northern Ireland and small communities in other parts of the world. Ian Paisley has always been Moderator of this anti-Catholic Church and it has strongly opposed any moves towards greater understanding among the churches. It is linked politically to the DUP.

)))➤ *Democratic Unionist Party, Ian Paisley*

FRENCH REVOLUTION (1789)

The French Revolution in July 1789 followed the American Declaration of Independence in 1776. Amongst other fears for established interests, the French event provoked fears in Britain that Ireland might follow in its footsteps, causing terror amongst the Anglican Ascendancy in particular. A modest relaxation of control to pre-empt a revolt benefited no-one except the Anglicans. Demands for reform became extensive and led to the emergence of the United Irishmen and revolutionary leaders in Ireland such as Theobald Wolfe Tone and the Sheares brothers. Frustration with a lack of progress meant they sought French assistance for an armed revolt, exploding disastrously in the 1798 Rebellion.

)))➤ *Henry and John Sheares, Theobald Wolfe Tone*

seventeenth century. Thereafter they declined, not fully recovering until the twentieth century, by which time their role as 'guerrilla friars' had been superseded.

)))➤ *Monasteries*

FREE DERRY CORNER

Focal point for Civil Rights and republican demonstrations. The name is given to a lone gable wall which stands in Derry's nationalist Bogside area. It is retained because of its important symbolism; local artists had painted 'You are now entering Free Derry' on the wall. The wall and its legend came to represent the defiance of the local people to the gerrymandered corporation and a focal point for Civil Rights meetings. It lay right in the heart of the 'no-go' area which the Royal Ulster Constabulary and British Army were not permitted to enter, and it was here that the ill-fated Civil Rights Movement march of 1972 ('Bloody Sunday') eventually finished.

)))➤ *Bloody Sunday, Civil Rights Movement, Royal Ulster Constabulary*

FREE PRESBYTERIAN CHURCH (1951)

Fundamentalist anti-ecumenical church established by Ian Paisley. When Paisley was refused the right to preach in Crossgar because of his reputation and the fact that he was a missioner, five members formed a new congregation and released the Free Presbyterian Manifesto, declaring its wish to be free from Presbyterian control. Paisley's Ravenhill church joined up and the church has

GAELIC ATHLETIC ASSOCIATION (1884)

Association formed in 1884 to promote the traditional Irish games of hurling, football, handball, rounders and camogie; known in Irish as *Cumann Luthchleas Gael*. Hurling is an ancient Gaelic game – similar to Shinty – played by men in teams of 15, using a ball (sliothar) and stick (cámán or hurley). The women's version of hurling is Camogie.

))))▶ *Gaelic League*

GAELIC IRELAND

Gaelic Ireland, especially before the Norman conquest, was a unique society with a highly developed administrative structure and legal code, known as the Brehon Laws. Regions or territories were controlled by different families and their associates, among them the Ó Néills in Ulster, the Ó Connors of Connacht and the Ó Briains of Thomond. The most powerful leaders became High Kings; the most prestigious of all was the king of Tara in County Meath. Brian Bóroimhe, a Munster king, was the first non-Ó Néill ruler to claim this position and in the century after his death in 1014, many different rulers vied for the title. Gaelic culture was so influential even after the Norman invasion that many of the Norman families became Gaelicized and elements of the Statutes of Kilkenny of 1366 were passed specifically to stem the spread of the Irish language and culture among them. Much of the Gaelic way of life remained intact until the Plantations of Munster and Ulster, with poets, clerics and lawyers following the hereditary

careers until they lost their patronage and prestige with the demise of the Gaelic ruling classes, especially after the Flight of the Earls in 1607.

))))▶ *Brehon Laws, Brian Bóroimhe, Conquest of Ireland, Flight of the Earls, Statutes of Kilkenny, Plantation of Ulster*

GAELIC LEAGUE (*CONRADH NA GAEILGE*) (1893)

Irish language organization founded in Dublin in 1893. Its leading members included Eoin Mac Néill and Douglas Hyde, who was its first president, and later Pádraig Pearse and Éamon de Valera. It differed in philosophy from earlier Irish language organizations in that rather than having an antiquarian interest in the language, it aimed to promote it as the everyday spoken language of the country. Its teachings therefore had a major influence on the growth of cultural nationalism at the end of the nineteenth

and beginning of the twentieth centuries. The Gaelic League sought to defend and expand the rights of Irish-speakers, to promote the language in the education system and to develop a modern literature in Irish. Initially non-political, its demands and campaigns inevitably brought it to challenge the government and by the time of the Easter Rising of 1916 – in which many members took part – it had become an important element in the struggle for national self-determination. It remains active to the present day as a language rights watchdog and promoter of literature and culture.

))))▶ *Éamon de Valera, Easter Rising, Douglas Hyde, Eoin Mac Néill, Pádraig Pearse*

GAELIC REVIVAL (14TH CENTURY)

Cultural and political movement of the later Middle Ages which saw Gaelic society in Ireland recover from the Norman invasions and gain strength both politically and culturally. There were a number of significant military reverses for the Normans, such as the defeat of the Fitzgeralds by the Ó Donnells in Sligo in 1257 and the revolts by the Leinster Irish in the latter half of the thirteenth century. At the same time many of the descendants of Anglo-Norman invaders became so assimilated that it was felt necessary to pass the Statutes of Kilkenny in 1366, which insisted on the use of the English language, names and customs in an attempt to stem this gaelicization. There was also a cultural revival at this time, as Irish kings reasserted their independence from Dublin rule and pointedly chose to reinstate the filí – the poets and the chroniclers – to their positions of power and influence. With such patronage restored, their art flourished and books such as the Book of Lecan date from this period.

The term 'Gaelic Revival', is also applied to the revival of the fortunes of the Irish language in the latter half of the nineteenth century and the beginning of the twentieth, especially in relation to the work of the Gaelic League.

))))▶ *Filí, Gaelic League, Statutes of Kilkenny, Book of Lecan*

GAELTACHT

Term used to describe the Irish-speaking areas of Ireland. While there were Irish-speaking regions in at least 23 counties in the period immediately after the Great Famine, the second half of the nineteenth century saw many of these areas disappear and the Irish language was increasingly found only on the western seaboard and in a few other isolated pockets. Although it is difficult to give an accurate figure of the number of people who use Irish as their everyday language today, the Dublin government recognizes parts of Counties Cork, Kerry and Waterford in Munster, Galway and Mayo in Connacht, Donegal in Ulster and Meath in Leinster as the official gaeltacht, which is partially administered by its own elected authority. There is also a significant Irish-speaking community in Belfast.

Galltacht is the term used for the English-speaking part.

))))▶ *Great Famine*

FAR LEFT: *Traditional Irish dancing.*
LEFT: *Gaelic shop sign.*
BELOW: *The Gaelic-speaking community at Muckish mountain.*

GALLARUS ORATORY (8TH–12TH CENTURIES)

Middle Ages place of prayer in County Kerry. Built sometime between the eighth and twelfth centuries, the Oratory is a famous landmark on the Dingle Peninsula in County Kerry, overlooking Smerwick Harbour. It is built out of unmortared drystone and has survived intact in its original form. It is an example of the flourishing monastic settlements which proliferated in Munster during this period, a time when Irish missionaries were becoming less welcome on the Continent. Legend says that its shape is that of an upturned boat, similar to that used by St Brendan who was supposed to have sailed to Newfoundland in the sixth century.

GALLOWGLASS (13TH–17TH CENTURIES)

Elite mercenaries of the thirteenth to seventeenth centuries. These mercenaries were usually in the pay of Scots and Irish chieftains. Noted for being exceptionally large men, the Gallowglass (an anglicized form of *gallóglach*, meaning 'foreign warrior') wore conical helmets and long coats of reinforced cotton or chain mail, and wielded large hand-held weapons such as the Claymore (*claiomh mór*) sword. They were descended from Viking settlers in the Hebrides. The Gallowglass became particularly important in the sixteenth century during the wars against the English, and they have been commemorated in monuments in churches.

GALWAY

Coastal city in the south of Connacht. Essentially an Anglo-Norman foundation dating from the early thirteenth century, Galway grew up around the castle built by Richard de Burgh in 1232. A charter of 1484 protected the city from the covetousness of neighbouring aristocrats and Gaelic warlords, and enabled the city's 14 English merchant families or 'tribes' to thrive in the French and Spanish trades. The city seemed set to grow and prosper until, captured by Cromwell after a nine-month siege in 1652, its structures were razed and its leading citizens expelled, those remaining then being decimated by an epidemic of Plague. The merchant city destroyed, Galway never entirely recovered as a trading centre: the industrial revolution that swept up Belfast, Dublin, and even Cork and Limerick, more or less passed it by. Now, Galway has found a role as a touristic 'gateway to the Gaeltacht': despite Cromwell, it is one of Ireland's most attractive provincial cities.
))))➤ *Richard de Burgh*

GANDON, JAMES (1742–1823)

London-born architect who designed some of the most important Georgian-era buildings in Dublin. Gandon came to Dublin in 1781 to build the new Custom House, and the following year he was commissioned to

design the extensions to the Irish parliament building, now the Bank of Ireland in College Green. He also built the Four Courts and the King's Inns and these all remain landmark buildings in central Dublin.
))))➤ *Custom House, Four Courts*

GENERAL POST OFFICE (1818)

Headquarters of the Irish Post Office – and of the Easter Rising of 1916. Impressively designed by Francis Johnston and first opened in 1818, the GPO would have been one of the sights of Dublin even had it not played such a vital role as historical stage-set. It was as much because of its grandiosity as its location at the very heart of central Dublin that it was selected it as the military headquarters for the Easter Rising. On Easter Monday 1916, Pádraig Pearse read out the proclamation of the Irish Republic there – and where 1,000 volunteers then hunkered down to defend it.

By the time Britannia's guns fell silent, the building was a blackened shell – even now its magnificent colonnade remains pitted by shellfire. Its interior restored, the GPO was re-opened in 1929: a statue of the fallen hero Cú Chulaínn commemorated those who had died in the uprising.

)))➤ *Easter Rising*

FAR LEFT: The Customs House, Dublin, designed by James Gandon.
LEFT: The General Post Office, gutted by fire during the 1916 Easter Rising.
BELOW: Bantry Bay in County Cork.

GEOGRAPHY

Ireland lies to the west of Great Britain and is separated from it by distances ranging from 18 to 193 km (11 to 120 miles), divided by the North Channel, the Irish Sea and St George's Channel. The seas surrounding Ireland are less than 198 m (650 ft) in depth and the island itself is 486 km (302 miles) from east to west and 114 km (71 miles) from north to south.

The island is host to lakes, large bog areas, low ridges and several mountain ranges, including the Blue Stack Mountains in the north, the Wicklow Mountains in the east, the Knockmealdown and Comeragh Mountains in the south, the Macgillycuddy Reeks in the south-west and the Twelve Pins in the west. Ireland's highest peak is Carrantouhill (1,040 m/3,414 ft) in the the Macgillycuddy Reeks. Ireland is known as 'the Emerald Isle' because of the exceptionally bright green shades that cover most of the island.

The shape of Ireland is often related to the shape of a saucer, with the edges representing the mountains and the centre of the island being much flatter. In the flatter, central areas the rivers widen out to form the lakes. The limestone plain is ringed by coastal highlands, all of which vary in geological structure. The mountain ranges in the west, north-west and east are mainly granite. Several large bays make up much of the coastline, particularly in the west and south-west, including Bantry Bay and Dingle Bay. These bays are former river valleys that have been drowned. The mountain ranges found in the west, north-west and east are granite, whereas in the south the mountains are usually formed of sandstone. A common feature of the landscape throughout Ireland is large areas of peat bogs. In the west of the island are extensive areas of bare limestone.

The sluggish and slow-flowing River Shannon runs for 258 km (160 miles) reaching tidewater at Limerick. The River Shannon broadens, in its middle course, into lakes but as it approaches the sea its gradient tends to become steeper. Many inland streams flow through the island and often these enter the sea by means of rapids and waterfalls. Many, such as the Slaney which enters the sea at Wexford, the Lagan which flows into Belfast Lough, and the Liffey at Dublin, the Boyne, the Nore and the Barrow are very slow-moving and therefore make perfect homes for the salmon which is fished here. The Suir, the Blackwater which reaches the coastline by making acute angled turns and passes through sandstone ridges, and the Lee are situated in the east-west valleys in the south of the island. The Bandon, the Clare and the Moy are also slow-moving. The slow flow of the rivers and inland streams has caused problems of flooding in the past because of the high levels of water retain-ed within the lakes. Government-sponsored projects have been established throughout the island's recent history in order to increase the flow of the rivers and inland streams, to eliminate the risk of the lakes flooding and to enhance the drainage programmes throughout the island. The majority of Ireland's running water is made up from alkaline rivers before joining the sea via winding marshy estuaries.

Ireland's plant and animal life tends to have resulted from the migration of the different species from elsewhere. Because Ireland was, during the Ice Age, covered with glaciers, one of which covered the whole of the country, and the other linking Limerick, Cashel and Dublin, it is unlikely that all of its plant and animal life are natives of the island. However, some are now unique to the island itself, such as the Irish orchid. Ireland's animals include the Irish stoat and the Irish hare, but does not include the snake or many reptiles; there is only one species of lizard. The natural resources of the island include zinc, lead, natural gas, barite, copper, gypsum, limestone, dolomite, peat and silver.

Ireland's climate is temperate and humid. This can be attributed to the fact that the prevailing south-westerly winds

ABOVE: The Ha'penny bridge over the River Liffey, Dublin.
ABOVE RIGHT: The Giant's Causeway.
RIGHT: William Ewart Gladstone.

and the warming effects of the Gulf Stream keep the island relatively warm during the winter. The mid-east of Ireland experiences less than 75 cm (30 in) of rain, with the south and west experiencing over 200 cm (80 in) of rain per year. The climate is classified as western maritime and the temperature tends to be uniform throughout the whole of the island. This trend is due to the island's situation to the Atlantic Ocean and the mild winds of the North Atlantic current. The coldest months of the year tend to be January and February when temperatures of four to seven degrees Celsius are experienced, and the warmest are July and August with temperatures of between 14 and 16 degrees Celsius or sometimes higher. The sunniest months are May,

with an average sunshine for 5.5 hours per day and June with average sunshine for 6.5 hours per day throughout the island. Snow is not often experienced, except in the mountain ranges and it is rare for snowstorms or prolonged periods of snow to occur.

GERALD OF WALES (GIRALDUS CAMBRENSIS) (1146–1223)

Anglo-Norman priest who visited Ireland on two occasions and wrote two highly political accounts of his impressions of the country. *Topographia Hibernica* is a description of the country and its people, while *Expugnatio Hibernica* (1189) details the events leading up to Henry II's invasion. In these books Gerald compared the native Irish unfavourably with his fellow Normans and thus sought to justify the Norman invasion.

))) ➤ *Henry II of England*

GIANT'S CAUSEWAY

A striking geological feature on the north Antrim coast between Portrush and Ballycastle, the Giant's Causeway was formed some 60 million years ago when molten basalt cooled rapidly, forming thousands of hexagonal columns which run from the cliff face into the sea. According to legend they are steps built by the giant, Fionn mac Cumhail, so that he could cross over to Scotland. Now managed by the British National Trust, the site is on the United Nations Educational, Scientific and Cultural Organisation (UNESCO) World Heritage List.

))))➤ *Fion mac Cumhail*

GLADSTONE, WILLIAM EWART (1809–98)

English statesman, Liberal prime minister (1868–74, 1880–85, 1886, 1892–94). A dominant presence in British politics for much of the second half of the nineteenth century, Gladstone had an enormous impact on the affairs of Ireland. Having disestablished the Church of Ireland and introduced a vital Land Act during his first term in office, he would later return repeatedly to the Home Rule question. His belief that the UK could only be saved by a constitutional reorganization which gave every indication of breaking it up did not convince his British contemporaries – although it was arguably prophetic.

))))➤ *Church Disestablishment Act, Home Rule, Land Acts*

GLEN MAMA, BATTLE OF (AD 999)

Battle which established the power of the High King Brian Bóroimhe. In AD 998 Brian Bóroimhe and Mael Seachnaill II, the two principal chieftains in Ireland, agreed a settlement which gave Brian the south and Mael Seachnaill the north. Mael Seachnaill then ousted his wife, Gormfhlaith, widow of the Viking leader, Olaf. Gormfhlaith sought help from her brother Mael Mordha, encouraging him to ally himself with her Viking son Sitric, the lord of Dublin, against Brian and Mael Seachnaill. The rebellion collapsed quickly at Glen Mama, when Brian's forces routed the armies of Mael Mordha and Sitric. Brian used diplomacy to settle the tension by marrying Gormfhlaith himself, reinstating Sitric in Dublin and offering him his daughter in marriage, and making Mael Mordha king of Leinster.

))))➤ *Brian Bóroimhe, Mael Mordha, Mael Seachnaill II*

GLENDALOUGH

Monastery in County Wicklow. When St Kevin died in AD 618, the pious world beat a path to his door, a significant monastery complex springing up where once had only been his hermit's cell. In 1111, in the aftermath of the Cashel Synod, a bishopric was established here. The atmospheric ruins include several churches and a round tower. The site was popular with pilgrims well into the nineteenth century; now new-age tourists flock to 'Ireland's Delphi'.

)))))➤ *Monasteries, St Kevin of Glendalough, Synod of Cashel*

GLENMALURE, BATTLE OF (1580)

Catholic rebellion against the English. Encouraged by papal support, and despite his lack of military judgement, Gerald Fitzgerald, 15th Earl of Desmond, led a rebellion against the English army and the English policy of scorched-earth settlement operated by Sir William Pelham and Lord Grey de Wilton. In November 1580 a force of Italians and Spaniards was wiped out at Dún an Óir. At this point, James Eustace, Viscount Baltinglass, entered the fray and defeated Lord Grey's forces at Glenmalure with the assistance of Fiach MacHugh O'Byrne. Despite this the English forces soon crushed the rebellion.

)))))➤ *Earls of Desmond*

GOOD FRIDAY AGREEMENT (1998)

Political settlement reached on Good Friday – 10 April – 1998, which allowed for the establishment of an all-party Assembly for the government of Northern

Ireland. Political progress within Northern Ireland be-came possible in the comparatively harmonious atmosphere that followed the Downing Street Declaration of 1993, an atmosphere eased further by the continuing ceasefire of the paramilitaries. There were still major sticking-points between the parties, though, as 1998 began, with the Unionists reluctant to sit down at the same table as Sinn Féin represen-tatives. Although the issue of how far or how finally the IRA had forsworn violence remains unresolved to this day, a formula was at last found which would enable Unionist leader David Trimble to participate. In the Assembly subse-quently elected, he became chief minister, while his deputy was Seamus Mallon of the SDLP. In a remarkable new order, Northern Ireland's education minister was the Sinn Féin member and former IRA commander Martin McGuinness.

))))▶ *Downing Street Declaration*

GORMFHLAITH

An extraordinary woman who was close to several of the main figures in Irish history at the end of the tenth and the beginning of the eleventh centuries. Her son, Sitric, was Viking king of Dublin for many years until 1036, though she was Irish, and sister to Mael Mordha, the Leinster ruler. She was also married to Mael Seachnaill, and later after his defeat to Brian Bóroimhe.

))))▶ *Brian Bóroimhe, Mael Mordha*

GOVERNMENT OF IRELAND ACT (1920)

Act which gave the 26 counties of southern Ireland limited independence. The Act was introduced by David Lloyd George after the election of 73 Sinn Féin MPs and by their subsequent refusal to sit in Westminster. Because of Conservative pressure in the coalition govern-ment, the six north-eastern counties were allowed to remain out of the Irish Free State, thus creating Northern Ireland as we know it. The Act was opposed most vehemently by southern Unionists and the nationalist population in the six counties of Northern Ireland were strongly against partition.

))))▶ *Dáil Éireann, David Lloyd George*

ABOVE LEFT: The Upper lake at Glendalough.
LEFT: Supporters of the Good Friday Agreement lobby outside the House of Commons.
RIGHT: Henry Grattan.

GRACES, THE (1626)

Privileges granted by Charles I to Ireland's 'Old English'. Those 'New English' settlers who arrived in Ireland in the course of the sixteenth and seventeenth centuries found it hard to know what to make of the 'Old English' they found already there. Embarked upon an aggressive programme of colonization marked by religious zeal and ideological fervour, they could hardly believe that there could be 'Englishmen' who, if not actually Gaelic-speaking Catholics themselves, seemed utterly at ease with a peasantry who were. The Old English, for their part, resented the new arrivals, fearing that they were about to become a subject race themselves. When Charles I asked them for financial support in his war with Spain, in 1626, they gave it on condition that he gave them certain assur-ances: the result was a list of 'Matters of Grace and Bounty to Ireland'. What to begin with seemed like assurances of the Old English's land rights and religion were actually watered down considerably as time went by. The Plantations still proceeding apace, Charles was coming under ever-increasing pressure from Ireland's Protestants. The 'Old Irish' were starting to be marginalized, just as they had feared.

GRATTAN, HENRY (1746–1820)

'Patriot' Politician. A 'patriot' in the specialized Irish eighteenth-century sense that, although born and bred a Protestant, he identified with Ireland, speaking out for his country's dignity as a separate kingdom – albeit one with a special relationship with Great Britain. Instinctively conservative, he was alarmed at the French Revolution, and felt his worst fears had been realized by the rebellion of the United Irishmen. Despite this, he con-tinued to argue for

Catholic Emancipation, though he felt a (Protestant) monarch should have a veto over appointments as a last resort.

))))▶ *Grattan's Parliament*

GRATTAN'S PARLIAMENT (1782–1800)

Name given to the Irish constitutional arrangement between 1782 and 1800. In 1782, in response to a move by patriot politician Henry Grattan, Westminster granted 'legislative independence' to the Dublin parliament. Though the heads of the executive remained English appointments, and the Privy Council had an ultimate veto on legislation (albeit rarely invoked), the arrangement still represented something resembling a system of self-government for Ireland. As such it was harked back to with great nostalgia by nineteenth-century nationalists, who drew great comfort from the unusual stability and prosperity of the time. More cynical historians have since suggested that, if the period was a golden age, it was because all could see the Act of Union was only an inevitable step away; others regard it as a matter of the merest happenstance.

))))➤ *Henry Grattan*

GRAY, BETSY (d. 1798)

One of the most romantic figures of the late-eighteenth century, Gray is also one of the most enigmatic, for although her story lives in poetry and legend historical facts about her are hard to find. A native of County Down, her brother and her sweetheart were on the rebel side in the Battle of Ballynahinch and, against their wishes, she joined them at their camp with a cartload of provisions. After the battle the defeated United Irishmen fled in different directions, pursued by the government forces. Several miles from the battlefield the yeomanry caught up with the trio and cut them down.

))))➤ *United Irishmen*

GREAT FAMINE (1845–49)

Worst famine to occur in Europe during the nineteenth century. The population of Ireland had increased by three million since the turn of the century and the price of grain had escalated following the wars between Britain and France. Traditionally the population of Ireland

ABOVE: Statue of Henry Grattan in St Stephen's Hall, Westminster.

(8,400,000 in 1844) had relied heavily on potatoes to make up a large part of their diet. Those living in secluded, rural areas – what amounted to almost half of the total population of the country – and particularly those on low incomes, used potatoes almost exclusively to feed themselves and their families. Because potatoes yielded more per acre than grain crops, the farmers only needed to use a small piece of land to feed their families.

In 1845, when a North American potato virus (the *Phytophthora* fungus) blighted most of their crops, a huge section of the Irish population was therefore at risk from famine. The potato blight had first been recognized in Canada and America, but in September 1845 it was observed in Wexford and Waterford then it rapidly spread through the whole of the country. To add to their difficulties, the weather in 1845 was unusually moist and cool – perfect conditions for the virus to thrive. During the next three years the crisis continued and each year the potato crop was insufficient to feed the population. Sir Robert Peel

(prime minister 1845–46) provided a degree of relief to those affected by the blight, watching their potato crops lying rotting in the fields. Peel set up a scientific commission to carry out research into the virus; little was of use because nobody knew enough about the blight and how or why it managed to spread so quickly. He appointed Charles Trevelyan, the assistant secretary to the Treasury, as administrator in charge of famine-relief measures in Ireland.

When Peel's parliament fell, Lord John Russell, the Whig prime minister who came to power in June 1846, maintained that the poorer section of the Irish population should become the financial burden of their own landlords, not the government, and established a policy of non-intervention. This policy proved impossible to execute as the peasants were unable to pay the landlords their rent and soon the landowners began to run out of money themselves. Help was summoned from Britain and America, who provided cornmeal, opened soup kitchens and provided employment on building sites and road works. By 1847 three million Irish

BELOW CENTRE: An evicted peasant and his family outside their cottage.
BELOW: Starving peasants in their hut.

people were being fed at Quaker-run soup kitchens throughout the country and eating the imported cornmeal from America as an alternative to potatoes. Relief funds were raised and the British government spent £8 million on famine relief. Some of the Irish population were still able to export grain and meat, but the poorer section did not have sufficient funds to be able to buy them for their own use. It is estimated that over one million people died as a direct result of the famine, either from starvation or from other famine-related illnesses such as typhus and dysentery.

The blight did not recur in 1847, but by then few potatoes had been planted and the crop yield was very poor. In June 1847 the Poor Law Extension Act ordered landlords to increase the Poor Rate and this money was used to support local workhouses. The blight did, however, strike again in 1848. By 1851 the total population of Ireland had fallen by 1,800,000 to 6,600,000, either as a result of death or due to emigration from the country. There was a considerable decline in the number of people employed as agricultural workers and those owning smallholdings, particularly in the counties situated to the west and south-west of the country. It is estimated that 1.5 million Irish people emigrated to Britain and North America in order to escape the situation in Ireland. Although there had been a tendency towards emigration in previous years, particularly to America, demand was so high for the regular departures from Liverpool that direct voyages from Ireland were organized to cope with the huge numbers fleeing their country. The famine destroyed the Irish economy and reversed the population increase. A problem that had always prevailed between tenants and their landlords escalated after the famine because poorer families felt unable to forgive landlords for their heartless behaviour. It also brought about the social changes

associated with emigration. Families were separated and many did not marry until much later in life. As it was obvious that only one child could inherit the family's farm on the death of their parents, this meant that the siblings often remained unmarried because they had no land of their own to farm, or they left the country altogether and emigrated to America or Britain. The Irish nationalists also felt resentment towards the British government for their handling of the famine.

))))➧ *Emigration*

GREAT TRANSPORT STRIKE (1913–14)

Lock-out leading to union defeat in Dublin. On 18 August William Martin O'Brien fired 40 members of the ITGWU (1909) and the union under James Larkin called for a general strike. O'Brien wanted to curb the strength of the unions. On 26 August the Employers Federation initiated a lock-out of employees and rioting broke out in Dublin. Larkin and James Connolly were jailed and the strikers endured great hardships. Despite aid from British unions the lockout resulted in a defeat for the unions.

))))➧ *James Connolly, James Larkin, William Martin O'Brien*

GREGORY, LADY AUGUSTA (1852–1932)

Irish writer and translator. Born into an upper-class Protestant background Lady Augusta lived at Coole in County Sligo and, after her elderly husband's death, she began to take an interest in Irish folklore and language, much influenced by W. B. Yeats. Politically she moved from being a unionist to a cultural nationalist and in the last years of her life she worked tirelessly, collecting and editing folk tales, running the Abbey Theatre, which she, Yeats and Edward Martyn had begun planning as early as 1897, and later writing many original plays herself. She also published translations of Irish poems and stories and her work was very influential in its time.

))))➧ *Abbey Theatre, W. B. Yeats*

GREY ABBEY (1193)

Monastic complex in County Down. Grey Abbey was founded in 1193 by Affreca, daughter of Godred, king of the Isle of Man, and the wife of John de Courcy, the Anglo-Norman lord of Ulster. Legend tells how she established it in gratitude for her deliverance from a storm at sea. The abbey is architecturally significant as the first fully Gothic church in Ireland.

))))➧ *John de Courcy*

GRIANÁN AILIGH ('GRIANAN OF AILEACH')

Ancient ring fort. Situated on a hilltop over 245 m (800 ft) above sea-level in north-east Donegal, this stone ring-fort was the power-base of a branch of the ruling Ulster dynasty, the Ó Néills. Its first chieftain was the fifth-century Eoghan, son of Niall Naoi nGiallach, who gave his name to the surrounding district Inis Eoghain/Inishowen ('Eoghan's Island') and it remained an important centre until its sacking by Brian, king of Munster, in 1101. It lay in partial ruins until it was reconstructed in the 1870s by the archaeologist Dr Bernard.

))))➧ *O'Neill Dynasty*

GRIFFITH, ARTHUR (1871–1922)

Republican politician, founder of Sinn Féin. A member of the IRB from 1893, Arthur Griffith established Sinn Féin in 1905 to campaign for a policy of abstentionism from all imperialist political institutions. He was imprisoned in 1916, despite his having played no part in the Easter Rising. Rearrested several times subsequently,

he was released in 1921 in time to head up the Irish delegation to the London talks. A signatory of the Anglo-Irish Treaty, he was elected president of the Dál in 1922, but died of a cerebral haemorrhage that same year.

))))➤ *Anglo-Irish Treaty*

GUINNESS (1799)

The national beer of Ireland. Guinness is a distinctive, dark, creamy stout that has been produced by the Arthur Guinness Company since 1799. At this time it was decided to concentrate on this popular dark beer with a rich head rather than supply the former variety of beers produced

in Dublin. The beer prospered and gained a strong following in Ireland. In 1855 Benjamin Guinness took over the brewery on his father's death and decided to try to sell the stout abroad. It is now sold in more than 120 countries.

GUNDESTRUPP CAULDRON
(1ST CENTURY BC)

Celtic artefact discovered in a bog in northern Denmark in 1891. It is a ritual vessel made of silver and measuring 69 cm (27 in) across; it dates from the first century BC. It has a number of highly decorated panels showing Celtic deities and other symbols associated particularly with the Celts of eastern Europe. It is not the only Celtic relic to have been found in Denmark, a country

LEFT: Grey Abbey, County Down.
ABOVE: An advert for Guinness.
RIGHT: The Gundestrup Cauldron.

normally regarded as being beyond Celtic territory, but it is the most famous, and it reminds us just how widespread Celtic influence in Europe must have been in pre-Christian times.

HALLSTATT CIVILIZATION

One of the first Celtic civilizations. In 1824 archeologists discovered a vitally important Celtic Iron Age cemetery at Hallstatt, a small village in upper Austria. Excavations were carried out from 1846 to 1963, during which time up to 2,000 graves were uncovered. What was significant about these finds was that it told us a great deal about what the Celts looked like, what they wore, how they fought and how their civilization was organized. The Hallstatt era corresponds with the late Bronze Age (1200–800 BC), the early Iron Age (800–600 BC) and the later period between 600–500 BC. It is from the later period that the richer graves have been found. Women wore jewellery, such as brooches and pins, and were often buried with bronze vessels, including bowls and cups. Other finds indicate that by 800 BC fortified settlements on hilltops were commonplace, as evidenced by the burial mounds, and that trade had been developed to such an extent that items from the Mediterranean were valued possessions. By the fifth century BC it appears that many of the hill forts had been abandoned and wealthy warrior societies were developing. The Hallstatt culture gave way to the more sophisticated La Tene.

))))➤ *Celts*

HAMILTON, WILLIAM ROWAN (1805–65)

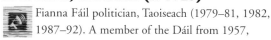 Astronomer and mathematician, most famous for his theory of quarternions in algebra. At the age of only 22, and an undergraduate, he was appointed professor of astronomy at Trinity College Dublin, and soon after became Astronomer Royal for Ireland. As well as being a scientific genius he was also a gifted linguist and a poet.

)))**➤** *Trinity College Dublin*

HAUGHEY, CHARLES (b. 1925)

Fianna Fáil politician, Taoiseach (1979–81, 1982, 1987–92). A member of the Dáil from 1957, Haughey went on to serve in the ministries of Justice, Agriculture and Finance, before the 'arms crisis' of 1970 sealed his fate. In the long run, Haughey benefited, acquiring a swashbuckling manner to go with his raffish air: he would go on to win notoriety as one of Irish politics' greatest survivors and most skilful 'fixers'. The gravity-defying

ABOVE: Charles Haughey.
CENTRE: Seamus Heaney.
RIGHT: Henry VIII.

housekeeping skills which for years allowed Haughey to maintain a millionaire lifestyle on a parliamentary stipend caused many in the Irish electorate to wonder where popular appeal ended and corruption began.

)))**➤** *Fianna Fáil, Jack Lynch*

HEANEY, SEAMUS (b. 1939)

Ireland's greatest living English-language poet. Seamus Heaney is a farmer's son from south County Derry. He worked briefly as a teacher before becoming a college lecturer. His first collection of poems, *Death of a Naturalist* was published in 1966. His poetry, which stems from his rural background, became increasingly influenced by the worsening situation in Northern Ireland through the 1970s, with *North*, published in 1975, being his darkest work. *Fieldwork* (1979) sees the poet coming to terms with the situation and striking a more positive note.

Through the 1980s and 1990s Heaney has continued to introduce new themes and to develop his art. As well as being very influential in Ireland his work also attracts considerable international attention and in 1995 he was awarded the Nobel Prize for Literature.

HEARTS OF OAK (1763)

South Ulster protest movement also known as 'The Oakboys'. Opposing increases in taxes for road building and tithes to the Church, the Hearts of Oak marched to the sound of blowing horns. Their name was derived from the fact that they wore sprigs of oak on their hats. They forced landlords and clerics to make public pledges to reduce the rates of the taxes and tithes. This was one of a number of short-lived, eighteenth-century agrarian protest groups.

)))**➤** *Tithes*

HEDGE SCHOOLS (1702 AND 1719)

Schools established following the introduction of the Penal Laws in 1702 and 1719. Irish Catholics set up institutions when the teaching of Catholic religion was banned. Illegal under English law, the lessons were paid for by the children's parents and were held by masters in places that were considered to be safe. Only those who could afford to pay would receive an education. In 1826, 403,000 children were being taught the 'three R's', classics and religion in Hedge Schools. The National School system, set up in 1831, provided free schooling, but the use of the Irish language was still prohibited.

)))◆ *Gaelic Ireland*

HENRY II OF ENGLAND (1133–89)

King of England (1154–89). Henry's territorial ambitions were threatened by Anglo-Norman power and adventurers in Ireland where, principally, Richard de Clare had supported the efforts of Diarmaid mac Murchadha to recover the crown of Leinster, and was himself crowned on mac Murchadha's death. In 1171–72 Henry led an expedition to Ireland to secure allegiance from de Clare and other Anglo-Norman lords, as well as the Irish Church. Henry split the land up into fiefdoms. He left Hugh de Lacy there as his royal vice-regent but failed to secure complete control in the face of resistance from lords such as John de Courcy. It is believed that Pope Adrian IV, the only English pope, granted Ireland to Henry as a papal fief through the bull *Laudabiliter*.

)))◆ *Richard de Clare, John de Courcy, Hugh de Lacy, Diarmaid mac Murchadha*

HENRY VIII OF ENGLAND (1491–1547)

King of England (1509–47). The power of the earls of Kildare as deputy lieutenants of Ireland was secure while the family kept control, but overtures from the earls of Desmond to the Emperor Charles V left Henry VIII doubtful of Kildare authority, especially when his divorce from Catherine of Aragon made an imperial threat likely.

In 1534, Gerald Fitzgerald, 9th Earl of Kildare, was summoned to England and his son Thomas Fitzgerald, 'Silken Thomas', led a rebellion, believing his father had been executed. His own execution in 1537 increased royal authority through the Irish parliament, which declared Henry king of Ireland. Property confiscation from rebels and monasteries helped unify Irish opposition to English rule. In the latter part of the reign property was awarded to lords who renounced papal authority, but the process was erratic and arbitrary.

)))◆ *Earls of Desmond, Gerald Fitzgerald, Earls of Kildare, Conn O'Neill, Shane O'Neill, Silken Thomas*

ANNO · ETATIS ·   · SVÆ · XLIX ·

HIGH CROSSES (9TH–10TH CENTURIES)

Monuments erected, for the most part, between the ninth and tenth centuries. Also known as Celtic crosses, the High Crosses of Ireland are quite distinct, their tall stone shafts topped by ringed cross-heads, decorated with looping, swirling ornamental designs – or, in some cases, scriptural scenes. The fashion for High Crosses was revived in the twelfth century, when the ornamentation became even more extravagant. Found for the most part at monastic sites, the original function of the High Crosses remains obscure.

))))▶ *Monasteries*

HIGH KING (1434 BC – AD 1318)

Celtic and early Christian Ireland was divided up into many small kingdoms, each with its own ruler. As time passed, certain groupings began to dominate particular regions and several major provincial rulers emerged. These rulers vied for supremacy with varying degrees of success. Brian Bóroimhe, king of Munster from AD 976, is generally regarded as the first true High King of Ireland; he consolidated his position by use of military might and strategic alliance, so that by 1002 he was able to travel to Armagh and proclaim himself emperor of the Irish. He ruled for 12 years until his death in victory at the Battle of Clontarf in 1014. His old rival Mael Seachnaill claimed the title of High King.

))))▶ *Brian Bóroimhe, Battle of Clontarf, Mael Seachnaill II*

HOME GOVERNMENT ASSOCIATION (1870–73)

Movement for self-government in Ireland. The Home Government Association was a movement founded by Isaac Butt in September 1870. Its aim was to repeal the Act of Union and bring self-government to Ireland. It was the first organization to be associated with Home Rule, the dominant political ideology up until 1916. Butt preferred not to be confrontational in his approach, but instead sought to win over the British parliament to the idea of having a subordinate Dublin government dealing with domestic affairs, while Westminster would still look after issues concerning both countries and international affairs. The movement declined in importance after the formation of the Home Rule League in November 1873.

))))▶ *Act of Union, Isaac Butt*

HOME RULE (1840S)

Dominant Irish political issue from the late-nineteenth century and the first half of the twentieth century, emerging first in the 1840s from Daniel O'Connell and the Young Ireland movement. Home Rule came to the fore in the 1880s under pressure from Charles Stewart Parnell, capitalizing on the reforming inclination of William Gladstone's Liberal government and the political machinations at Westminster, where Irish support played a vital role in the power struggle between Tories and Liberals. World War I suspended the issue and led to an outbreak of violent sectarianism during and after the war. Settlement ultimately created an independent southern Ireland while most of Ulster was retained by Britain.

Following the Great Famine of the 1840s, ordinary Irish people became interested in more radical methods of reform. The Fenian Movement was founded in 1858, with the intent to exploit any moment when Britain was engaged in a major war elsewhere. Fenian uprisings in 1865 and 1867 sustained the tradition of armed rebellion in pursuit of independence. The disastrous winter of 1878–79 revived fears of another famine. It propelled land reform to the forefront of Irish politics.

Michael Davitt, a Fenian leader, was committed to religious diversity and the interests of all workers. Eventually captured, he was imprisoned for seven years. Undeterred, Davitt founded the National Land League on his release in 1879 and set about pursuing abuses against tenant farmers. Although lawful methods were used, the Land League also resorted to violent intimidation. This produced individual victories over landlords, but not any wholesale achievement of land reform.

Charles Stewart Parnell, a Protestant landowner, inherited a family tradition of Irish nationalism. His strident pursuit of Irish independence characterized his reputation in parliament from the moment he took his seat in 1875. He remained committed in spite of the opposition he incited amongst his own class. With Davitt's help, Parnell was re-elected in 1880 with a number of supporters and took leadership of the Irish Party in parliament. Under pressure from Parnell, Gladstone's government passed the radical Land Act of 1881. It forced fair rents, prevented unfair evictions, and allowed tenants to control sale or transfer of their leases. Further reform culminated in the Wyndham Land Act allowing tenants to purchase their farms over 68 years.

The Franchise Act (1884) brought in around half a million poorer Catholic new voters, and allowed Parnell to manipulate Home Rule into being the central issue of the 1885 election. Conservatives feared the British Empire would break up. Catholic supporters of Home Rule, 'Nationalists', saw this is as the only way forward. Ulster Presbyterians, 'Unionists', feared the inevitable Catholic domination of any Home Rule settlement.

In 1885, Gladstone's Liberals won 335 seats. The Conservatives took 249 seats. Parnell and his supporters took 86 seats. To ensure the Irish Party worked with him, Gladstone agreed to introduce a Home Rule Bill in 1886 in spite of some Liberal opposition. This opposition was enough to ensure that the bill was defeated, though that it had been drafted at all was a political triumph for Parnell.

FAR LEFT: High Cross, Ahenny, County Tipperary.
ABOVE: Cartoon of Parnell and Home rule.
RIGHT: Cartoon for Home Rule.

Disaster followed in 1890 when Parnell's adultery with Kitty O'Shea was exposed. The colossal spiritual power of the Catholic Church in Ireland guaranteed that it would destroy Parnell's political career, and also split the Irish Party. Gladstone made Parnell's expulsion as leader of the Irish Party a condition of further support for Home Rule. In the meantime, Ulster Unionism consolidated its opposition to Home Rule, organizing a 12,000-strong convention in 1892 and providing the Conservatives at Westminster with a cause.

The second Home Rule Bill passed the Commons in 1893 but fell in the Lords. Parnell's death in 1891 extinguished the zeal which had driven the movement. With land-reform measures continuing, and British investment in Irish higher education, communications and other public works, Home Rule lost momentum. Irish intellectual society became more interested in developing the Irish Celtic tradition, generating a more subtle Irish sense of identity. In the longer term, this had a decisive influence on wider Irish nationalism, for example the creation of Sinn Féin in 1905.

British political expediency revived Home Rule in the inconclusive election of 1910. Asquith's Liberals bought power by promising the Irish party a Home Rule Bill. As the 1912 Bill progressed through parliament, Ulster Presbyterians determined to defeat it or demand their exclusion from any settlement. Nationalists and Unionists created, in anticipation of violence, paramilitary groups: the Irish Volunteers and Ulster Volunteers respectively. Meanwhile, as Liberals and Conservatives began to agree on the exclusion of Ulster, so the Irish nationalists saw the prospects of a wholly free Ireland fade.

The outbreak of war in August 1914 suspended Home Rule and the Ulster question was put on hold. This was the chance radical republicans had been waiting for. Terrorism and armed rebellion (the Easter Rising of 1916) now characterized the conflict, polarizing loyalties and leading to the political annihilation of the Irish Party in 1918 as Sinn Féin came to the fore. The explosion of sectarianism produced the War of Independence, the Government of Ireland Act (1920) which brought separate restricted Home Rule for Northern Ireland and southern Ireland, and finally the Peace Treaty (1921) which split Ireland in two. The separation of Northern Ireland generated an anti-Treaty faction and the bloody Irish Civil War of 1922–23, ending in the establishment of the Irish Free State which declared full independence from Britain in 1948.

))⟩➤ *Fenian Movement, Irish Civil War, Land League, Daniel O'Connell, Charles Stewart Parnell, Young Ireland*

HOME RULE BILL (1886)

 Constitutional arrangement by which Ireland would control its own domestic affairs from Dublin, as part of an overarching United Kingdom. Not for the first time in Irish history a political formula has gained success by its very vagueness. The beauty of the phrase, thought to have been first used by 'Home Government' campaigner the Reverend Joseph A. Galbraith, was that it soothed middle-class Protestant anxieties while raising Catholic nationalist hopes, few taking the time to read the small print that said what sounded like full independence would really be something more along the lines of the 'devolved' government to be found in Wales and Scotland today. A mounting groundswell of support through the 1870s, built up by Isaac Butt and then by Charles Stewart Parnell, found its first important British champion in William Gladstone,

who introduced a Home Rule Bill in 1886. This failed, as did subsequent efforts in 1893, 1912 and 1914, the special interests of the Ulster Protestants proving an impassable sticking point.

))⟩➤ *Isaac Butt, William Gladstone, Charles Stewart Parnell*

HOWTH GUN-RUNNING (1914)

On 26 July 1914 the Volunteers armed themselves in a gun-running episode at Howth near Dublin. The guns were bought in Germany and shipped in by nationalist sympathizers Darrell Figgis and Erskine Childers, in Childers' yacht, *Asgard*. Police and soldiers were sent to seize the guns, but were unsuccessful. Most of the guns were safely landed further down the coast so the incident at Howth was largely a publicity stunt aimed at humiliating the authorities.

))⟩➤ *Roger Casement, Robert Erskine Childers*

HUMBERT, GENERAL JOSEPH AMABLE (1755–1823)

Commander of the French troops sent to Ireland in 1798. At Ballinamuck Humbert was compromised by outnumbered and exhausted troops. He secured Shanmullagh Hill but in spite of resilient defence he was forced to retreat from a cavalry charge into cannon fire and surrendered soon after. In 1803 he left France to fight in the Mexican War in the United States.

)))))➤ *Battle of Ballanimuck*

HUNGER STRIKE (1981)

A method of protest used mostly to make a political statement. The use of hunger strikes by Irish protestors has a long history. In Celtic Ireland, a person with a grievance would fast outside the perpetrator's door until, through shame, the perpetrator was forced to make amends. During the struggle for independence, the hunger strike was used by republican prisoners, and the deaths of Thomas Ashe in 1917 and Terence MacSwiney in 1920 had a huge influence on public opinion and on later generations of protestors. Indeed, such was the impact of MacSwiney's death that the tactic was adopted by civil rights groups across the world, especially by proponents of passive resistance and non-violent protest such as Gandhi in India.

In 1981 a group of republican prisoners in the H-blocks of Long Kesh (later the Maze prison), near Belfast, began a hunger strike in demand of better conditions. Led by Bobby Sands this was really an ideological struggle between the Republican prisoners and the British authorities. The British prime minister, Margaret Thatcher, was never going to submit to pressure and so despite Sand's by-election victory in Fermanagh-South Tyrone, he and nine other hunger-strikers died before the protest was called off. The huge impact of this campaign, and in particular the election success it brought, can now be seen as a turning point in the conflict, with Sinn Féin recognizing that there was now potential for progress through democratic means.

)))))➤ *Irish Republican Army, Bobby Sands*

LEFT: Isaac Butt, founder of the Home Rule Association.
CENTRE: Terence MacSwiney's death following a hunger strike.
BELOW: Bobby Sands.

HYDE, DOUGLAS (1860–1949)

One of the founding fathers of the independent Irish state. Although not involved in political activity in the way that Pádraig Pearse or Éamon de Valera were, Hyde's contribution was significant. He was born in County Roscommon, where his father was a Church of Ireland minister. He came into contact with Irish as the language of the people among his rural neighbours and when he went to Dublin to study divinity he met with others interested in preserving and promoting the language. In 1892 he gave an influential address on 'the necessity for the de-Anglicization of Ireland' and the following year became the first president of the newly founded Gaelic League. He was an innovative and capable Irish scholar and a man whose vision inspired others. He became first professor of modern Irish at University College Dublin in 1909. It was a sign of the esteem in which he was held that he was chosen with all-party support as first president of Ireland in 1938.

)))))➤ *Éamon de Valera, Gaelic League, Pádraig Pearse*

INTERNMENT

The holding, without charge or trial, of those suspected of subversive activity. *Habeas Corpus* ('that you might have the body') has been a cornerstone of British justice since 1679, stipulating that an arrested prisoner must be charged and brought to trial or else given his freedom. The temptation to suspend it has, however, always been strong in times of trouble, and it was set aside at various points through the eighteenth and nineteenth centuries. The events of 1916 and thereafter saw internment on a larger scale than ever before by the British, though the government of the Free State would leave their record far behind. By 1923, in the aftermath of the civil war, they held over 11,000 Republicans, imprisoned yet uncharged, and they would not be slow to reintroduce the policy in the future. The term 'internment' today is most immediately associated with the Northern Ireland of the 1970s, when several thousand (largely innocent Catholics) were detained as suspected terrorists.

)))**⟩ *Irish Civil War***

INVINCIBLES (1881)

Violent sub-group of the Fenian Movement. A short-lived splinter-group of Fenians formed in 1881, the Invincibles' single serious action came the following year with the Phoenix Park Murders: in the frenzy of police activity that followed they were unable to function further.

The group proved all too vincible when tracked down and arrested, the evidence of leader James Carey sending five erstwhile comrades to the scaffold and eight others to prison. He was set free, only to be shot dead by yet another former henchman.

)))**⟩ *Fenian Movement, Phoenix Park Murders***

IRISH CITIZEN ARMY (1913)

Socialist militia. Deployed aggressively by the authorities during the Dublin Lockout of 1913, the Dublin Police did their violent best to frustrate the workers' protest. Two men were killed in one baton charge on what is now O'Connell Street, and it seemed as though the Union might simply be beaten into submission. The Irish Citizen Army was formed to offer protection to the strikers: Sandhurst-educated anarchist Captain Jack White took charge of assembling and training what Lenin later praised as the first Red Army. In 1914 the ICA came under the leadership of James Connolly. Countess Constance Markiewicz was lieutenant-commander in the Citizen Army, which went on to play a key role in the Easter Rising of 1916.

)))**⟩ *James Connolly, Dublin Lockout, Easter Rising, James Larkin, Constance Markiewicz***

IRISH CIVIL WAR (1922–23)

War between former members of the IRA. Following the Treaty establishing Home Rule, and Arthur Griffith and Michael Collins as its leaders in December 1921, the IRA split between those who accepted the Treaty and those who opposed it. The opposition was led by Éamon de Valera, president of Sinn Féin, but remained armed and organized. The opponents regarded the new state as British rule covertly continued, especially as British troops were incorporated into the Free State army alongside former IRA members.

Collins found himself arming Catholics to protect themselves in Ulster, while his authority was challenged by anti-Treaty Republicans based in the Four Courts in Dublin. Fighting broke out and the Dublin anti-Treaty Republicans capitulated. Collins then embarked on an Ireland-wide

LEFT: Members of the Invincibles committing the Phoenix Park Murders.
ABOVE RIGHT: A delegation against the 1921 Treaty.
RIGHT: Sackville Street; the Republicans last stand.

led by the Protestant landowner and MP William Smith O'Brien. Although at the beginning the movement was committed to peaceful reform, it could hardly fail to be influenced by the climate of Revolution abroad in Europe as 1848 began: O'Brien himself admitted that the situation had changed and that violent solutions might have to be considered. No sooner had the Confederation agreed upon this aim, however, than the authorities were moving in to shut the organization down: the rising of that July collapsed ignominiously, going down in history as 'the Battle of Widow McCormick's Cabbage Patch'.

campaign against anti-Treaty Republicans. Griffith's death from a brain haemorrhage was rapidly followed by Collins' assassination on 22 August 1922. The new administration under William Cosgrave passed an Emergency Powers Bill and operated a ruthless programme of executions against widespread terrorism until the IRA collapsed in May 1923.
))⟩▶ *Michael Collins, Arthur Griffith, Home Rule, Irish Republican Army, Sinn Féin, Éamon de Valera*

IRISH COLLEGES (17TH–18TH CENTURIES)

Colleges set up for the training of secular clergy abroad. Before the reigns of Elizabeth I and James I of England the clergy received their training in monastic schools in Ireland. When these were suppressed training colleges were opened on the Continent in Rome, Spain, Portugal, Belgium and France and priests were prepared in these colleges in an attempt to preserve the faith in Ireland during the seventeenth and eighteenth centuries. Several of these colleges, most notably Rome, still function, and others such as Paris and Louvain have recently been renavated and are used as Irish academic and cultural centres. The college in Rome is a popular venue for Irish marriages and also serves as an unofficial cultural embassy.

IRISH CONFEDERATION (1840S)

Nationalist organization of the late-1840s. Formed in 1847 by members of the Young Ireland movement disillusioned at what they felt was O'Connell's readiness to compromise with the English Whigs, the Confederation was

IRISH FREE STATE (1922)

Following the Anglo-Irish Treaty the new Irish state had dominion status within the British Commonwealth similar to that enjoyed by Australia, Canada, New Zealand and South Africa. Working with these countries, as well as independently, the Irish sought to enhance their position by building diplomatic relations and participating in

the League of Nations. It was clear that Fianna Fáil which came to power in 1932, and Éamon de Valera in particular, did not regard the Treaty as a final settlement and in 1937 he introduced a new constitution, Bunreacht na hÉireann, which changed the state's name to Éire (Ireland). The term 'Free State' is still used in Northern Ireland as a derogatory term for the Irish republic.

)))➡ *Anglo-Irish Treaty*

IRISH LANGUAGE

The earliest records of the language come from Ogham inscriptions and modern Irish is closely related to Scots Gaelic and Manx and less closely related to Welsh, Cornish and Breton.

Irish (or Gaelic) is a Celtic language which at one time was spoken across Ireland and most of Scotland, reaching its strongest position at the beginning of the eleventh century following Brian Bóroimhe's defeat of the Norse in 1014 and Malcolm's defeat of the Northumbrians four years later. After this time the Anglo-Normans exerted increasing influence and the predominant language in many areas became English.

Although it is estimated that there were over four million Irish speakers in Ireland at the time of the Great Famine, most of these were among the poorer classes who were most badly affected by the famine and the subsequent emigration. Thus the decline in the use of the language, which had been gradual before then, increased rapidly and today Irish is spoken primarily in a number of clearly defined geographical regions known as the Gaeltacht.

Despite many predictions of its demise the language remains vibrant and recent years have seen the growth of Irish medium education, the introduction of an Irish-language television channel (TG4) and a daily newspaper based in Belfast (*Lá*). It also has a strong literary culture, with many books published annually.

)))➡ *Gaeltacht, Great Famine, Ogham*

IRISH NATIONAL LIBERATION ARMY (1974)

Armed Republican group. Formed in 1974 by former members of the Official IRA and Sinn Féin disillusioned by their organizations' continuing inaction, the Irish National Liberation Army (and its political wing the Irish Republican Socialist Party, IRSP) committed themselves to the struggle to create a specifically socialist united Ireland. Never more than a few dozen strong, the INLA has still succeeded in pulling off a number of notable coups over the years, most recently the assassination of Loyalist leader Billy Wright inside the top-security Maze Prison at the end of 1997. This action arguably broke the terms of a ceasefire which until then had held since 1994; another ceasefire was announced the following August.

)))➡ *Irish Republican Army, Sinn Féin*

transcend its specifically rural roots. Though the issues of tenants' rights and land ownership would always remain a central concern, it was soon campaigning on a more broadly based nationalist agenda, with different emphases in different areas. After 1882 it was taken in charge by Charles Stewart Parnell, who rebuilt and renamed it as the highly centralized National Party.

)))⮞ *Charles Stewart Parnell*

IRISH REPUBLICAN ARMY (1916)

Armed Republican group. The name by which the Irish Volunteers were increasingly known after 1916, the IRA came to the fore during the War of Independence, although as uncompromising Republicans they found themselves on the losing side in the ensuing civil war. While Éamon de Valera and his Fianna Fáil managed to reach some grudging accommodation with the new dispensation from 1925 onwards, eventually becoming the Free State's leading constitutional force, a rump remained implacably opposed. De Valera's harnessing of republican rhetoric to his own political ends left the actual arms-bearing heirs to Connolly and his followers essentially marginalized. Sporadic campaigns of sabotage and assassination along the Northern Irish Border and in Britain from the 1930s onward left the IRA no closer to attaining any sort of relevance to the lives of the mass of the Irish people. Hence the shift towards non-violent political action that had come to characterize the organization by the 1960s.

Not until the end of the 1960s and the violent crackdown on the Civil Rights Movement in Northern Ireland was a role offered the IRA as protectors of the Catholic citizens of the Orange State. By that time, however, the organization's hierarchy was largely committed to left-wing political, rather than to military action.

)))⮞ *Provisional IRA, War of Independence*

IRISH PARLIAMENTARY PARTY (1851)

Political party of the nineteenth century. Founded in 1851 by Frederick Lucas as an alliance of Tenants' Rights associations, the Irish Parliamentary Party went on to

LEFT: The first National Army Guard of Honour at the Senate House, 1922.
ABOVE: The earliest records of the Irish language date back to inscriptions on Ogham stones.

IRISH REPUBLICAN BROTHERHOOD (1867)

Nineteenth-century Republican group. The Fenian Brotherhood as overhauled after the fiascos of 1867 and its aftermath, notably by Jeremiah O'Donovan Rossa and John Devoy. For some considerable time the IRB remained marginal, thrust into the sidelines by the success of Parnellism, though when constitutional nationalism foundered in the new century, the revolutionary spirit would once more come into its own.

)))⊪ *John Devoy, Fenian Movement, Jeremiah O'Donovan Rossa*

IRISH SOCIALIST REPUBLICAN PARTY (1896)

Political party. The ISRP was founded by James Connolly in 1896 and could claim to be Ireland's first Marxist communist party. The latest in a long line of high-minded attempts to transcend the stubborn sectarianism of Ireland's prevailing political discourse, it fell apart on Connolly's departure for America in 1903.

)))⊪ *James Connolly*

IRISH VOLUNTEERS (1913)

Armed nationalist organization. A nationalist militia created in Dublin in 1913 in response to the for-mation of the Ulster Volunteer Force by northern

Protestants the previous year. Seen as an armed wing of the Home Rule movement, it had well over 100,000 members by 1914, but the involvement of leading Fenians made constitutional nationalists like John Redmond increasingly nervous. Disagreement over how best to respond to the outbreak of World War I left the Volunteers split from top to bottom, most following Redmond's call for nationalists to support the British. The radical core which remained were built into a 15,000-strong force by Eoin MacNeill, though an IRB cadre beneath him had their own plans for the organization. MacNeill – and the bulk of his Volunteers – were kept completely in the dark about the role they were destined to play in the run-up to the Easter Rising.

IRON AGE (c. 1000 BC–c. AD 50)

Period of history characterized by the use of iron in metalwork. There have been between 30,000–50,000 Iron Age sites called ring forts identified. Despite the disturbance of the land over the years, the Iron Age has still left its mark in Ireland. Excavations have shown that some of the sites are defensive in nature, with circular embankments around them. However, it has been discovered from the 150 sites have been excavated so far, that many of the rings were enclosures for cattle and sheep, and not defensive at all. The Iron Age people were the early Irish farmers; they created elaborate field systems and introduced mixed farming based on wheat, barley, cattle and sheep. They sowed winter crops on their network of small, rectangular plots, lived in circular houses, stored grain in raised buildings and built underground silos for seed corn. This was the period of the hill fort into which the farmers would move in times of danger.

)))⊪ *Celts*

JACOBITISM

Name given to supporters of the deposed James II of England and his descendants; from the Latin for James, *Jacobus*. Jacobites attracted broader support from disaffected British politicians and soldiers and generating an alliance between Catholic dynastic supporters and Anglican Tories. Jacobites posed an arguably legitimate threat to the crown from 1689 until the mid-1700s. James

LEFT: Eamon de Valera, featured on an Irish Volunteers banner.

Stuart, the 'Old Pretender' (1688–1766), tried to return in 1706 and 1715. Charles Stuart, the 'Young Pretender' (1720–88), posed the most dangerous threat in 1745 but failure of French and Scottish support led to defeat at Culloden. The event and the man were romanticized out of recognition, guaranteeing Jacobitism an enduring legacy as a political fancy.

⟫⟫ *James II of England*

JAMES II OF ENGLAND (1633–1701)

King of England (1685–88). A Catholic, James's sympathies and promotion of Catholics provoked outright opposition in England, leading to his deposition in December 1688 after the birth of his son threatened the Protestant succession. His daughter Mary and her husband William of Orange were invited to take the throne. The suppression of the Confederates by Cromwell in 1649–50 left much of Ireland inclined to support James's attempts to win back his throne.

He landed in Ireland in 1689, but his failure to take Derry, and the defeat at the Boyne in July 1690 destroyed his chances and he fled to France. His remaining forces were finally defeated at Aughrim in 1691.

⟫⟫ *Battle of Aughrim, Battle of the Boyne, Confederate War, Siege of Derry, William III of England*

JARLATH, ST (c. AD 445–c. 540)

Saint and monastic founder, also known as Iarla. A noted teacher in his day, Jarlath is now best known as founder of the monastery at Cloonfush in County Galway. According to tradition Jarlath's student, St Brendan the Navigator, was told in a vision that his master must set out on a journey eastward: where his chariot-wheel broke, he was to establish his second monastery. All turning out as Brendan had prophesised, Jarlath set up a second foundation at Tuam. The 'School of Tuam' would in time rival Clonmacnoise as a centre of art and learning.

LEFT: *James II of England.*
BELOW: *The relief of Londonderry, 1689, following a two–month siege by the Jacobites.*

JERPOINT ABBEY (1160)

Monastic complex, situated south of Thomastown in County Kilkenny. Originally a Benedictine monastery, founded in 1160, Jerpoint Abbey was taken over by the Cistercians in 1180. After the dissolution of the monasteries

in 1540, James Butler, Earl of Ormond, leased the Abbey from the Crown – its spiritual function may have been forgotten, but its fields, fishponds, weirs and watermills remained of very real economic value. Although it has long since fallen into atmospheric ruin, enough of the structure survives to provide an extraordinary sense of the working life of a medieval monastery.

⫸ **Benedictine Order, Cistercian Order**

ABOVE: Jerpoint Abbey.
ABOVE RIGHT: James Joyce.
FAR RIGHT: A page from the Gospel of St Mark in the Book of Kells.

JOYCE, JAMES (1882–1941)

Irish novelist. Dublin-born Joyce was one of the most influential novelists of the twentieth century. Works such as *Ulysses* and *Finnegans Wake* continue to attract huge critical attention and both the subject matter and the style of writing have been the subject of much debate. *Ulysses*, which takes its structure from Homer's great work, is set in Dublin on 16 June 1904, and recreates life in the city with great attention to detail. It tells of the various doings and misadventures of Leopold Bloom, a Dublin Jew, on that day. *Finnegans Wake,* an even more ambitious work, took 17 years to complete. It is written primarily in English, Irish and Norwegian, but includes words and phrases from many other languages and is packed full of literary and historical allusions. He also wrote an autobiographical novel, *Portrait of the Artist as a Young Man,* in which he sets out his artistic beliefs, and a book of short stories, *Dubliners,* as well as some poetry and a play. He lived most of his adult life in continental Europe and died in Zurich in 1941. Joyce and his work are now commemorated annually on Bloomsday.

⫸ **Bloomsday**

KAVANAGH, PATRICK (1904–67)

Poet and author from Inniskeen, County Monaghan. Kavanagh celebrated rural Ireland in an honest and unromantic way, and although he spent much of his working life in Dublin and collaborated with many of his literary contemporaries he remained fiercely independent in his attitudes. His autobiographies, *The Green Fool* (1938) and *Tarry Flynn* (1948) remain popular. His posthumous epic poem, *Lough Derg,* is regarded as a poetic analysis of Irish Catholicism.

KELLS, BOOK OF (c. 8TH–9TH CENTURIES)

Ireland's most famous medieval manuscript. The Books of Kells is a Latin copy of the four Gospels and was produced in the eighth or ninth centuries. It is written on calf vellum and has been well preserved, although it is estimated that about 10 per cent of the original leaves have been lost over the centuries. It has long been associated with the monastery at Kells in County Meath, which was founded in AD 807 by St Colm Cille following Viking attacks on Iona. It is possible, therefore, that it may have been compiled at Iona and brought to Kells at that time. Regarded as the high point of Celtic monastic art, many of its pages are richly decorated using vegetable dyes and mineral pigments. The artwork shows a variety of influences and motifs from the book continue to influence Irish design to this day. Today the book is kept in Trinity College Dublin, where it is on public view with a different page shown every day.

))))➤ *St Colm Cille, Trinity College Dublin, Vikings*

KELLS, SYNOD OF (1152)

Assembly of the early Church. Held at Kells, County Meath, in 1152, then afterwards adjourning to Mellifont Abbey, County Louth, this gathering completed the work initiated half a century earlier by the Cashel Synod, adding two further archbishoprics, Dublin and Tuam, to those already established at Cashel and Armagh.

))))➤ *Synod of Cashel*

KELLY, MICHAEL (1764–1826)

Dublin-born opera singer. Kelly became principal tenor at the Vienna Court opera in 1783 and appeared in the first production of Mozart's *Marriage of Figaro*. He published his *Reminiscences* in 1826 and reputedly taught Mozart a number of Irish tunes, echoes of which can be heard in his compositions.

KEVIN OF GLENDALOUGH, ST

Hermit who lived in a cave at Glendalough in County Wicklow. Such was Kevin's fame and following that a major monastic site later developed here. In 1111 the importance of the site was so significant that it was granted its own bishop. St Laurence O'Toole was also an abbot here. As part of the recent millennial celebrations a new hermitage in honour of St Kevin has been opened which is proving popular with modern-day pilgrims.

))))➤ *St Laurence O'Toole*

KICKHAM, CHARLES J. (1828–82)

Tipperary-born writer and political activist. Kickham is best-remembered for his nationalist writings, especially the novel *Knocknagow* (1873). An active member of the Tenant League and a regular contributor to *The Nation*, he later joined the Fenians and strongly promoted their aims and methods in his writings. He was arrested in 1865, along with James Stephens, and jailed for treason. While in jail he wrote *Sally Cavanagh*, a novel that deals with the difficulties faced by the small farmers and the evils of emigration. On his release he continued to take a militant stand and although his political influence declined, his writings remained very popular.

))))➤ *Fenian Movement*, **The Nation**, *James Stephens*

KILDARE, EARLS OF

The family of Fitzgeralds, or Geraldines, who ruled Kildare from the fourteenth to sixteenth centuries. The Earls of Kildare were descendants of Maurice Fitzgerald, who landed in Ireland in 1169 during the Anglo-Norman invasion. Through a series of inter-marriages they ultimately established supremacy as leaders and lord deputies of Ireland. Their kingdom was re-established after 1318 by the forming of the Kildare, Desmond and Ormonde earldoms and they went on to build many castles. This creation of earldoms brought about a revival of political power and an increase in lands during the fourteenth century. Despite giving support to Lambert Simnel, pretender to the English throne, in 1487, Thomas, the 7th Earl, was not displaced. When he showed support to another pretender to the throne, Perkin Warbeck, he was substituted with Sir Edward Poynings, an Englishman, by Henry VII. Poyning passed an act called Poyning's Law, however, and Thomas was restored in 1496. The title passed through the generations to Gerald, 8th Earl (Gerald Mór) and then his son, Gerald (Gerald Óg) 9th Earl until Henry VIII and James, 10th Earl of Desmond, afraid of imperial intervention, ousted Gerald and executed his son, Silken Thomas.

)))➤ *Red Piers Butler, Sir Edward Poynings*

KILDARE SUPREMACY (1318–1534)

After the Battle of Faughart in 1318, the English reasserted their control of Ireland by creating three Anglo-Irish earldoms. The Fitzgeralds were given Kildare and Desmond and the Butlers were granted the territory of Ormond. Over the following century the Kildares dominated and were the virtual rulers of Ireland. When Edward IV succeeded the English throne in 1461 he executed the Earl of Desmond and Thomas, 7th Earl of Kildare was made lord deputy in 1471, the title passing to his son, Garret More, 8th Earl and then to Garret Óg, 9th Earl. Henry VIII removed Garret Óg's son Silken Thomas in 1534.

)))➤ *Earls of Kildare, Garret Fitzgerald, Silken Thomas*

KILKENNY CASTLE (1172)

Norman stone keepless castle situated above the River Nore. Originally Kilkenny Castle was built by Richard de Clare, but it was later destroyed by Donald O'Brien, king of Thomond and rebuilt by his son-in-law, William Marshall, in 1204. In 1391 it was sold to the earls of Ormond, who lived in it until 1967. It was damaged during Cromwell's siege of 1650 and after the Restoration of 1660 it was rebuilt. It is now a national monument and is open to the public.

)))➤ *Richard de Clare*

KILKENNY, STATUTES OF (1366)

Legislation governing conduct of life in the medieval English colony. Alarm at what was seen as creeping Gaelicization within what was nominally the English colony in Ireland led to the enactment in 1366 of a set of laws relating to every aspect of social and cultural life. Not only was English to be spoken and English names used, but resort was to be made to English legal traditions for settling disputes – it was even stipulated that horses had to be ridden in the English manner. Relations with the Irish peoples outside the colony were also covered: no horses or weapons

ABOVE: Kilkenny Castle.
RIGHT: Parnell is interviewed in Kilmainham jail.
FAR RIGHT: Map showing the town of Kinsale during the siege.

were to be sold to them, lest they be used against the English in future risings. Given the tendency to relax these rules in quiet periods, the statute had to be reintroduced several times thereafter, before it was finally superseded in the early seventeenth century.

KILMAINHAM TREATY (1882)

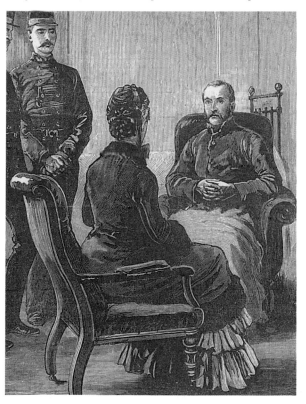 Agreement between Irish nationalists and the British government that ended the Land War in 1882. Not a written 'treaty' as such, but an important accommodation nevertheless, the Kilmainham Treaty helped take some of the acrimony out of what had been becoming a highly volatile situation. The arrest of Parnell and other leaders of the Land League had only inflamed the passions of the rural poor:

Gladstone agreed to release them, and make other concessions, in return for their help in settling the situation. No sooner had they started, though, than the Phoenix Park Murders sent them back to square one.

))➤ *Land Wars, Charles Stewart Parnell, Phoenix Park Murders*

KILMICHAEL (1920)

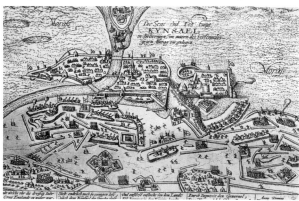 Ambush of Auxiliaries at Kilmichael, County Cork, by the IRA on 28 November 1920. Paid twice as much as Black and Tans, Auxiliaries were recruited for the Royal Irish Constabulary from among English soldiers, and were noted for their aggression and courage. Tom Barry, a British ex-soldier, led an IRA flying column to ambush 18 Auxiliaries in trucks. At 4 p.m. Barry spotted the column and signalled it to stop. His men then threw bombs and fired rifles, killing nine Auxiliaries. The rest surrendered but shot IRA men who came forward. Barry then ordered the Auxiliaries to be killed, leaving only one wounded survivor.

))➤ *Black and Tans, Irish Republican Army*

KINSALE, BATTLE OF (1601)

English victory against the Ó Néill and Ó Dónaill rebels in 1601; the climax of the rebellion which broke out in 1594, led by Aodh Rua Ó Dónaill and Aodh Ó Néill. The 2nd Earl of Essex's comprehensive failure against the rebels strengthened their resolve. They earned support from the pope, Clement VIII and Philip III of Spain, who saw this as an opportunity to pursue the ambitions of the Counter-Reformation against England. Philip III sent a small force of about 3,000 Spaniards to Ireland under the command of Juan del Aguila. Kinsale welcomed them on 22 September.

In 1601, however, Charles Blount, Lord Mountjoy, was appointed lord deputy of Ireland in Essex's place and immediately besieged Kinsale. By December Mountjoy had increased his forces to about 7,000 but was cut off by Ó Néill and Ó Dónaill, who had marched south. A surprise attack failed due to storms and flooding and on 24 December 5,000 Irish troops faced 3,000 English soldiers (the remainder sustained the siege). The Irish were rapidly pushed back and defeated, with many of Ó Dónaill's troops fleeing. The Spaniards surrendered Kinsale several days later. Although Ó Néill held out until 1603, the prospects of a Spanish-sponsored expulsion of the English from Ireland were ended.

▶▶ *Aodh Rua Ó Dónaill. Elizabeth I of England, Lord Mountjoy, Red Hugh O'Donnell*

KNOCK

Place of pilgrimage in County Mayo. The scene of a Marian vision in 1879, the Virgin's appearance attested to by no fewer than 15 local people, Knock has been an official pilgrimage site since the 1930s. Bucking the apparent trends of an age of secularism – and of modernization even within the Roman Catholic Church – the shrine of Knock has continued to attract pilgrims in ever-increasing numbers. The Basilica of Our Lady, Queen of Ireland, was completed in 1976, while an international airport was opened to serve it 10 years later.

LA TENE CIVILIZATION

One of the earliest Celtic civilizations. The Celtic La Tene culture is named after a lakeside site found in La Tene in Switzerland by archeologists in the nineteenth century. La Tene is as a term used to compare the craftsmanship of other Celtic finds during their various stages of occupation. The La Tene tile was cold cast in bronze, a favoured method of Celtic handmade art. There are examples of La Tene culture in Ireland that draw upon Greek, Etruscan and Sythian abstract designs in metal, pottery and wood. The culture flourished in Ireland whilst it was extinguished in other parts of Europe by the growing Roman Empire.

▶▶ *Halstatt Civilization*

LABOUR PARTY

Political party in the Irish Republic. The exasperation of those idealists who feel the Irish really ought to have been able to see beyond sectarian and nationalist loyalties to more universal questions of social justice finds an echo in the perplexity of those scholars who have considered the historical record. Although the Irish Trades Union Congress and Labour Party took no part in the election

campaigns of 1918 and 1921, it scored an impressive 21.3 per cent of the vote in 1922 and won 17 seats in the Dáil. Since then, though, the urgency of the nationalist issue would appear to have abated, it only seems to have dominated Irish politics all the more, and – except as a minor player in the coalition game – Labour has never looked like making its way back from the margins.

LACY, HUGH DE, THE ELDER (d. 1186)

Hugh de Lacy, 5th Baron Lacy and 1st Lord of Meath, Anglo-Norman soldier, castle builder and one of the conquerors of Ireland. Lacy accompanied Henry II to Ireland in 1171 on the expedition to challenge the power of the Anglo-Norman adventurer Richard de Clare, by then king of Leinster. In 1172 he was created constable of Dublin and justiciar. From 1176 he was made procurator-general of Ireland, but his personal ambitions aroused suspicions that he planned to become king of Ireland himself after he apparently married the daughter of Ruairí Ó Conchubhair, king of Connacht. He seems to have been permanently removed from his post by 1184, but was accused by prince John, lord-lieutenant of Ireland from 1185, of plotting against his authority. In 1186 he was assassinated.

▶▶ *Richard de Clare, Henry II of England*

ABOVE: The Irish rebels' encampment on Vinegar Hill.
RIGHT: William Gladstone, who introduced the first Land Act in 1870.

LACY, HUGH DE, THE YOUNGER (d. 1242)

Younger son of Hugh de Lacy the Elder, soldier and Anglo-Norman lord. Hugh de Lacy the Younger fought for the Crown in Ireland against the rising power of Anglo-Norman adventurers. In 1204 he captured John de Courcy, and was awarded his lands in Ulster and Connacht and was created 1st Earl of Ulster in 1205 (the first Anglo-Norman Irish peerage). Disputes over his authority caused King John to come to Ireland in 1207, expelling Hugh de Lacy, who fled to Scotland. He fought in France until 1221 but then allied himself with the O'Neills in Ireland. Restoration of his lands in 1227 restored his loyalty to the Crown until his death.

))))➤ *John de Courcy*

LAKE, GENERAL GERARD (1744–1808)

English general who led English forces against rebels and French invaders in Ireland in 1798. Lake saw service during the American Revolutionary War in 1781, and in the French Revolutionary Wars in 1793–94. In 1798 Lake was placed in command of the British Army in Ireland and conducted a savage campaign against the rebels and anyone thought to be synpathetic to their cause. He engaged the Irish rebel encampment at Vinegar Hill near Wexford on 21 June, securing a decisive defeat. Lake also led the defeat of Humbert's French forces at Ballinamuck, following the landing at Killala Bay. Lake was subsequently promoted to commander-in-chief in India.

))))➤ *Battle of Ballinamuck, General Humbert, Battle of Vinegar Hill*

LAND ACTS (1870–1909, 1923)

A series of legislative measures passed by the British parliament and then by the Free State government (1923) designed to rationalize landlord–tenant relationships in the Irish countryside. Beginning with Gladstone's Land Acts of 1870 and 1881, the Land Acts were a response to ceaseless agitation by Irish campaigners, calling for an end to the abuses of what had become a tradition of high-handed landlordism in Ireland. While the act of 1870 restricted the circumstances in which tenants could be evicted, successive acts set up bodies to supervise the imposition of fair rents and loans which enabled tenants to buy their own properties. The Irish Land Act of 1903 went as far as offering encouragements to landlords and tenants to agree such sales, making explicit the government's bias in favour of a system of owner-occupancy. It was left to the Free State government to take the process to its logical conclusion, its Land Commission compulsorily purchasing land from landlords for redistribution to their tenants.

))))➤ *William Gladstone*

LAND LEAGUE (1879)

Organization campaigning for reform in Irish landholding laws. The creation of Michael Davitt, the Land League was set up in Dublin in 1879 under the presidency of Charles Stewart Parnell, who proved an inspirational leader for a movement which suited the needs of the hour. Its declared objective was an improvement of the lot of the rural poor through fairer tenancies – or, better yet, a system of peasant proprietorship. The Land League offered a political home for individuals with far more radical nationalistic agendas. British critics were quick to claim that the League was merely a front for more generalized sedition, while even disinterested commentators were struck by an apparent imbalance between the patriotic ardour it generated and the mundanity of its stated aims. For many in the countryside there could really be no more important cause than that of fair rent and security of tenure – yet there may well have been an increasing tendency to see the Crown as the ultimate landlord.

))⟩⟩ **Michael Davitt, Land War, Charles Stewart Parnell**

LAND WAR (1880)

Although ostensibly a peaceful organization, the Land League was nevertheless intimidatory in its tactics. However far, and however sincerely, the leadership chose to distance itself from those criminal acts carried out in the organization's name, the League undoubtedly depended to a considerable degree on the implicit threat of force. The 'boycott' (named for the Mayo land-agent who fell foul of the League's supporters in 1880 and was duly ostracized), the threatening letter, the rent strike, the obstruction of evictions: all these weapons were freely used – as was actual violence on occasion. The situation gradually worsened and the movement gathered momentum. Gladstone's Land Act of 1881 (his second) and his Kilmainham Treaty with Parnell in 1882 were both attempts to draw the sting of the unrest in rural areas. To some extent he was successful, although the discontent would rumble on, finding expression in the continuing rise of Parnell through the early 1880s.

))⟩⟩ **William Gladstone, Kilmainham Treaty, Land Acts**

LANDLORDS AND TENANTS

Following the Battle of Kinsale in 1601 and the subsequent Flight of the Earls, 1607, the old Gaelic order of Ireland was ended. During the period 1608–91 successive transfers of land from the predominantly Catholic population to the Protestant immigrants from Scotland and England pushed around 85 per cent of the population into poverty. The Plantations system can be likened to 'ethnic cleansing': Catholic land was confiscated and the population evicted and resettled. Effectively the Plantations (Ulster 1609, Cromwellian 1652 and the Williamite 1693), deprived the dissident Irish aristocracy of their source of power. Many of the Irish peasants were retained as farm labourers or tenant farmers and were paid low wages and charged high rents. Many of the major landowners were absentees, whose interest was purely financial. Tenants had little security of tenure and were often at the mercy of the agents who managed the estates. As the population grew, farms were subdivided and making a living became increasingly difficult. Evictions were common and the small farmers, who also had to pay tithes to the Established Church, became increasingly aggrieved. The agrarian unrest of the eighteenth century developed into major political movements in the following century, with the Tithe War and the efforts of the Land League bringing major change in the relationship between landlord and tenant.

))⟩⟩ **Cromwellian Plantation, English Civil War, Plantation of Ulster, Williamite Plantation**

LEFT: Charles Boycott, a victim of ostracism by Irish Land League agitators, harvests his corn under police protection.

LARKIN, JAMES (1876–1947)

Leader of Irish trade unionism; also known as 'Big Jim'. James Larkin was the founder of the Irish Transport and General Workers Union and its general secretary from 1909–24, becoming the general secretary of the Workers Union of Ireland in 1924–47. He played an influential and heroic role in laying the foundations of the trade-union movement in Ireland. He was jailed for sedition following his activities in the General Strike in 1913. During World War I he went to the USA and tried to raise funds for the Irish to fight the British. As a Communist he was convicted of criminal anarchy but pardoned in 1923 and deported back to Ireland. He remained active in trade unionism and represented the Labour Party in Dáil Éireann.

))))▶ *Trade Unionism*

LARNE

Small seaport on the coast of County Antrim. A thriving harbour settlement as long ago as the seventh century, Larne would be key to the Scots-Irish connection well into modern times. The traffic that poured through Larne not only commercial but also cultural and demographic – helped cement the bonds across the water ever more firmly through medieval times. The MacDonnell family, dominant locally, were also powerful in Scotland, and instrumental in organizing the Ulster Plantation of the seventeenth century. It was through Larne that the Scots settlers came – and from here that, in the eighteenth century, almost a quarter of a million Ulster Scots set out in search of religious toleration and economic opportunity in colonial America.

Larne has long been a Loyalist stronghold, and it was there that an agent of the Ulster Unionist Council arranged to have a shipment of 25,000 rifles and three million rounds of ammunition landed from Germany in April 1914 for the use of the Ulster Volunteer Force (UVF) in an attempt to influence the British government's policy on Home Rule, and thus bringing the gun into Loyalist politics where it remains to the present day.

))))▶ *Howth Gun-running*

LEFT: James Larkin.
BELOW: River Lee, Cork.

LEABHAR BREAC (15TH CENTURY)

Manuscript compiled at Clonmacnoise and several other centres at the beginning of the fifteenth century. It is one of the sources consulted by Micheál Ó Cléirigh when he was compiling the *Annals of the Four Masters*. The *Leabhar Breac* ('Speckled Book'), which is now in the library of the Royal Irish Academy in Dublin, consists mainly of religious and historical material.

))))▶ **Annals of the Four Masters,** *Clonmacnoise,* **Micheál Ó Cléirigh**

LEE, RIVER

River in County Cork. Running from east to west across the interior of County Cork, the Lee breaks up into a marshy, many channelled delta as it reaches the sea. Thus the fact that, though a coastal city, Cork has never itself been a significant port: its real harbour has, in recent centuries, been along the coast at Cobh.

LEINSTER

Province of Ireland. The most south-easterly of Ireland's provinces, and its second largest, Leinster has also been its most accessible from England. As such it was the centre for English conquest and settlement in medieval times, the Viking city of Dublin providing a colonial capital around which spread the original area of 'civilization', the English Pale.

Yet Leinster already had a long and fascinating history before the first colonists arrived, enjoying a more equitable commerce across the Irish Sea. While Romano-British monks are believed to have established foundations in Leinster well before the arrival of St Patrick in the north, there is also evidence of Irish monastic activity in Britain, especially in Wales, where it is believed Irish rulers may have held territory at times. St David, patron saint of Wales, features in a number of Irish chronicles, while Irish monks are known to have taken an interest in Welsh history. At one time, then, the relatively narrow and sheltered strait between south-east Ireland and the Pembroke–Carmarthen coast seems to have been a busy, two-way highway for cultural (and commercial) traffic. The onset of the Viking raids in the tenth century apparently interrupted this trade, while the Anglo-Norman invasion and English colonization would irrevocably alter the balance of power between the two islands. The long-term English presence in large parts of Leinster did not, of course, necessarily make the province as a whole more loyal – anything but: hence, for example, the particular bitterness of the insurrection of 1798 in the area round Wexford.

Today's four provinces are the result of seventeenth-century mapping – though this largely only confirmed much earlier divisions. Prior to the Anglo-Norman conquest, though, much of Leinster's northern part (including Meath, Westmeath, Offaly, Longford, and areas of Louth and County Dublin) had in fact belonged to a fifth province, the ancient territory of Mide, a distinction which is still to some extent made by historians.

))))▶ *Conquest of Ireland, Monasteries*

ABOVE: Leinster House.
ABOVE RIGHT: Seán Lemass.
FAR RIGHT: The Siege of Limerick.

LEINSTER, BOOK OF (12TH CENTURY)

Major manuscript anthology dating from the early twelfth century. *The Book of Leinster* contains copies of such important works as the *Book of Invasions*, *The Cattle*

Raid of Cooley, many literary works, genealogical and historical material. It was compiled under the patronage of Diarmaid mac Murchadha and consists of 187 vellum folios.

))))▶ **Cattle Raid of Cooley, Book of Invasions,** *Diarmaid mac Murchadha*

LEINSTER HOUSE (1745–51)

Georgian Palladian mansion, home of the Irish parliament's Dáil (chamber of deputies) and Seanad (senate). It was built by the German-born Huguenot architect Richard Castle (*c.* 1690–1751) between 1745–51 as a central hall with cupola and flanking wings for James Fitzgerald, 1st Duke of Leinster, on an undeveloped rural site. The design resembles elements of Vanbrugh's Castle Howard in Yorkshire (1699–1712). Leinster House rapidly became the centre of the most fashionable part of Georgian Dublin. In 1815 it was bought by the Royal Dublin Society, who sold it in 1925 to the Irish government. The original wings have been replaced with the National Library and Museum buildings.

LEMASS, SEÁN (1899–1971)

Irish nationalist and politician. Lemass took part in the Easter Rising of 1916, when the Irish Volunteers and the Irish Citizen Army seized control of Dublin. Lemass was a founding member of Fianna Fáil in 1926, and served in a number of ministerial posts. He was Taoiseach between 1959 and 1966; an era which saw great economic progress in Ireland. He also initiated dialogue with Northern Ireland prime minister Terence O'Neill.

))))➤ *Easter Rising, Fianna Fáil*

LIFFEY, RIVER

River in east of Ireland. Rising in Sally Gap, in County Wicklow, the River Liffey curves round to the north-west through County Kildare before flowing eastward to reach the sea at Dublin Bay. The deep pool at the river's mouth, after which the city of Dublin ('dark pool') was named, was carved away by repeated dredging in modern times.

LIMERICK

City at the mouth of the River Shannon in south-west Ireland. Like so many Irish cities, a Viking foundation, Limerick was from the tenth century the capital of the O'Brien kings of Munster, though in the twelfth century the Anglo-Norman lords would make it a centre for their conquest of the west. To this day a Shannon tributary, the Abbey River, divides off a northerly 'English Town' (complete with castle and cathedral) from an 'Irish Town' district in the south of the old city. Apart from the comic rhymes called 'Limericks' (whose connection with the place, if any, is obscure), the city is most famous for the Treaty signed here in 1691 to ratify the victory of William III in his war with James II, and whose terms permitted that exodus of Irish Catholic gentry which would become known as the 'Flight of the Wild Geese'. More recently, the city's early twentieth-century slums have become infamous throughout the world thanks to the surprise success of Frank McCourt's memoir *Angela's Ashes*.

))))➤ *Flight of the Wild Geese, Treaty of Limerick*

LIMERICK, TREATY OF (1691)

Treaty ending the Siege of Limerick in 1691. Limerick's castle and medieval fortifications made it one of the most important strongholds in Ireland, and its control of the mouth of the River Shannon meant James II's troops installed there could be easily supplied. Following the Battle of the Boyne, French troops left, but the resistance to William III's army was determined and was aided by bad weather. An assault on 27 August 1691 was fought back with such ferocity that William had to negotiate the town's surrender. Then on 3 October the Treaty of Limerick was signed, permitting Jacobite defenders to go to France, thus ending the war in Ireland.

))))➤ *Battle of the Boyne, James II of England, William III of England*

LINEN

Material produced from flax plant fibres. Produced since antiquity, linen production was ideally suited to small farmsteads. An Irish tradition of fine linen developed, particularly in Ulster where most Irish linen is now produced. Today, 20 per cent of Europe's linen is made in Ireland, at around 2,000 tonnes per annum, but almost all the flax is now imported.

LLOYD GEORGE, DAVID (1863–1945)

British statesman, Liberal prime minister (1916–22). More non-conformist than nationalist, Lloyd George's Welsh background seems to have inclined him to sympathize far more with Ireland's northern Protestants than with the overwhelmingly Catholic advocates of the Home Rule movement. Hence his robust line when entrusted by Herbert Asquith with the negotiation of a Home Rule agreement to exclude Ulster, at the start of 1916, and his toughness on assuming the premiership himself later that same year. British victory in World War I – and the heroic contribution made by the Ulster regiments – did nothing to soften his uncompromising position in the talks leading up to the Anglo-Irish Treaty of 1921.

)))▶ *Anglo-Irish Treaty, World War I*

LOCAL GOVERNMENT

Administration of the country at local level. British-ruled Ireland, like Britain itself, was divided up into counties (from the Norman-French *comté*), although such urban centres as Dublin, Galway and Carrickfergus had a quasi-county status. Through the modern age the importance of the urban councils has grown, while the twentieth century saw the state assuming responsibility for many social services (health, social security, etc.) in both Free State and Northern Ireland. Local government in the North has been a matter of far more than local significance, becoming a vital tool for maintaining Protestant power. The 'gerrymandering' of electoral boundaries to ensure the disproportionate return of Unionist councillors, as well as discrimination in local-government services (most crucially housing) would be among the major grievances of the Civil Rights Movement in the 1960s.

)))▶ *Civil Rights Movement*

LOMBARD, PETER (1554–1625)

Catholic cleric. Born into Old English stock in Waterford, Peter Lombard went abroad to study in Europe. A brilliant thinker, he came to the attention of Pope Clement, who appointed him to the archbishopric of Armagh. Ireland's leading Catholic clergyman, Lombard remained a major figure on the European stage at a time when the Church was attempting to strike back against Protestant gains through its own 'Counter-Reformation'.

LOUGH DERG

Also known as St Patrick's Purgatory and Station Island, this is the site of a pilgrimage which dates back to early Christian times. The original site was a cave (now destroyed) at Station Island on Lough Derg, near Pettigo in County Donegal. Nowadays pilgrims come to the island and stay for several days, fasting and

ABOVE: David Lloyd George.
RIGHT: St Patrick, who is said to have fasted at Lough Derg for 40 days.
FAR RIGHT: The Lusitania *sailing from New York, 1915.*

praying. Although only open for the summer months it attracts many thousands of visitors annually. St Patrick is reputed to have fasted here for 40 days; the significance of the site was recognized by continental Christians from the twelfth century and was a popular medieval pilgrimage for them. It has also influenced the work of many Irish writers including Seamus Heaney and Patrick Kavanagh.

)))➤ *Seamus Heaney, Patrick Kavanagh, St Patrick*

LOUTH

Eastern Irish county. The most northerly county of Leinster from the mouth of the River Boyne to the borders of Monaghan and Armagh, Louth belonged in pre-Conquest times to the province of Mide. Today the county is perhaps most famous for its warlike history, for Cromwell's massacre at Drogheda (1649) and for the victory won in 1690 'King Billy' (William III) at the Battle of the Boyne. The highlight of the Orange Order's ceremonial year, commemorations of this occasion are held on 12 July annually, though the battle was actually fought on 11 July (1 July under the old calendar then in use).

)))➤ *Battle of the Boyne, Siege of Drogheda*

LUNDY, ROBERT (d. c. 1716)

Garrison commander, Derry City, 1688–89. His role in the events of the Siege of Derry apart, the details of Robert Lundy's life are more or less unknown. A Scottish Protestant, Lundy was given command of forces in the city by James II, who hoped to allay the fears of Protestant citizens that their lives were in danger. In March 1689

Lundy accepted a commission from William III – only to advocate surrender after after Jacobite victories in the surrounding area. He finally fled the city that same summer. His name living on as a byword for betrayal, Lundy is burned in effigy by Derry loyalists each year.

)))➤ *Siege of Derry*

LUSITANIA (1915)

British liner, sunk on 7 May 1915 by a German submarine off the coast of Ireland. The crew ignored instructions to zig-zag following a series of submarine attacks on merchant shipping off Ireland. The ship was carrying a cargo of munitions, but nearly 1,200 passengers drowned, including 128 Americans. The sinking of the *Lusitania* hastened US entry into World War I.

LYNCH, JACK (b. 1917–2001)

Fianna Fáil politician, Taoiseach (1966–73, 1977–79). As Taoiseach through the years following the onset of the Ulster 'Troubles' – and as leader of a political party whose republican traditions, at least in theory, were still

strong – Lynch had to perform a difficult balancing act, but did so with some skill. Though he can be said to have cynically scapegoated Charles Haughey in the 'arms crisis' of 1971, all would end happily for Haughey – and for Fianna Fáil – their nationalist credentials underlined.

))))▶ *Fianna Fáil, Charles Haughey*

MAC GRIANNA, SEOSAMH (1901–90)

Irish writer. From the Rann na Feirste Gaeltacht in County Donegal, Mac Grianna is considered one of the most important prose writers in modern Irish, even though all his creative work was done in a 10-year period before 1935. He had qualified as a teacher in 1921 but because of IRA involvement during the civil war he was initially barred from permanent employment and had to struggle to make a living in a succession of short-term appointments and by writing. Later he was employed by the civil service in Dublin translating European literary works into Irish. His creative work which includes influential

ABOVE: Jack Lynch with Margaret Thatcher during the EEC summit in Dublin, 1979.

essays, short story collections, novels and an autobiography was written around the same time. The pressure of this work and possibly the residual effects of a hunger strike affected in his mental health. By 1935 he realized that the 'well' of inspiration had gone dry and that he would write no more. He spent the last 30 years of his life in hospital.

))))▶ *Gaeltacht, Irish Civil War*

MAC LOCHLAINN, MUIRCHEARTACH (d. 1166)

King of Ireland and warrior; also known as Muircheartach Ó Lochlainn. A series of campaigns won him power across Ireland. In 1139 he defeated the Ó Dubhdas in Ulster and in 1147 the Ulidians at Dundrum, County Down. Within two years the Vikings of Dublin and Leinster had capitulated to him, followed by the O'Connors of Connacht the next year. In 1154 the Dublin Vikings accepted him as king, and from 1155 until his death in battle against the Ulidians he was High King of Ireland. In 1161 Diarmaid mac Murchadha and Ruairi Ó Conchubhair submitted to him. A Christian, Mac Lochlainn went to the synod of Mellifont in 1157 and founded the Cistercian monastery at Newry.

))))▶ *Diarmaid mac Murchadha*

MAC MURCHADHA, ART CAOMHÁNACH (1357–1415)

Irish chieftain and warrior, the natural son of Diarmaid Mac Murchadha, Art constantly pursued his own interests by attacking the English. Richard II, who visited Ireland in 1394–95 and 1399, offered a reward for his capture.

))))▶ *Richard II of England*

MAC MURCHADHA, DIARMAID (DERMOT MAC MURROUGH) (c. 1110–71)

King of Leinster from 1126, Diarmaid overcame his disputed succession by blinding or killing his rivals in Leinster in 1141. He was forced into exile in 1166 after carrying off Dearbhla, wife of Tiarnán Ó Ruairc, king of Breifne (now Counties Leitrim and Cavan) in 1154, which instigated a long-running feud. Diarmaid then sought help from Henry II, promising his vassalship in return. Henry approved and allowed Richard de Clare and other Anglo-Norman lords to intervene. The campaign was successful. Strongbow married Aoife, Diarmaid's daughter, and became king of Leinster on Diarmaid's death.

)))➤ *Aoife, Tiernan O'Rourke*

MACALEESE, MARY

Politician, president of the Irish Republic (since 1997). After the overwhelmingly positive impression made on the world stage by the defiantly secularist, modernist Mary Robinson, some feared that the election of the avowed nationalist and Belfast born Mary MacAleese was a reversion to Fianna Fáil type. Within weeks of her appointment, however, she had shocked traditionalists by receiving Holy Communion at a Church of Ireland service, sending a clear signal to the Protestant North that she was interested in 'building bridges'.

MACBRIDE, MAUD GONNE (1865–1953)

Actress and nationalist campaigner. The daughter of an English army officer of Irish descent, Maud Gonne was educated largely in France where, as a young woman, she established the French-language Irish nationalist paper, *L'Irlande Libre*. It was in Paris that she met W. B. Yeats, in whose play *Cathleen ni Houlihan* she would take the starring role; she remained his lifelong muse, even after her marriage to Major John MacBride.

)))➤ *W. B. Yeats*

MACBRIDE, SEÁN (1904–88)

Revolutionary and politician. The son of Maud Gonne and Major John MacBride, Seán MacBride grew up to fight in the War of Independence; an opponent of the Treaty, he was imprisoned by the Free State government, 1923–24. IRA chief of staff from 1936–38, he chose to take a constitutional path from 1939, eventually, in 1946, founding Clann na Poblachta. His position of minister for external affairs in the coalition government of 1948–51 led to his admission into the ranks of the international great and good. A founder-member of Amnesty International and co-author of the UN Declaration of Human Rights, he was awarded the Nobel Peace Prize in 1974.

)))➤ *Clann na Poblachta, War of Independence*

MACCURTAIN, THOMAS (1884–1920)

Rebel and politician. An inspirational leader of the Easter Rising in Cork, MacCurtain managed to hold off the military authorities for a week, before a dignified surrender and orderly handover of weapons was agreed. As commander of the IRA in Cork, he was elected mayor of the city in 1920, only to be assassinated – it is believed by the police – a few weeks later.

)))➤ *Easter Rising, Terence MacSwiney*

MACDIARMADA, SEÁN (1884–1916)

Revolutionary. A member of the IRB from 1906, MacDiarmada revitalized what had been an exhausted organization and took a revolutionary core with him into the Irish Volunteers. Owing their allegiance primarily to him, rather than to the organization's nominal leader, Eoin MacNeill, MacDiarmada's volunteers would be the main force involved in the 1916 Easter Rising.

)))➤ *Easter Rising, Irish Volunteers, Eion MacNeill*

MACDONAGH, THOMAS (1878–1916)

Poet and revolutionary. No more than a minor poet himself, MacDonagh did much to promote Irish literature – indeed it was in publicity (what we might now call 'spin') that his real genius arguably lay. The organizer of O'Donovan Rossa's funeral in 1915, at which his friend Pádraig Pearse had such an enormous oratorical triumph, MacDonagh was one of the leaders (and, subsequently, one of the martyrs) of the Easter Rising.

)))➤ *Easter Rising*

ABOVE LEFT: Maud Gonne.
ABOVE: Seán MacBride.

MACDONNELL, SORLEY BOY (c. 1505–90)

Gaelic chieftain in Ulster; also known as Somhairle Buídhe. Although his claims to territories in Antrim were initially recognized by the English Crown, he found these rights effectively cancelled in grants made to settlers by the 'Enterprise of Ulster' (1571). Warring with the Earl of Essex and Henry Sidney (for whose Rathlin Island Massacre he took revenge), MacDonnell managed to hold up, if not actually prevent, the process of English colonization in Ulster.

))))➤ *Rathlin Island Massacre*

MACKEN, SIMON (c. 1760–1836)

A native of Kells, County Meath, Macken lived most of his life in County Fermanagh, and in his later years became a prosperous schoolmaster in Enniskillen. He was also a noted Irish scholar who transcribed many important manuscripts of poetry and prose, and was probably the last of the traditional scribes in County Fermanagh.

MACNEILL, EOIN (1867–1945)

Nationalist and academic. A founder of the Gaelic League, Eoin MacNeill earned a considerable reputation as a historian, being appointed the first Professor of Early and Medieval Irish History at University College Dublin in 1908. Having first suggested the creation of the Irish Volunteers following the formation of Carson's Ulster Volunteer Force in 1912, he became the organization's chief of staff, but was kept in the dark about many of the decisions of its IRB-infiltrated inner circle. Preparations for the Easter Rising accordingly passed him by completely – though on discovering what was afoot, he stood down his men, causing chaos throughout the organization around the country. A supporter of the 1921 Treaty, he represented the Free State on the Boundary Commission, resigning when it became clear that it was going nowhere. He subsequently retired from active politics, concentrating once more on his career as a scholar, heading the Irish Manuscripts Commission from 1927.

))))➤ *Anglo-Irish Treary, Boundary Commission, Gaelic League, Irish Volunteers*

MACSWINEY, TERENCE (1879–1920)

Politician and hunger striker. A leader of the Irish Volunteers in Cork, he heeded MacNeill's order to stand down in 1916, but played an important role in bringing about a negotiated settlement between those who did rise up with MacCurtain and the military authorities. The Sinn Féin mayor after MacCurtain's murder, he was arrested in 1920 and died in London's Brixton Prison after a 74-day hunger strike.

))))➤ *Irish Volunteers, Thomas MacCurtain*

MAEL MORDHA (d. 1014)

King of Leinster, also known as Mael Mora. Mael Mordha opposed Brian Bóroimhe's rule and led rebellions against him to assert his rights as king of Leinster, soliciting support from the Dublin Vikings. Mael Mordha was defeated at Glen Mama in AD 999. Brian tried a

diplomatic solution, reinstating the Dublin Viking king Sitric Silkenbeard, and marrying Mael Mordha's sister Gormfhlaith himself (although he eventually rejected her). This triggered the Mordha and Viking campaign to destroy Brian Bóroimhe, which climaxed in the Battle of Clontarf in 1014, during which Mael Mordha was killed, alongside most of the Leinster chiefs.

))))➤ *Brian Bóroimhe, Battle of Clontarf, Battle of Glen Mama, Sitric Silkenbeard*

MAEL SEACHNAILL I (d. AD 863)

King of Ireland from AD 842 (also known as Malachy I and Mael Sechlainn I). His reign was characterized by constant fighting against the Vikings, whom he defeated in AD 844, 847 and 859. He also invaded Munster on three occasions.

))))➤ *Vikings*

MAEL SEACHNAILL II (AD 949–1022)

Uí Néill tribal leader, king of Meath and later king of Ireland from AD 980; also known as Malachy II and Mael Sechlainn II). He defeated the Vikings at Tara in AD 980 and 1000, but was beaten by his rival Brian Bóroimhe and forced to concede the kingship in 1002. However, the death of Brian and his son in the Battle of Clontarf (1014), which ended Viking ambitions, allowed Mael Seachnaill to restore his authority.

))))➤ *Brian Bóroimhe, Battle of Clontarf*

MAGRATH, MILER (c. 1523–1622)

Cleric. Magrath started his religious life as a Franciscan friar and was granted the bishopric of Down and Connor in 1565. Five years later, however, he accepted the authority of the Anglican Church of Ireland, and was appointed Bishop of Clogher by Elizabeth I. As Archbishop of Cashel and Bishop of Emly – with responsibility at times for the bishoprics of Waterford and Lismore as well – Magrath raised eyebrows with his eager accumulation of titles and increasingly blatant nepotism. While his original apostasy may at first have helped contribute to better understanding between Ireland's Gaelic population and their English governors, it would ultimately undermine his position as spiritual leader.

))))➤ *Elizabeth I of England*

MAGUIRE DYNASTY (c. 1300–1607)

Ruling dynasty of Fermanagh. One of the major Gaelic dynasties, the Maguires dominated life in Fermanagh from *c.* 1300 until 1607, when chieftain Cú Chonnacht Mag Uidhir left Ireland in the Flight of the Earls. They often played a role of power-balancing and mediation between the O'Donnells of Donegal and the O'Neills of Tyrone as they had close connections with both these families. Their dominance of political and ecclesiastical affairs in Fermanagh ended with the Plantation of Ulster but several branches of the family, most notably the Tempo Maguires, managed to hold on to some of their lands and they continued to influence local affairs into the nineteenth century.

))))➤ *Flight of the Earls, Plantation of Ulster*

MALACHY, ST (d. 1148)

Prelate and church-reformer. Designated Archbishop of Armagh in 1129, Malachy found himself effectively unable to take up office, so deeply rooted had the scions of the Clann Sínaich dynasty become in what was supposed to be a spiritual position. Thanks to the Irish

Church's rules on married clergymen, the abbots of this family had been able to hand down this and other key positions for almost 200 years. This was the immediate, personal motivation for what became a wholesale campaign for reform within the Irish Church which would culminate in the Synods of Cashel and Kells and the introduction of the Cistercians.

))))➤ *Synod of Cashel, Synod of Kells*

LEFT: Eoin MacNeill.
ABOVE: Lavabo Cistercian Abbey, County Louth.

MANCHESTER MARTYRS (1867)

Group of Fenians hanged in 1867. The abortive uprising of 4–5 March 1867 was quickly suppressed by the British authorities, who had in fact pre-emptively arrested the most likely leaders. There were important repercussions, however, when a group of Fenians ambushed a prison van in Manchester, in which two of their comrades were being taken to trial; a policeman was fatally injured in the process. Although there was no question of his having been intentionally murdered, the British court was unrelenting and three men, who became known as the 'Manchester Martyrs', were sent to the scaffold. Once again, operational fiasco was transmuted by British ineptitude into rebel triumph: the episode would live long in the annals of Irish Republicanism.

)))▶ *Fenian Uprising*

MARKIEVICZ, COUNTESS CONSTANCE (1868–1927)

Republican activist and politician. Born in London, Constance Gore-Booth, she acquired her title on her marriage to Count Casimir Markievicz in 1900. He left her in 1913, returning home to the Ukraine. A Sinn Féin

ABOVE: The surrender of the Countess Markievicz.
RIGHT: Lord Thomas Fitzgerald renounces his allegiance to Henry VIII.

member since 1908, she joined James Connolly's Citizen Army and fought in the Easter Rising: afterwards she was condemned to death, but had the sentence revoked because she was a woman. Elected as a Sinn Féin candidate in Dublin in 1918, she became the British parliament's first female MP, though in line with her party's abstentionist line she would never take up her seat. The same applied to the Dáil seat she won for Sinn Féin in 1923, although she had been minister of labour in the unrecognized Dáil of 1919–22.

)))▶ *Citizen Army, James Connolly, Easter Rising*

MATHEW, FATHER (1790–1856)

Father Mathew was appointed Provincial of the Capuchin Order in Ireland. In 1838 he began temperance work by holding a meeting of the Cork Total Abstinence Society in his own schoolhouse. He is quoted as stating 'Here goes in the Name of God' before signing his pledge in a large book. Over the succeeding years his following grew as he began to tour the country in his

attempts to convert the population. In 1843 he wrote: 'I have now, with the Divine Assistance, hoisted the banner of Temperance in almost every parish in Ireland.'

MAYNOOTH, BATTLE OF (1535)

Maynooth was a stronghold of Kildare power in Ireland. It was besieged during the rebellion of Lord Thomas Fitzgerald, known as 'Silken Thomas', which began in 1534 in support of his father Gerald, who had been recalled to England. Silken Thomas was defeated here by Lord Leonard Grey, marshal of the English army in Ireland under the lord deputy, William Skeffington. Survivors were executed, an event known ironically as the 'Pardon of Maynooth'. Silken Thomas escaped but was later captured and executed in 1537.

))))➤ *Gerald Fitzgerald, Pardon of Maynooth, Silken Thomas*

MAYNOOTH COLLEGE (16TH CENTURY)

St Patrick's College, Maynooth, is Ireland's national seminary for the training of priests. It was set up in 1795 by an act of parliament at a time when the Penal Laws were being relaxed. This was also the period when a number of continental colleges had been forced to close, particularly those in France which had been affected by the French Revolution. Although government support for this institution was vigorously opposed by some Protestant elements, the government believed that by founding the college and having some input in to it they could influence the clergy and gain the support of moderate Catholics at a time when the demands for Catholic rights were growing.

MAYNOOTH GRANT (1845)

Award of state funding to St Patrick's College, Maynooth, County Kildare in 1845. A generous (over £30,000) increase in the funding given to Ireland's leading seminary for training priests, the Maynooth Grant was in principle an attempt to take some of the heat out of the Repeal campaign. By showing his support for Catholic Ireland's cultural institutions (he also established a series of 'Queen's Colleges' open to all), British prime minister Robert Peel sought to drive a wedge between moderate, middle-class Catholics and the nationalist firebrands. In the event, it would be the extremism of his own anti-Catholic supporters he had to fear: the payment caused a split among English Conservatives and, ultimately, the collapse of Peel's government.

))))➤ *Maynooth College, Robert Peel*

MAYNOOTH, PARDON OF (1534)

Following Thomas Fitzgerald's imprisonment in the Tower of London for renouncing his allegiance to Henry VIII, the English king's armies attacked Maynooth Castle. Forcing Fitzgerald's army to surrender, Henry VIII's men offered the survivors of the battle 'The Pardon of Maynooth' – they were all executed.

))))➤ *Henry VIII of England*

MCCORLEY, RODDY (d. c. 1800)

Rebel. Although the famous song states with confidence that 'Young Roddy McCorley goes to die on the bridge at Toome today', the actual date of his death – even the year – remains shrouded in mystery. Thought to have been one of the 'Defenders', an informal grouping created to fight the Peep o'Day Boys in Armagh in the early 1790s, and only loosely associated with the United Irishmen's insurrection of 1798, McCorley's case has been fought over by those who would either play up or play down his national significance, hence the contention over whether his execution took place in 1799 (i.e. in the immediate aftermath of the events) or a year later (which suggests a more local notoriety).

)))➤ *Defenders, Peep o'Day Boys*

MCCORMACK, JOHN (1884–1945)

Irish opera singer. The greatest lyric tenor of his time, John McCormack was born in Athlone and studied in Italy. The start of his career coincided with the advent of recording technology and he made over 500 recordings of operatic and popular Irish songs which sold well on both sides of the Atlantic. He toured in the United States and in Australia, singing with major operatic companies as well as enjoying great success in his native country. He was the archetypal Irish tenor and has had many imitators even to this day.

MCCRACKEN, HENRY JOY (1767–98)

Irish Presbyterian nationalist, rebel, and leader of the United Irishmen. Born into a business family of Huguenot descent responsible for the oldest English language newspaper (the *Belfast Newsletter*), McCracken was a successful Ulster cotton manufacturer with a personal commitment to social reform, non-denominational education, and universal democratic rights.

In 1795, McCracken joined the Belfast United Irish Society but his radical views led to his imprisonment. Following release he was instructed by the Ulster Executive of the United Irishmen to co-ordinate the 1798 Rebellion, which depended on the simultaneous outbreak of regional risings. McCracken believed he could organize a rising of United Irishmen and Catholics with French aid. However, the rebellion broke out sporadically and early. Disarmament by the English forces left the rebels largely toothless. Few Catholics joined McCracken in the Antrim rebellion and he was easily defeated, which he attributed to treachery. He was executed on 17 July 1798.

)))➤ *United Irishmen*

MCGEE, THOMAS D'ARCY (1825–68)

Poet and political campaigner. McGee's international fame rests on his espousal of the cause of confederation in his adoptive homeland of Canada from 1857 onwards, but his background in Irish politics would return to haunt him. After one spell in North America (1842–45) he returned to campaign as a Young Irelander, emigrating again after the abject failure of the 1848 Rising. Throwing all his energies into Canadian politics, he was a member of parliament there from 1858: he was assassinated after some outspoken attacks on Fenianism.

MCHALE, JOHN (1791–1881)

Known as the Lion of Tuam, where he was archbishop from 1834, McHale was a Catholic clergyman who took a strong public stand on political questions of the day. He strongly opposed the tithes paid to the Church of Ireland, supporting Daniel O'Connell's Repeal movement, and criticizing the British government's policies on Ireland. He was a native speaker of Irish, a supporter of the language, and the author of a number of books, including Irish translations of the *Illiad* and Thomas Moore's *Melodies*.

)))➤ *Church of Ireland, Thomas Moore, Daniel O'Connell, Tithe War*

MCMAHON, HEBER (1600–50)

Catholic cleric and soldier. Trained as a priest on the continent, Heber McMahon was one of a group of Catholic clergy who, at the Synod of Kells of 1642, gave their blessing to the Ulster Rising of the preceding year, which has been described as a 'lawful and pious undertaking'. Though the causes – and even the events – of that insurrection had been highly complex, the bishops' statement had the effect of simplifying it in retrospect; it was subsequently seen as a straightforward revolt against Plantation and Protestantization. Appointed bishop of Clogher in 1643, he was already a key advisor of Eoghan Rua Ó Néill's death in 1649. McMahon, who was a member of the Gaelic aristocracy of County Monaghan, was chosen to lead the Irish forces. He was wounded and captured by Cromwellian troops, following the defeat at Scarrifhollis in County Donegal in 1650, and was brought to Enniskillen where he was later executed, and his head displayed on a spike above the castle.

))))▶ *Synod of Kells, Ulster Plantation*

LEFT: *Count John McCormack in 1934.*
ABOVE: *Henry McCracken was the leader of the United Irishmen, shown here in training.*

MCMANUS, TERENCE BELLEW (1823–60)

Revolutionary. A veteran of the abortive rising of 1848, McManus was arrested and transported to Van Diemen's Land (Tasmania); he escaped to San Francisco, where, however, he died in poverty. The repatriation of his remains was the first major project of the Fenian Brotherhood in 1861, generating enormous publicity and sympathy for the nationalist cause.

))))➤ *Fenian Brotherhood*

MÉADHBHA (QUEEN MAEVE OF CONNACHT)

A legendary pre-Christian leader who features prominently in the *Táin Bó Cuailgne* (Cattle Raid of Cooley). In every area Méadhbha competes and tries to dominate her husband, Ailill. He, however, has a brown bull to which there is no equal, exept for the Brown Bull of Cooley (now in County Louth). The owner of the Brown Bull of Cooley would not yield his beast, so Méadhbha launches an attack against them, but her army is repulsed by Cú Chulainn. Apart from this epic tale, Méadhbha appears in a number of other tales and legends, and a large cairn in County Sligo has traditionally been pointed out as her grave.

MEATH

County in central Ireland. The ancient territory of Mide was broken up by successive waves of conquest in medieval times, but the name survives in that of Meath

and neighbouring Westmeath. The county of Meath itself, lying well eastward, was among the first to feel the impact of invaders: the town and castle of Trim bear magnificent testimony to the years of Anglo-Norman rule. Colonization was more or less complete in Meath by the start of the sixteenth century, much of the modern county falling into the area marked out by the English Pale.

))))➤ *The Pale, Tara*

MELLIFONT, TREATY OF (1603)

Since Conn O'Neill first made his peace with Henry VIII, the O'Neills had been the Tudors' favourite Irish chieftains, seen as a force for order among what were otherwise an unruly people. The son of Conn's illegitimate son, Hugh O'Neill, 2nd Earl of Tyrone, having been similarly indulged to begin with, fell out of favour with Elizabeth I when he started intriguing with the Spanish Crown. In the Nine Years' War that resulted, O'Neill proved an unexpectedly difficult adversary, both militarily and politically, although his attempts to win Old English support under the banner of *patria* (Latin for 'fatherland') were unavailing. Defeated at Kinsale in 1601 (along with a Spanish expeditionary force), he finally surrendered to the Old English commander Mountjoy at Mellifont Abbey, though he was allowed to keep the patent to his original earldom.

))))➤ *Lord Mountjoy*

MELLOWS, LIAM (1890–1922)

Irish Volunteer leader. Mellows joined a republican youth movement, Na Fianna, and was imprisoned in 1915. He took part in the Easter Rising of 1916, after which he escaped to the US. In the Irish Civil War of 1922–23, he fought for the anti-Treaty faction, surrendering in Dublin to the Free State forces. In November 1922 he was dragged from his cell and executed without trial.

))))➤ *Irish Civil War*

MERRIMAN, BRIAN (c. 1740–1805)

Poet and schoolmaster. Merriman was born in County Clare and is best remembered for his humorous epic poem on the themes of clerical celibacy and female passions *Cúirt an Mheán Oíche* ('The Midnight Court'), which was written around 1780. Although little is known of the poet, his 1,200-line masterpiece survived in the oral tradition in County Clare until the use of Irish declined in the mid-twentieth century, as well as in numerous manuscript copies. It has been translated into English a number of times.

MESOLITHIC PEOPLE (c. 5000 BC)

Nomadic Stone Age people. The Mesolithic people did not have any sophisticated tools or particular skills but constructed their huts from hazel and animal hides. There is believed to have been a small Mesolithic population in Ireland, based in County Antrim and County Offaly. Evidence of their existence has been found at Mount Sandal.

)))⯈ *Mount Sandal*

METHODISM (18TH CENTURY)

Religious movement established by John Wesley at the end of the 1720s and brought to Ireland a few years later. The spiritual sensation of the eighteenth century, the Methodist movement in England galvanized an apathetic

population of nominally adherent poor, largely forgotten until then by a genteel Church of England. Given the ethnically and ideologically charged religious feelings to be found in Ireland, it could hardly hope to have the same effect there, and indeed its followers only ever numbered in their tens of thousands. Yet Methodism would prove influential in setting a standard for other creeds which had grown complacent: a revival in worship and an upsurge in charitable activity can both be indirectly attributed to its example. As in England, the movement would be weakened by the debate over whether or not to break with the established Church, though the split of 1816 would be healed again in 1878.

MILESIANS (c. 1000 BC)

According to the *Book of Invasions* the Milesians were the ancestors of the Gaels and they came from Spain. Most notable among them were the brothers Eber and Eremon who, according to legend, divided Ireland between them. Taking a harpist with him, Eremon went north and Eber, taking a poet, went south. After a peaceful year Eber's wife wanted the northern hill of Tara. Eremon, who claimed sovereignty of the whole island, won the ensuing battle.

)))⯈ **Book of Invasions**

FAR LEFT: Standing stones at Loughcrew in County Meath.
LEFT: John Wesley, the founder of Methodism.
ABOVE: The Hill of Tara.

MITCHEL, JOHN (1815–75)

Writer and political activist. Mitchel was born in Dungiven, County Derry, the son of a Presbyterian minister, and qualified as a lawyer before starting to write for *The Nation*. He became editor of the paper in 1847, but his militancy brought him into conflict with more moderate nationalists and he left later that year to found his own newspaper, *The United Irishman*. The horrors of the Famine led him to exhort the people to revolution. In May 1848 he was convicted by a packed jury of treason-felony and sentenced to transportation. While on the prison ship he wrote his very influential *Jail Journal*, which was published in 1854 following his escape from Van Dieman's the previous year. He actively supported the Confederate side in the American Civil War and later worked for the Fenians in Paris, before falling out with them. He returned to Ireland in 1875 and, after first being disqualified as an undischarged felon, was elected MP for County Tipperary in the subsequent by-election. He died shortly afterwards in Newry, County Down.

))))➤ *Fenian Movement, Great Famine,* **The Nation,** *Transportation*

MONAGHAN AND DUBLIN BOMBING (1974)

Terrorist incident. The killing of 33 people by car bombs detonated without warning in Monaghan and Dublin streets on 17 May 1974 represented the largest number killed in a single day in the history of the modern Troubles. Identified as the work of the northern Loyalist group the UVF, the attacks were assumed to be an attempt to undermine the Sunningdale Agreement and power-sharing executive, which duly collapsed some 10 days later. Few believed that the UVF had acted unassisted: accusations of collusion between the northern security forces and the Protestant paramilitaries were by now routine, and clear

evidence seemed to support the claims in this case. More sensational by far have been the persistent allegations that the attacks were organized by elements in the British intelligence services determined to destroy the peace agreement.

))))➤ *The Troubles, Ulster Volunteer Force*

MONASTERBOICE (6TH CENTURY)

Monastery complex north-west of Drogheda in County Louth. Literally the 'monastery of Boice', Monasterboice was established by St Buithe (or Boice) in the sixth century, although the physical fabric of that foundation has long since been lost. Those church buildings that remain seem to date from the thirteenth century, though a fine

round tower would appear to have been built three centuries previously. The chief attraction here, however, is a fine group of tenth-century high crosses, including the Muiredagh Cross – 5 m (15 ft) tall and carved on both sides with stunning biblical scenes.

))))➤ *Monasteries*

MONASTERIES

Religious foundations for work, prayer and often power. Communities of monks, presided over by abbots, monasteries were originally intended as places of

ABOVE: John Mitchel.
ABOVE RIGHT: The monastery at Monasterboice.
FAR RIGHT: The grounds of Trinity College, where Thomas Moore studied.

prayer and contemplation, though learning – the copying of scripture, the recording of Church history – was also important. The monasteries' emergence as institutions of power was in large part the result of their evolution as economic centres. Work, for the monks, was something to be offered up to God as a form of prayer, but it was also a means of achieving self-sufficiency: vital to what was generally an isolated community. It was of course but a small step from getting by to generating what might in time be considerable surpluses; while many monasteries were further enriched by lavish endowments from pious individuals. Yet the importance of the monasteries in the economic and political history of medieval Ireland, though clearly profound, can be overstated. In particular, recent studies have called into question the view that the abbots were an ecclesiastical law unto themselves.

MOORE, THOMAS (1779–1852)

Popular romantic nationalist poet whose *Melodies* had a huge impact when they first appeared and many of which are still well-known and enjoyed. As a student at Trinity College Dublin he became friendly with Robert Emmet and, although never overtly political, there was much in Moore's work that appealed to the national spirit of his times. In the *Melodies* he put English words to versions of the airs which had been collected by Edward Bunting at the Belfast Harp Festival.

))))➤ *Belfast Harp Festival, Edward Bunting, Robert Emmet, Trinity College Dublin*

MOUNT SANDAL

Mount Sandal, on the banks of the river Bann near Coleraine, is regarded by archeologists as the site of the earliest settlement in Ireland found so far. This is a Mesolithic site, dating back about 9,000 years. The Mesolithic people are the earliest known inhabitants of Ireland and their stone axes, flint-headed spears and arrows have been found at a number of sites. Although they are regarded as being nomadic, this site shows signs of continued occupancy, and excavations have yielded a great amount of evidence about their lives.

))))➤ *Mesolithic People*

MOUNTJOY, CHARLES BLOUNT, LORD (1563–1606)

Eighth baron Mountjoy, and soldier. Mountjoy fought in the Netherlands, Brittany and against the Armada, and accompanied Essex to the Azores in 1597. This raised suspicions about his loyalty when Essex was tried for treason, but he was freed. In 1601 he was made lord deputy of Ireland and sent against the Tyrone rebellion, inflicting a wholesale defeat at Kinsale in 1601. Mountjoy retained his post under James I, and put down further resistance to English military control by Aodh ó Neill, Earl of Tyrone, before returning to England in 1603 where he became master of ordnance and master of Portsmouth Castle.

))))➤ *Elizabeth I of England, Battle of Kinsale*

MULCAHY, RICHARD (1886–1971)

Politician. A veteran of the Easter Rising and the War of Independence, during which he served as IRA chief of staff, Richard Mulcahy was a supporter of the Treaty in

1921. As general officer commanding forces for the provisional government in the ensuing civil war, he was a natural choice for defence minister 1923–24. Leader of Fine Gael from 1944–59, he was also minister of education 1948–51 and 1954–57.

))))▶ *Fine Gael, Irish Civil War, Irish Republican Army*

MULLAGHMAST MASSACRE (1577)

Famous battle that took place on New Year's Day 1577. Under Mary I of England, the O'Moore and O'Connor lands in Laois and Offaly were confiscated and were planted with English settlers. A type of guerilla war ensued and the English, unable to defeat the Irish, sum-

moned them to a conference at Mullaghmast in County Kildare. There Morris O'Moore and at least 40 other Irish were treacherously slaughtered by the soldier-colonists Francis Colby and Robert Hartpole.

MUNSTER

Province of Ireland. Including not only the south-west of Ireland, but much of the south, Munster is by some distance the largest of the four provinces. In its western areas it is also among the most recently colonized. Yet while Munster's distance 'beyond the Pale' would lead to its characterization as wild and barbarous by later English commentators it was, through the pre-Conquest period, by far the most stable of the Irish provinces. Their kingdom centred in the plains of Tipperary and eastern Limerick but also extending up the adjacent river valleys, the Eóganacht dynasty held sway here without interruption from *c.* AD 600 for several centuries. Further west, the family's Locha Léin branch dominated the Kerry lowlands, while vassals of the

IRELAND
just before
THE ENGLISH INVASION

Eóganacht were ensconced in all the upland areas. The arrival of the Vikings in the ninth and tenth centuries led to the foundation of trading cities at Limerick, Cork and Waterford, but had comparatively little impact on the lives of the inhabitants of the interior.

The relaxed regimes of the Anglo-Norman lords and 'Old English' settlers who ruled much of Munster up until the time of the Tudor kings meant that, even under occupation, Gaelic language and traditions could continue more or less unhindered. That this only deferred an inevitable problem is suggested by the bitterness eventually surrounding the Munster Plantation of the sixteenth century – and an eventful subsequent history of unrest and rebellion. The land agitators of the nineteenth century found a ready ear among the people here, while a good many Fenians (including John O'Leary and Jeremiah O'Donovan Rossa) hailed from Munster. The long-standing presence of a significant Protestant population, far from moderating nationalist feeling in the city of Cork, seems only to have motivated many in what became the second city of the Easter Rising.

MUNSTER PLANTATION (1580S)

Aggressive colonization of lands in Munster from 1580s onwards. The difficulties the Crown had experienced in finally putting down the second Desmond Revolt left it determined to prevent any reoccurrence. Hence the appointment of 35 'undertakers' to clear vast tracts of confiscated land of its Irish tenants and to settle it instead with English incomers. The reality on the ground was not quite so draconian as this may sound, many of the undertakers finding it easier simply to exact rents from existing tenants. Many of those dispossessed, moreover, were able to mount convincing cases for the restoration of their lands, citing royal pardons or long-established freeholds. Further complications were caused by the Nine Years' War, which saw many of the settlers temporarily dislodged, though they would for the most part be able to return on the war's conclusion.

))))➤ *Desmond Rebellion*

MURPHY, FATHER JOHN (c. 1735–98)

Parish priest of Boolavogue, County Wexford, and hero of 1798 Rebellion. Modern scholars are sceptical about the revolutionary bona fides of this celebrated priest, suggesting that his role was built up by nationalist historians bent on salvaging some Catholic kudos from what was a triumph (albeit ultimately a tragic one) of secular radicalism. Father Murphy seems initially in fact to have discouraged his parishioners' participation in the insurrection of the godless United Irishmen. His call to arms was almost certainly given only in response to violence from local Protestants and government troops: whatever his motives, though, he joined the rebellion and was hanged by the authorities.

))))➤ *United Irishmen*

FAR LEFT: Richard Mulcahy.
LEFT: Ireland before the English invasion.
RIGHT: Father Murphy during the 1798 rebellion.

MUSIC IN IRELAND

The origins of Irish traditional music are lost in antiquity, but clearly it is a very old tradition which has undergone many changes over the years. Harpists were prominent in the courts of the Gaelic chieftains but their tradition was virtually extinct by the time of the Belfast Harp Festival in 1792. The works of the early poets were written to be sung and, through their connection with particular poems, it is possible to show that certain airs are several hundred years old. Traditional singing was usually solo and unaccompanied, and often highly complex. This form of singing, which is found mostly in Irish, is known as *sean-nós* or 'old-style' singing.

Apart from the harp, other instruments which are regarded as distinctly Irish are the *uilleann* ('elbow') pipes, which are blown by a pair of bellows under the piper's elbows and the *bodhrán*, a small one-sided drum. Close contact with continental Europe led to the introduction of other instruments and influences so that some of the compositions of the harpist Turlough O'Carolan, for instance, have a baroque feel to them.

While the harp was used primarily to accompany the poet's songs other instruments, as they were introduced, provided music for dancing. Chief among these is the violin, or fiddle, followed by the flute, the accordion and the concertina. Irish dance music, most usually reels or jigs, has a strict rhythm. The jig may have a continental origin and the reel is also associated with Scotland.

While instrumentalists of the past usually performed solo, the early twentieth century saw the development of groups, such as céilí bands which were able to provide music for large public dances where previously most entertainment took place in the home.

Recording technology gave traditional music a new impetus as many emigrant musicians made records in the United States in the 1920s to 30s where there was a ready market for them. Traditional music however went into decline in the 1940s to 50s until the renewed interest in folk music that swept the western world in the 1960s gave an international platform to performers such as the Dubliners and the Clancy Brothers and triggered a revival in Ireland as well.

Since then the music has developed in many different directions, with some musicians staying close to their traditional roots and others developing new forms of the music which were unimaginable 20 years previously.

⫸ Belfast Harp Festival, Turlough O'Carolan

LEFT *Traditional music festival, County Mayo.*
ABOVE: *Uileann piper.*
RIGHT: *The capture of Theobald Wolfe Tone in 1798.*

NAPOLEONIC WARS

Principally the European wars of 1803–15, but forming part of a longer-term conflict between Britain and France, including the French Revolutionary Wars. The French Revolution provoked Irish revolutionary movements as well as offering France a potential base from which to attack England.

Theobald Wolfe Tone led a movement to unify Ireland's Catholics and Presbyterians in an attempt to force reform. In 1796 and 1798 he persuaded France to send forces in support of his movement. Bad weather ended the 1796 invasion almost before it had begun. In 1798, a popular rising collapsed when General Gerard Lake destroyed the rebels at Vinegar Hill and then defeated a further French invasion at Ballinamuck. Wolfe Tone was intercepted en route from France and imprisoned. The outcome was the Act of Union in 1800 which incorporated Ireland wholesale into the United Kingdom, with no Catholic representation. Ireland found itself contributing considerable manpower and revenues to the fight against Napolean.

)))**➤** *General Gerard Lake, Theobald Wolfe Tone, Battle of Vinegar Hill*

NATION, THE (1842–48 AND 1849–96)

Influential political and cultural weekly paper published by Thomas Davis, Charles Gavan Duffy and John Blake Dillon to promote the ideals of the Young Ireland movement. It encouraged cultural as well as political nationalism and gave a platform to many of the leading Irish poets of the time, publishing a wide range of political essays. Its suppression in May 1848 led to the production of several other revolutionary papers. A more moderate and less popular series began the following year.

)))**➤** *Thomas Davies, Charles Gavan Duffy, Young Ireland*

NATIONAL SCHOOLS SYSTEM

System of free primary education for Irish children, inaugurated by an Act of Parliament in 1831. It may seem odd that the introduction of universal elementary education to Ireland has gone down in the list of British outrages, but it is on account of the particular linguistic prejudices embedded in the philosophy of the National Schools. Established at a time when the speaking of Irish seemed to halt progress, an isolating influence preventing

participation in the 'modern' world of technology and trade, they did quite consciously (at times no doubt brutally) set out to produce a nation of English-speakers. Despite the schools contribution to the destruction of Gaelic culture, they did offer mass literacy and widespread economic opportunity in return. While clearly not the unproblematic panacea their creators thought, the National Schools System was hardly the 'murder machine' that Pádraig Pearse claimed.

NATIONALISM

Doctrine stating that a people can find political fulfilment only in the attainment of their own sovereign nation state. Nationalism in its softest sense can be said to have existed throughout Irish history, and certainly since the first tribesmen offered resistance to the Viking and Anglo-Norman raiders. But this was an age of local loyalties, of chiefdoms and aristocracies – in Ireland as elsewhere, any notion of overarching nationhood, was late in developing. Something of the sort appears to have arisen at the end of the sixteenth century in Hugh O'Neill's appeal to an idea of *patria* to unite native Irish and Old English – although its originator's obvious opportunism did the doctrine no great service. Not until the 'patriots' of the eighteenth century – and, pre-eminently, the United Irishmen, do we see the modern idea of an all-embracing, non-sectarian Irish nationalism truly taking shape. Though the passionate adherence of the vast majority to an authoritarian Roman Catholic Church would be a source of constant tensions for the nationalist movement through the nineteenth century and beyond, this ideal of an Irishness that could be shared equally by Protestants and Catholics in an independent Ireland has remained, in theory at least, the goal of Irish nationalism.

)))**➤** *Hugh O'Neill*

NELSON'S PILLAR (1808)

 Nelson's Pillar in
O'Connell Street,
Dublin was a 41-m (135-ft)
high column commemo-
rating Lord Nelson's victory
at Trafalgar in 1805. Work
began on 15 February 1808
when the Duke of
Richmond, lord lieutenant
of Ireland, laid the first
stone. It was destroyed
on the fiftieth anniversary
the Easter Rising by
militant republicans.

))))) *Dublin*

NEOLITHIC PEOPLE

 Stone Age farmers of ancient Ireland. The Neolithic
Revolution that took place between around 3900
and 3000 BC was not spontaneous to Ireland; rather, the
techniques of cultivation and pastoralism were introduced
by immigrants from abroad. Inaugurated in the Middle
East around 7000 BC, the revolution expanded northwards
and westwards through the millennia that followed, existing
hunter-gatherer societies being either displaced or assimilated
as its practitioners spread. Neolithic settlers are thought to
have arrived in Ireland across the Antrim–Scotland link: they
brought with them cattle, sheep and goats (of the traditionally
farmed livestock only wild pigs were native to Ireland),
as well as skills in making pottery and superior stone tools.
With these they set
about clearing the
forests, beginning
with more sparsely-
wooded upland, and
establishing the larger,
more permanent
settlements which
were a feature of the
Neolithic lifestyle.
Excavations at the
'Céide Fields' in
County Mayo suggest

that sizeable communities may have worked quite extensive
areas of land. Boundary stones found here by archeologists
suggest that a single village had up to half a square kilometre
of ground under cultivation.

))))) *Céide Fields*

NEUTRALITY (WORLD WAR II)

Ireland's policy of staying officially removed from the
conflict in World War II (1939–45). If the Free State's
detachment from what it called the 'Emergency' has been
much misunderstood in Britain, this reflects a certain degree
of confusion within Ireland itself. The old feeling that
'England's difficulty is Ireland's opportunity' remained sufficiently strong in the independent state giving rise to a certain
reluctance to be seen as rallying to Britannia's banner. There
was also, as the Anglo-Irish novelist Elizabeth Bowen noted,
a widely held (if seldom articulated) belief that, having
experienced colonial suffering, an independent Ireland had a
certain national 'spirituality' that must set it apart from the
sordid business of world war. At the same time, the ties with
Britain were long-established and not easily disregarded.
Hence the ambivalence that, on the one hand, saw Ireland
sending its firecrews to the assistance of Belfast in the Blitz
of 1941 and, on the other, led de Valera to dispatch his
notorious telegram to Hitler after his defeat of 1945. The
'spiritual' tradition survived the War to inform Ireland's
subsequent activities on the world stage: Ireland refused to
line up with the Western Cold War powers in NATO, but
has worked tirelessly on behalf a range of international good
causes from human-rights to famine-relief and has been a
major contributor to UN peacekeeping forces.

NEW IRELAND FORUM (1983)

Conference bringing together political representatives
from constitutionalist nationalist parties from North
and South. At the suggestion of SDLP leader John Hume,
then-Taoiseach Garret Fitzgerald convened a series of
meetings at Dublin Castle in May 1983, at which the full
gamut of constitutionalist nationalist opinion, from all parts
of Ireland, could be heard. Over the next 12 months,
delegates roughed out possible programmes for increased
cross-border co-operation between the UK and Irish
Republic, as well as more ambitious schemes involving
possible federalist solutions that might allow Ireland's

thus-far intractable constitutional problems to be transcended. An avowed friend of the Ulster Unionists, British prime minister Margaret Thatcher was initially dismissive, but the work of the Forum would make possible the Anglo-Irish Agreement of 1985, as well as helping to pave the way towards the current peace process.

))))➤ *Anglo-Irish Agreement, Garret Fitzgerald, John Hume*

NEWGRANGE

Monument in County Meath. A celebrated 'passage tomb' – its central chamber reached by a stone-slab passage and it is roofed over by a circular mound of earth – Newgrange is one of Ireland's most venerable constructions; at 4,500 years old it may even pre-date the Egyptian pyramids. The fact that its main passage lines up perfectly with the Sun at the winter solstice suggests that it may have had a ritual significance above and beyond its importance as a tomb. The eye motifs among the swirling carvings on the great entrance stone have provoked fevered speculation as to what the structure's precise astronomical or astrological function may have been: all one can really do with any safety, though, is marvel at the richness and accomplishment of Neolithic art.

))))➤ *Bronze Age, Neolithic People*

NÍ RUAIRC, DEARBHLA (DEVORGILL O'ROURKE) (1108-93)

Dearbhla was the daughter of Aodh Ó Ruairc, and wife of his cousin Tiernan O'Rourke. In 1152, Dearbhla eloped to Leinster with Diarmaid Mac Murchadha. Tiernán's kinsman, Tarlach Ó Conchubhair, attacked Diarmaid mac Murchadha's stronghold and recaptured Devorgill. Devorgill became devoted to the church, endowing a nunnery church at Clonmacnoise. After Tiernán's death, she retired to the Cistercian abbey at Mellifont.

))))➤ *Diarmaid Mac Murchadha, Mellifont, Tiernán Ó Ruairc*

FAR LEFT: Nelson's Pillar, Dublin.
BELOW LEFT: A passage grave at Newgrange.
BELOW: Newgrange tomb.

NIALL GLUNDUBH (c. AD 870–919)

King of Ireland from AD 916, succeeding Flann Sinna. Glundubh rose to power after fighting in Connacht and seizing the crown of Aileach in AD 911. In AD 919 Sitric the Viking took Dublin and then set sail for England to assist his brother Ragnald in his claim on the kingdom of Mercia. Niall Glundubh, styled 'King of Ireland', took the opportunity to attack Dublin. At Coill Moramocc, now Kilmashogue, near Rathfarnham and about 10 km (6 miles) from Dublin, Sitric's sons met him with an army. The Irish suffered a catastrophic defeat. Glundubh was killed along with his stepson and heir, Conchobhar, and many of the other chieftains.

))))➤ *Battle of Dublin, Flann Sinna*

NIALL NAOI NGIALLACH (NIALL OF THE NINE HOSTAGES) (r. AD 383–409)

First High King of Ireland; a descendant of Conn Céad-Chathach. The extent of Niall's power is unknown but is unlikely to have been comprehensive. He ruled from Tara, probably acting as the leader of a confederation of chieftains, and led raids against Roman Britain. Dynastic power was extended when his sons Eoghan and Conall Gulban conquered parts of Ulster. After his death another son, Laedhaire, succeeded him. Niall's dynasty, the Uí Néill, dominated Irish kingship for much of the first millennium.

))))➤ *High King*

NIGHT OF THE BIG WIND (1839)

Hurricane wind that wrought havoc all over Ireland in January 1839. Tales of the Night of the Big Wind have been handed down through generations and have become part of Irish mythology. On the night of 6 January 1839, following a snowstorm, the winds increased through gale to hurricane force and heavy rain began to fall. The hurricane continued for five hours before decreasing again to gale force. Over 700 people are estimated to have been killed across the county, and many others suffered serious injury. Animals, their enclosures and buildings were severely damaged.

NINE YEARS' WAR (1688–97)

European power struggle, also known as the War of the League of Augsburg. French support for the deposed Catholic king James II demonstrated that England was involved in a more widespread European conflict. Ireland's Catholic population guaranteed that it would be a potential power–base for Catholic forces. The Battle of the Boyne in 1690 might have ended James's campaign, but he never abandoned hopes of a restoration.

BELOW :King William III.

Parliamentary grants of vast sums of money to William III to enable him to prosecute the war came with conditions of supervision. In 1692, a French fleet was defeated at Cap de la Hogue, destroying the hopes of a French invasion fleet made up of 30,000 troops loyal to Louis XIV and James II which had gathered at Brest. In 1693 William III's army was defeated at Landen, emphasizing the escalating cost of the conflict. The Bank of England was founded in 1694 to fund the national debt, but costs continued to mount. In 1697 the Peace of Ryswick ended the war, with Louis XIV recognizing William III's right to be king. This terminated James II's prospects of ever mounting a French-sponsored invasion of England via Ireland again.

NORMANS

Having conquered England in 1066, the Normans, who originated in Normandy and northern France, invaded Ireland a century later. The Irish were left without a strong leader because of fighting between the Irish and the Vikings, and between different Irish chiefs. Diarmaid mac Murchadha, king of Leinster, had been defeated and he travelled to France to seek the aid of Henry II. Henry II had been interested in taking Ireland for some time, but war with France meant that he could not become directly involved. Henry promised aid, and on mac Murchadha's return journey he met with Richard de Clare ('Strongbow') in Wales who agreed to lead an expedition to Ireland and restore mac Murchadha to his kingdom. There was, however, a heavy price to pay. Strongbow would marry mac Murchadha's daughter Aoife, and on mac Murchadha's death the kinship of Leinster would pass to him and his descendants. mac Murchadha was briefly restored to power in 1167 and under the settlement made with the High King, Ruairí Ó Conchubhair: the Norman mercenaries left the county. However, in 1170 the Normans returned, landing near the Norse city of Waterford, which they soon captured. Aoife and Strongbow were wed as agreed and Strongbow marched on Dublin. The Norse were defeated before the main Irish forces arrived, and although they regrouped and joined forces to lay seige to Dublin, the

Normans held the city, and in 1171 Henry II landed with a large army, securing the Norman position. By the Treaty of Windsor (1175) Ó Conchubhair recognized Henry's rule in Dublin, Leinster, Waterford and Wexford. The Normans continued to expand the territory under their control as the years passed and as they moved out from Dublin, a certain amount of assimilation took place, and many of them adopted Irish lifestyles and customs. It was to stem this trend that the Statues of Kilkenny were passed in 1366. The Normans built towns and castles and had a major cultural impact on the country. They later became known as the Old English, so as to distinguish them from the sixteenth century English invaders, at whose hands they often suffered a similar fate as the Gaelic Irish.

ABOVE: Replacing a simple wooden chapel, the Normans built St Patrick's Cathedral in 119:. it was rebuilt again in the thirteenth century.
RIGHT: Knight of Kilfane at the Norman castle of Kilkenny.

NORTHERN IRELAND

Under the Government of Ireland Act of 1920, six of the Ulster counties remained part of the United Kingdom while the rest of Ireland went on to gain dominion status under the terms of the Anglo-Irish Treaty of 1921. For the Unionists, led by Dublin-born Edward Carson who had vigorously opposed Home Rule, this was the lesser of two evils since it meant that the majority of the predominantly Unionist Protestant population remained under British rule. Carson would have preferred to see the whole of Ireland remain this way, while nationalists, who were deeply divided by the arrangement, regarded it as a temporary situation, with the possibility of at least some of the territory changing hands following the deliberations of the Boundary Commission, especially counties such as Fermanagh and Tyrone which had nationalist majorities.

A regional parliament was set up in Belfast which moved to the purpose-built Stormont building in 1932. Sir James Craig was the first prime minister and the slogan 'a Protestant parliament for a Protestant people' became a reality, even though more than one-third of the population of Northern Ireland were Catholic. Sir Dawson Bates, the minister of

home affairs until 1943, was particularly influential and his draconian Offences Against the State Act, and Special Powers Act gave the Royal Ulster Constabulary, and their much-feared auxiliaries, the B-Specials, powers which were

Unfortunately the authorities, not used to such opposition, reacted against these early protest with too much force on the streets and not enough action in parliament, and with the involvement of Protestant paramilitaries the situation rapidly went out of control. The ineptitude of the Northern Irish government, and especially the shocking events of Bloody Sunday, finally led to the suspension of local government in 1972 and the introduction of direct rule from Westminster, effectively ending half a centruy of one-party rule.

))))➤ **Sir Edward Carson, Eatser Rising, Irish Republican Army, Republic of Ireland, Sinn Féin, Ulster Unionists, Ulster Volunteer Force**

FAR LEFT: Stormont, Belfast.
CENTRE: Violence erupts at a protest rally in Londonderry, 1972.
BELOW: Ian Paisley.

reputedly the envy of the apartheid regime in South Africa. The Catholic population which had endured much during the Belfast pogroms of the 1920s felt isolated and abandoned by the authorities in Dublin. They believed that gerrymandering and discrimination in the allocation of housing and jobs was rife. In a parliament that was likely to have a permanent Unionist majority there was little that they could do to change the situation.

Northern Ireland's traditional industries, shipbuilding, linen and agriculture, as well as a new manufacturing industry, which was introduced especially around Belfast, together with the parity of treatment insisted on by Craig with the rest of the United Kingdom, ensured that the standards of living for most people was higher than that experienced by people of the same class in the Free State. Therefore people in Northern Ireland enjoyed the benefits of the welfare state when it was introduced after World War II and free education following the 1947 Education Act. This act may have been at least partly responsible for the development of the new generation of articulate Catholic leaders who emerged in the 1960s, beginning a campaign for civil rights which gained much of its inspiration from the Black Civil Rights Movement in the United States.

O'BRIEN, MURROUGH, 1ST EARL OF INCHIQUIN (1614–74)

O'Brien was a soldier and controversial Munster political figure, also known as Murcha na dToiteán ('Murrough of the Burnings') because he built a huge turf fire against the defences of the Rock of Cashel which he captured in 1647. Raised as a Protestant and married to a daughter of the lord president of Munster he fought on the English side against the Irish during the 1641 rebellion. Despite further actions against the Catholics and his appointment by the English parliament as president of Munster, he later made peace with Ormond and the Confederate forces. Shortly after, however, Cromwell and his forces landed in Ireland and made steady progress against the Irish. O'Brien took refuge in Brittany in 1650 and was made governor of French-controlled Catalunya. He converted to Catholicism and went to England in 1663, hoping to be restored to the Munster presidency, but as a Catholic he was barred from holding the position. However, he was given a substantial estate, where he lived peacefully for the rest of his days.

O'BYRNE, FIACH MACHUGH (c. 1544–97)

Chief of the O'Byrnes of Wicklow and Irish rebel. Together with Viscount Baltinglass, he defeated the English army at Glenmalure in 1580, near his stronghold of Ballinacor, during a campaign characterized by the burning of property and plundering. He negotiated a pardon by agreeing to renewable submissions to the Crown, which he maintained until he was charged with the responsibility for his son's crimes. Although he secured a further pardon he joined the Desmond rebellion, during which he was captured and executed.

)))⏵ *Battle of Glenmalure*

Ó CADHAIN, MÁIRTÍN (1906–70)

Irish-language writer and activist from the Conamara Gaeltacht. His most famous novel, *Cré na Cille* (1948) consists of excerpts of the unending conversations between the corpses in a west Ireland graveyard. He was a member of the IRA and was interned in the Curragh Camp during World War II. He later became professor of Irish at Trinity College Dublin.

)))⏵ *Gaeltacht, Irish Republican Army, Trinity College Dublin*

O'CAROLAN, TURLOUGH (1670–1738)

Blind harpist from County Meath. O'Carolan was one of the most popular musicians of his time. He travelled around the country enjoying the patronage of both the planters and the Gaelic nobility, and he dedicated many of his compositions to them. His music – while firmly within the Gaelic tradition – also draws on continental European influences. Bunting recorded about 50 of his works at the Belfast Harp Festival and on his subsequent travels. Many of his most popular works are still regularly heard in the traditional repertory today.

)))⏵ *Belfast Harp Festival, Edward Bunting*

O'CASEY, SEAN (1880–1964)

Dublin-born writer. A self-educated Dublin labourer, O'Casey wrote three plays which have had lasting appeal, *The Shadow of a Gunma,* (1923), *Juno and the Paycock* (1924) and *The Plough and the Stars* (1926), all of which were produced at the Abbey Theatre. He then moved to London but none of his subsequent works had the same success as the first three plays, which drew heavily on his own experiences of life in Dublin before and after the Easter Rising, the Civil War and the War of Independence.

)))➤ **Abbey Theatre, Easter Rising, Irish Civil War**

Ó CLÉIRIGH, MICHEÁL (c. 1590–1643)

Chief compiler of the *Annals of the Four Masters*. Ó Cléirigh was born near Ballyshannon in County Donegal. After studying as a traditional historian he became a lay Franciscan brother at the Irish college in Louvain. From there he was sent back to Ireland in 1626 to gather information for the Franciscans' historical projects. With three others he made the compilation of all available Irish records of ecclesiastical, political and family history, which is known to us today as the *Annals of the Four Masters*. He visited different monasteries, schools and individuals and made copies of their manuscripts, which he sent back to Louvain and, in doing so, saved many valuable records which otherwise would have been lost. He returned to Louvain in 1637 and compiled an Irish dictionary. He died there in 1643.

)))➤ **Annals of the Four Masters,** *Franciscan Order*

Ó CONAIRE, PÁDRAIC (1882–1928)

Modernist writer. Galway-born Ó Conaire was among the first modernist writers in Irish. He wrote one of the first novels *Deoraíocht* (1910) and many short stories. He is commemorated today with a statue in Eyre Square in Galway, and his work remains widely known through its use in schools.

O'CONCHUBHAIR, AODH (HUGH O'CONNOR) (d. 1067)

Irish chieftain. O'Connor led the northern Irish resistance to Anglo-Norman expansion. Recognizing the shortcomings of Irish military skills and equipment, he employed gallowglass mercenaries from Scotland. When the Anglo-Norman Walter de Burgo advanced deep into Ulster, O'Connor's army met and routed them at Áth an Chip.

)))➤ *Gallowglass*

LEFT: Sean O'Casey.
RIGHT: Daniel O'Connell.
ABOVE RIGHT: Robert Peel, leader of the Conservative Party with whom Daniel O'Connell clashed.

Ó CONCHUBHAIR, RUAIRÍ (RORY O'CONNOR)

The last High King of Ireland, Ruairí Ó Concubhair had succeeded his father as king of Connacht and was recognised as High King following the death of his main rival in 1166. He made two unsuccessful attempts to drive the Normans out of Ireland in 1169, and although he did not submit to Henry II, he agreed to the Treaty of Windsor in 1175, which supposedly guaranteed his rule over the unconquered part of Ireland. This did not stop the advance of the Normans however, and with his territory shrinking, he abdicated in favour of his son in 1183.

O'CONNELL, DANIEL (1775–1847)

Politician, campaigner for Catholic Emancipation and repeal of the Union; popularly known as 'The Liberator'. A Catholic lawyer, and thus a member of a class directly disadvantaged by restrictions placed on Catholics holding office, O'Connell was an active campaigner for Emancipation from 1805 onwards. His unique contribution, however, was to transform the Emancipationist cause into a mass movement with the creation of the Catholic Association in 1824. Riding high on a tide of public support, he fought the Clare by-election of 1828 to win a parliamentary seat which, however, he was forbidden by law to occupy. As leader of the 'Repealers' – a group of Irish MPs calling for the repeal of the 1800 Act of Union – O'Connell found himself increasingly in conflict with Robert Peel's Conservative government. That O'Connell envisaged the repeal of the coercive union *strengthening* his country's ties with England has all too frequently been forgotten by later nationalists. The English government sent a battleship to back up their prohibition of a great mass-meeting at Clontarf, County Dublin, in 1843. Although O'Connell had respected the ban he was nonetheless arrested and imprisoned for sedition. Released after 14 weeks, he attempted to take up where he had left off, but his movement was derailed by the crisis of the Great Famine.

))))▶ *Catholic Association, Catholic Emancipation*

O'CONNOR DYNASTY

The Ui Conchobhair (O'Connors of Connacht) were descended from Brión, brother of Niall of the Nine Hostages. The name originates with Conchobhair (d. AD 973), who could trace his descent from Duach Galach (d. AD 438), who was converted to Christianity by St Patrick. The dynasty dominated the High Kingship in the twelfth century. The O'Connors rose to major power with Tarlach (r. 1106–56) and his son Ruairí (Roderic) acceded in 1156, and was made High King in 1166.

By the sixteenth century, the O'Connor dynasty had three branches: Roe, Don and Sligo. The first two had constantly disputed the kingship. The English administration was destroying Irish dynasties by offering earldoms and knighthoods in return for traditional titles. O'Connor resistance ended with the Composition of Connacht (1585) which extinguished O'Connor titles in return for knighthoods.

))))▶ *Niall of the Nine Hostages, St Patrick, Ruairi Ó Conchubhair*

ABOVE: Feargus O'Connor.

O'CONNOR, FEARGUS (1794–1855)

Politician. In the course of two distinct political careers, Feargus O'Connor first campaigned beside O'Connell for Repeal, then emigrated to Leeds in England, where he established the Chartist newspaper, the *Northern Star*, in 1837. A radical – though non-violent – organization committed to the attainment of a 'Charter' offering universal (male) suffrage and the secret ballot, Chartism became the major focus for working-class discontent in an England which, as the novelist-statesman Benjamin Disraeli put it, now comprised 'two nations, the rich and the poor'.

))))▶ *Daniel O'Connell*

O'CURRY, EUGENE (1796–1862)

Gaelic scholar and academic. O'Curry was born in County Clare but spent most of his working life in Dublin, where he was employed by the topographical section of the Ordnance Survey. There he came into contact with scholars such as John O'Donovan and George Petrie. An expert on Irish manuscripts, he was appointed professor of Irish History and Archeology at the Catholic University, Dublin, in 1854. Together with O'Donovan he laid the foundations of Celtic studies in Ireland.

))))▶ *John O'Donovan, Ordnance Survey, George Petrie*

Ó DÍREÁIN, MÁIRTÍN (1910–88)

Irish poet. Although he spent most of his adult life as a civil servant in Dublin, as a poet Máirtín Ó Díreáin continued to draw on his native Aran Islands for inspiration. In his later work he compares the moral barrenness of modern urban society unfavourably with the strong social structures of island life. Often using a deceptively simple vocabulary his was one of the most significant voices in Irish language poetry in the twentieth century.

)))))➡ *Aran Islands*

O'DONNELL DYNASTY (CLANN DÁLAIGH)

Although the O'Donnells of Tir Chonaill (County Donegal) can claim descent from Niall Naoi nGiallach, it was at the beginning of the thirteenth century that the family came to prominence. Most significant of the early chieftains was Aodh Rua I (Red Hugh I) (1427–1505), who built his Norman-style castle in Donegal town. Better

known is the second Aodh Rua (1572–1602) who fought alongside Aodh Ó Néill at the Battle of Kinsale in 1601. Following his death in Spain where he had gone to seek support, his brother Ruairí became chief and continued the struggle until he left Ireland in the Flight of the Earls in 1607.

)))))➡ *Flight of the Earls*

CENTRE: *Eugene O'Curry became an expert on Irish manuscripts such as the Book of Kells.*
BELOW: *The Aran Islands provided the inspiration for Máirtín O Díreáin's poetry.*

O'DONNELL, PEADAR (1893–1986)

Political activist and writer. O'Donnell was born on a small farm in County Donegal and he became a life-long political activist and a writer of some significance. He trained and worked as a teacher in his native county before becoming a trade union activist and organizer. He joined the IRA and fought in the War of Independence. He opposed the Anglo-Irish Treaty and was editor of the IRA newspaper *An Phoblacht* from 1925–31. O'Donnell later split from the IRA and concentrated on socialist politics. He was also editor of the influential literary publication *The Bell* from 1946–54. He wrote a number of novels and autobiographical works and remained politically active into old age.

⟫➤ *Anglo-Irish Treaty, Irish Republican Army, War of Independence*

O'DONNELL, RED HUGH (c. 1571–1602)

Hugh Roe O'Donnell, 'Red Hugh', Lord of Tyrconnell. Imprisoned in Dublin in around 1587 by Sir John Perrot, lord deputy of Ireland, Red Hugh escaped in 1592. After driving out English adventurers from their base in Donegal monastery, Red Hugh took control across Connacht before becoming embroiled in the Tyrone rebellion led by Hugh O'Neill. He played a decisive part in the victory over the English at Yellow Ford in 1598. In 1601 Red Hugh led a lightning march to help the O'Neill and Spanish forces besieged by Mountjoy at Kinsale. The battle was a disaster. Red Hugh fled to Spain where he died, reputedly from poison administered by an English agent.

⟫➤ *Battle of Yellow Ford*

O'DONOVAN, JOHN (1809–61)

Important nineteenth-century Irish scholar. O'Donovan's work with the Ordnance Survey took him to every parish in the country and brought him into contact with many local experts. His letters during this period amount to some 50 volumes which are full of valuable information and observations about place names, language, topography and customs throughout the land.

RIGHT: Eoin O'Duffy.
FAR RIGHT: The papal visit of 1979, when Tomás Ó Fiaich was head of the Roman Catholic Church in Ireland.

He also transcribed and edited the *Annals of the Four Masters* (1848–51) and in 1852 he was appointed professor of Celtic at Queen's University Belfast.

))))▶ **Annals of the Four Masters,** *Ordnance Survey*

O'DONOVAN ROSSA, JEREMIAH (1831–1915)

Fenian revolutionary. A grocer from Skibbereen, County Cork, where he founded the proto-Fenian Phoenix Society in 1856, O'Donovan Rossa went on to join – and substantially shape – the Fenian Brotherhood proper. Imprisoned in 1865, he was released in 1871 and went to America, where his 'skirmishing fund' helped resource revolutionary activities back in Ireland. From 1881 to 1885 O'Donovan Rossa directed the first Irish nationalist bombing campaign in Britain. His 1915 funeral was a great publicity coup for Pádraig Pearse, whose eloquent graveside speech can be seen in hindsight as the opening propagandistic volley of the Easter Rising.

))))▶ *Fenian Brotherhood, Fenian Movement, Pádraig Pearse*

O'DUFFY, EOIN (1892–1944)

Soldier and politician, leader of the 'Blueshirts'. A veteran of the War of Independence, Eoin O'Duffy supported the 1921 Treaty and was chief of staff for the pro-Treaty forces in the civil war. Commander of the newly-formed Garda Síochána (Free State police) from 1922 to 1933, he was dismissed when de Valera came to power and became leader of the Army Comrades' Association, which took on a recognizably fascist quality along with the blue shirts for which they became known.

))))▶ *Blueshirts, Irish Civil War, War of Independence*

Ó FIAICH, TOMÁS (1923–90)

Cardinal Tomás Ó Fiaich was head of the Roman Catholic Church in Ireland from 1979 until his death in 1990. A native of south Armagh and a noted historian, he was unashamedly nationalist in his politics. He welcomed Pope John Paul II to Ireland in September 1979. Prior to his appointment as archbishop of Armagh he had been president of Maynooth College and professor of history. He was the author of a number of significant works on Gaelic Ireland and on Irish monastic influence on continental Europe.

))))▶ *Maynooth College*

OGHAM

 Early Irish alphabet. The first alphabet used in Ireland, ogham (or 'ogam' in old Irish) is found primarily on early stone monuments, where letters are represented by strokes or notches cut into the edge of the stone. Most surviving examples can be found in Cork and Kerry, but they have also been recorded in Wales and Cornwall. Because of its cumbersome nature, most inscriptions are little more than the names of the people commemorated by the stones on which the notches are found.

Ó hEODHASA, EOCHAIDH (c. 1560–1612)

Chief poet to three successive Maguire rulers of Fermanagh. Ó hEodhasa's work gives us a valuable insight into Gaelic society in the period just before the Flight of the Earls. He accompanied his chieftain to the Battle of Kinsale in 1601 but was wounded in a skirmish and had to return to Fermanagh. Over 50 of his poems have survived in manuscript form; some of these are strictly conventional while in others the poet expresses his personal feelings in a much more open manner.

⟫⟫ *Flight of the Earls, Battle of Kinsale, Maguire Dynasty*

O'HIGGINS, BERNARDO (c. 1777–1842)

Liberator of Chile. Born to an Irish emigrant family in Chile, Bernardo was educated in Peru and England, while his father rose to be viceroy of Chile. In Europe Bernardo met Latin American liberationists, returning to his inheritance on his father's death in 1801, soon joining a revolutionary junta until the Spanish viceroy of Peru destroyed the new government and its forces in 1814. Bernardo fled into exile. In 1817 he returned, defeated the Spaniards at Chacabuco and became interim supreme director. But he relied too much on personal prestige and alienated support. In spite of establishing a republican government, fears of monarchical tendencies forced his resignation in 1823 and exile to Peru.

O'HIGGINS, KEVIN (1892–1927)

Politician. A member of the first Dáil, O'Higgins won notoriety in the aftermath of the civil war as a ruthless scourge of the Free State's Republican enemies. As minister of justice and external affairs and vice president of the executive he became chief apologist for the execution of 77 Republicans in 1922–23. O'Higgins made no secret of his contempt for his opponents, and seemed to have little time for the nationalistic pieties to which even his own colleagues in Cumann na nGaedheal paid lip-service. His assassination by an IRA gunman (apparently acting unofficially) seems not to have occasioned any outpouring of national grief.

⟫⟫ *Cumann na nGaedheal*

ABOVE: Stones with ogham inscriptions.
RIGHT: Kevin O'Higgins.

OISÍN

Mythological hero. In ancient Irish literature and contemporary folklore Oisín is son of Fionn mac Cumhail. He was also the central figure in James MacPherson's bogus Celtic epic *Ossian*. Apart from his many adventures in the company of Fionn he was also lured to Tír na nÓg – the land of eternal youth – for several centuries by Niamh Cinn Óir. On his return he met St Patrick, and the discussion they are thought to have had has become symbolic of the coming together of the pagan and Christian traditions in Ireland.

)))► *Fionn mac Cumhail, Tír na nÓg*

O'KELLY, SEÁN T. (1882–1966)

Politician, president of Ireland (1945–52, 1952–59). One of the founders of Sinn Féin, Seán Thomas O'Kelly fought in the Easter Rising and was afterwards imprisoned. He became speaker in the first Dáil, 1919–21. An opponent of the 1921 Treaty he rose to power with Éamon de Valera's Fianna Fáil, serving as minister for local government and minister for finance and education before being elected to the presidency in 1945.

)))► *Sinn Féin*

Ó LAOGHAIRE, ART (1747–73)

Gaelic nobleman and the subject of a famous lament written by his widow Eibhlín Dubh Ní Chonaill, *Caoineadh Airt Uí Laoghaire*, following his murder. He had recently returned to Ireland after serving as a captain in the Hungarian Hussars. The high sheriff of Cork attempted to try Ó Laoghaire as an outlaw, but failed and later suffered the indignity of being beaten by Ó Laoghaire in a horse race. He offered Ó Laoghaire £5 for the horse which, as a Protestant he was entitled to do under the Penal Laws, but rather than submit to this Ó Laoghaire went on the run. He survived one ambush but was shot at Carraig an Ime in County Cork and, according to the poem, his blood-stained mare made its way back home, thus raising the alarm.

)))► *Penal Laws*

OLD ENGLISH

Term used to describe the former Norman-Irish lords to distinguish them from the 'New English' settlers and the 'Gaelic Irish'. After the Plantations the Old English

BELOW: Sean O'Kelly.

found themselves victims of the New English discoverers who enforced the forfeiture of their lands to the Crown. In an attempt to retain their land they contributed to Charles I's war with Spain in exchange for 'the Graces' confirming their rights to land titled for 60 years or more.

)))► *The Graces*

O'LEARY, JOHN (1830–1907)

Fenian writer. O'Leary trained in law and medicine but did not qualify in either. He joined the Fenian movement, promoting its position as editor of the *Irish People*. Betrayed in 1865, he was imprisoned for 20 years but released after nine and ordered to leave Ireland until 1885. On his return he influenced the poet and proponent of the Irish Gaelic tradition, W. B. Yeats.

)))► *Fenian Movement, W. B. Yeats*

OMAGH

Town in County Tyrone. A centre for the Ulster Plantation (though there are signs of settlement long before), Omagh only really took its place in Irish history very recently. Twenty-nine people were killed, and many more wounded, by the bomb placed here on 15 August 1998, by members the 'Real IRA', a republican splinter-group unprepared to join the 'cessation of violence' agreed by the Provisionals and Sinn Féin. The greatest single act of slaughter in 30 years of the Northern Ireland conflict, there were grounds for hope that the Omagh bomb would at least be the concluding atrocity of the 'Troubles'. A clear 'own-goal' for the Real IRA (who had delivered a misleading warning), the outrage was uncompromisingly condemned by Sinn Féin's Gerry Adams. Tragic as the episode had been, it had positive consequences, many felt, in giving enormous moral momentum to the peace process.

))⧫ *Plantation of Ulster, The Troubles*

O'MALLEY, GRACE (c. 1530–c. 1603)

Chieftain and pirate (Irish, Granuaile ot Gráinne Uí Máille). The O'Malleys were renowned seamen, trading with Spain and Scotland. In around 1546 Grace married Donal O'Flaherty, chief of Ballinahinch. Her political acumen and use of piracy to blackmail traders, meant her influence soon exceeded his. After his death in battle she married Richard-an-Irainn, chief of the Burkes of County Mayo. In 1576 she submitted to Sir Henry Sidney, the lord deputy of Ireland. In 1577 she was seized by the Earl of Desmond while on a raid, and imprisoned until 1578. Released on good behaviour, she continued to raid and was pursued relentlessly by Sir Richard Bingham, governor of Connacht, causing Grace to petition Elizabeth I for a pardon.

Ó NÉILL, AODH MÓR (GREAT HUGH), 2ND EARL OF TYRONE (c. 1550–1660)

Grandson of Conn Bacach and a skilled politician and soldier. Raised in the Pale, and outwardly favourably disposed to the English, he became increasingly involved in a miltary campaign against them, especially after 1595 when he was recognized as leader of his clan and enjoyed the allegience of a large section of Gaelic Ireland. He suffered a major setback at the Battle of Kinsale in 1601 and

left Ireland in 1607 in the Flight of the Earls. Ó Néill died in Rome in 1616 without ever returning.

))⧫ *Flight of the Earls, Battle of Kinsale*

O'NEILL, BRIAN (d. 1574)

Sir Brian MacPhelim O'Neill was chief of the O'Neills of Clanaboy, surrendering his title to Sir Philip Sidney for a knighthood in 1567. He turned against the English when he learned of plans for imposed settlement. Walter, 1st Earl of Essex, forced him to submit. O'Neill rebelled again. Hundreds of his people were massacred, and he was executed.

))⧫ *O'Neill Dynasty*

Ó NÉILL, CONN, 1ST EARL OF TYRONE (1480–1559)

Conn Bacach (the Lame) became chief of the Tyrone branch of the Ui Néill in 1520 and was the first of his name to lead the Irish against England's attempt to subjugate Ireland. He supported the Kildare rebellion, and on its collapse, had to give up his traditional title and accept an English one instead in order to hold his territory. Henry VIII made him earl of Tyrone after he made his submission in person, a move which made him deeply unpopular with his own people. Ó Neill was deposed by his son, Shane the Proud.

))))➤ *Henry VIII of England, O'Neill Dynasty*

O'NEILL DYNASTY (15TH–16TH CENTURIES)

Reputedly the oldest traceable royal lineage in Europe, the O'Neills are descended from the fifth century Niall Naoi nGiallach (Niall of the Nine Hostages). This dominant Gaelic family produced a number of kings, soldiers and influential individuals who have played their part in Irish history, almost to the present day, as even Terence O'Neill, prime minister of Northern Ireland (1963–69), was one of their number. In early Christian Ireland the O'Neill's were kings of Tara, and from then until the fall of Gaelic Ireland at the beginning of the seventeenth century, they were the dominant family in the northern half of the island. Their last major chiefs were Aodh Mór Ó Néill (Great Hugh O'Neill) of Tyrone, who left Ireland in the Flight of the Earls' and his nephew Eoghan Rua Ó Néill (Owen Roe O'Neill) (c. 1582–1649) who was a leading Irish military commander and political strategist during the rising of 1641.

))))➤ *Flight of the Earls*

Ó NÉILL, EOGHAN RUA (OWEN ROE O'NEILL) (1590–1649)

Rebel commander against English rule in Ireland. Returning from his 30 years' service in the Spanish army, Eoghan Rua replaced Phelim O'Neill as commander in the north in 1642, after the outbreak of the insurrection. He routed England's Scottish ally, General Hector Munro, at the Battle of Benburb in June 1646 and helped the papal nuncio Giovanni Battista Rinuccini to force the confederacy to rescind their peace agreement with the English. Eventually he had to ally with the Royalists against the Parliamentarians. Eoghan Rua was the nephew of the Irish chieftain Aodh O Néill, 2nd Earl of Tyrone.

))))➤ *Battle of Benburb*

O'NEILL, PHELIM (1604–53)

Roman Catholic rebel. Appearing to support Charles I, O'Neill, a member of the Irish parliament, seized Charlemont Castle in Ulster, initiating the major revolt of 1641–52 against English rule in Ireland. O'Neill claimed that Charles I had initiated the seizure. Losing his command to Eoghan Rua Ó Néill, he held Charlemont until 1650 when he went into hiding; he was betrayed in 1653.

))))➤ *Rebellion of 1641*

Ó NÉILL, SEÁN AN DIOMAIS (SHANE THE PROUD O'NEILL) (1530–67)

Eldest legitimate son of Conn Bacach, Seán and Diomais Ó Néill killed his half-brother, Matthew, whom his father had nominated as his successor and was regarded by the Ó Néill's as their rightful chieftain. The Earl of Sussex engaged in three costly and unsuccessful campains against Ó Néill. In 1562 he submitted to Elizabeth I on the understanding that he would be granted the title and even attacked the mac Donnells of Antrim to illustrate his loyalty. The appointment of Sir Henry Sidney as lord deputy signalled a change in English policy and Ó Néill found himself under pressure once more. Increasingly desperate, he even appealed to the Mac Donnells of Antrim for assistance, but they killed him, possibly in revenge for his earlier attack on them.

))))➤ *Elizabeth I of England, Conn Ó Néill*

LEFT: The Grianon of Ailech, once home to the O'Neill dynasty.
ABOVE: Eoghan Rua Ó Néill.

O'NEILL, CAPTAIN TERENCE (1914–90)

Unionist politician and prime minister of Northern Ireland and later Lord O'Neill of the Maine. He was minister for finance in 1956 and succeeded as prime minister in 1963. He called an extraordinary general election in 1968 following civil rights demonstrations, stating that 'Northern Ireland was at a crossroads'. He called for

a mandate for reform at this time and when one was not forthcoming he retired as prime minister. He was made a life peer in 1970.

Ó NUALLÁIN, BRIAN (1911–66)

Irish writer; also known as Flann O'Brien and Brian O'Nolan. He was born in Strabane, County Tyrone, and apart from a long-running satirical column in the *Irish Times*, he is best remembered for the novels *At Swim Two Birds, The Third Policeman* and *An Béal Bocht*. Although most of his work was written in English he draws heavily on the Gaelic tradition for its sense of magic and mischievous word-play.

ABOVE: Terence O'Neill with Lord Antrim at the Giant's Causeway.
RIGHT: Orangemen hold a short religious service after police refuse to allow their march to continue.

ORANGE ORDER (1795)

Militant Protestant society, established Loughgall, County Armagh in 1795. For over two centuries the Orange Order has been at the organizational heart of Ulster Loyalism, its meetings and parades allowing ordinary Protestants a place to 'stand up and be counted'. Spreading quickly through southern Ulster in the years after its foundation, the Orange Order played a key role in mobilizing armed opposition to the United Irishmen's insurrection. So successful was it in the decades that followed in establishing itself in both the yeomanry (local militias) and the Army proper, that the British government – fearing divided loyalties – ordered its suppression as an 'unlawful society'. Never successfully stamped out on the ground, the Order grew ever stronger from 1867 onwards, its rise reflecting Protestant fears at the gathering strength of the Home Rule movement.
))))▶ *Orangeism*

ORANGEISM

Ideology of the Orange Order. For many people the most instantly recognizable image of Protestant Ulster, the Orange March seems to sum up a certain strong ambivalence in Unionist attitudes. Standing at once for elaborate, formal ritual and for the ugly threat of violence, it is an organization associated equally with regimented discipline and with outbreaks of affray. This ambivalence was in fact present in the Order from the very first, when it was established by the Loyalist winners of the Battle of the Diamond in 1795. Formed after what had been little more

known it and vigorously attacks the new rulers. As well as having considerable poetic merit, therefore, his work also gives us a valuable historic insight into life in Kerry at the time.

))))▶ *Battle of the Boyne*

ORDNANCE SURVEY (1825–41)

County-by-county survey of Ireland carried out between 1825 and 1841. The survey resulted in detailed large-scale maps of the whole country and were the first of their kind. Men such as John O'Donovan and George Petrie were employed and a huge amount of additional cultural and social information was collected and collated. Place names in particular were examined and standardized English versions were set out. This major survey is a unique record of Ireland before the Great Famine.

))))▶ *Great Famine, John O'Donovan, George Petrie*

than a glorified riot, the Order was solemnly dedicated to the memory of a grander triumph, William III's victory at the Battle of the Boyne in 1690, hailed as the achievement that had inaugurated the era of Protestant supremacy in Ireland. The commemoration of this victory became the centrepiece of the Order's ceremonial calendar, its eternal glory lending lustre to innumerable shabby street-battles. With their dignified ritual, meanwhile, the Order's quasi-masonic lodges became a meeting-place for an eminently respectable (if not necessarily very tolerant) Protestant middle class.

The Order retains these contradictions – and a great deal of its importance – to this day.

))))▶ *Battle of the Boyne, William III of England*

Ó RATHAILLE, AODHAGÁN (c. 1670–1729)

Munster poet whose work is full of vitality and energy. His own landlord and patron lost his lands following the Battle of the Boyne in 1690, so Ó Rathaille witnessed at first hand the passing of the old Gaelic order which had given his work its context and provided him with patronage. He laments the passing of society as he had

Ó RIADA, SEÁN (1931–71)

Hugely influential composer. Ó Riada developed new ways of orchestrating and setting traditional Irish music. He also wrote film scores and masses and brought Irish traditional music to a whole new audience. He worked as musical director of the Abbey Theatre and as a lecturer in Cork University.

))))▶ *Abbey Theatre, Music in Ireland*

Ó RÍORDÁIN, SEÁN (1916–77)

Major Irish-language poet. Ó Ríordáin suffered from tuberculosis for most of his adult life. For him poetry was a form of meditation and prayer, and his periods of illness were often his most creative. He worked for a time as a civil servant before gaining a part-time lectureship at Cork University, where he had a major influence on the upcoming generation of poets.

ABOVE: Orange Parade, Belfast city centre, 1996.

ORMOND, DUKES OF

James Butler, 1st Duke of Ormond (1610–88), supported the Earl of Strafford in his stern government of Ireland, and thereafter represented the Crown's interests during the Confederate War which broke out in 1641. Ormond defeated the rebels in 1641 and 1643, but negotiated peace deals so that Royalist troops could fight in England. Cromwell destroyed his forces in 1649 and he joined the exiled court of Charles II. After the Restoration he reinstated the Anglican Church in Ireland and was made lord lieutenant 1661–69, 1677–82 and 1684. He was a supporter of the deposed James II of England.

James Butler, 2nd Duke of Ormond (1665–1745), fought for William III against James II at the Boyne, taking Dublin and Kilkenny Castle afterwards. Further military service under William III followed. He was made lord lieutenant of Ireland under Queen Anne in 1703–05, 1710–11 and 1713. He came to support the Jacobite cause, eventually fleeing to France and losing his estates in 1715. In 1719 he was offered command of a Spanish fleet intended to restore the Stuart line.

⟫ *Battle of the Boyne, Confederate War, Oliver Cromwell*

ABOVE: The sixteenth century mansion of the Ormonds.
LEFT: James Butler, Duke of Ormond.

O'ROURKE (d. 1591)

Sir Brian-na-Murtha, chief of the Uí Ruairc, gave up his title for an English knighthood and was allowed to repossess Leitrim. In 1580 he rebelled and invaded Connacht. Shipwrecked Spaniards from the Armada were offered his protection. In 1589, Sir Richard Bingham forced him to flee into exile in Scotland where James VI (later James I of England) seized him and handed him over for execution.

Ó RUAIRC, TIARNÁN (TIERNAN O'ROURKE) (d. 1172)

King of Breifne. O'Rourke fought in Meath and Connacht but the abduction of his wife Dearbhla in 1152 by Diarmaid Mac Murchadha brought him into alliance with Tarlach Ó Conchubhair and the broader struggle for the High Kingship. With Ó Conchubhair he quickly recovered Dearbhla, but found himself facing the Anglo-Norman threat from soldiers invited by Diarmaid Mac Murchadha in his war with Tarlach's son, Ruairí. Tiarnán Ó Ruairc was killed in 1172 by Hugh de Lacy who arrived in Ireland with Henry II in 1171.

))))➤ *Conquest of Ireland, Hugh de Lacy*

O'SHEA, KITTY (1846–1921)

Wife of Captain William O'Shea, a Home Rule MP, Kitty O'Shea had a long affair with the nationalist leader Charles Stewart Parnell, which led to his political downfall following a divorce case instigated by her husband. The case affected not only Parnell's political career, but the course of Irish history, as the scandal split the Home Rule party, as well as removing its most capable leader. Parnell had three children by her before they married in June 1891 after her divorce was granted, and just a few months before his death.

))))➤ *Charles Stewart Parnell*

Ó SUILLEABHÁIN, AMHLAIBH (1780–1838)

First Irish-language diarist. Ó Suilleabháin lived in Callan, County Kilkenny. His diary, which covers the period 1827–35, is a valuable record of life in pre-Famine Ireland. In it he records his observations of nature as well as daily life in a small provincial Irish town.

))))➤ *Great Famine*

Ó SUILLEABHÁIN, EOGHAN RUA (1748–84)

Munster poet whose life and work is still remembered in the folklore of the district. He moved from place to place, working as a schoolmaster and a labourer before falling foul of a man called Nagle and taking refuge in Fermoy barracks. From here he was press-ganged into the British Navy, with whom he served in the West Indies before being transferred to the British army. He was eventually dismissed after a feigned illness. He returned to Kerry and announced that he was opening a school. He died after being injured in a brawl with the servants of a local landowner he had satirized in one of his poems.

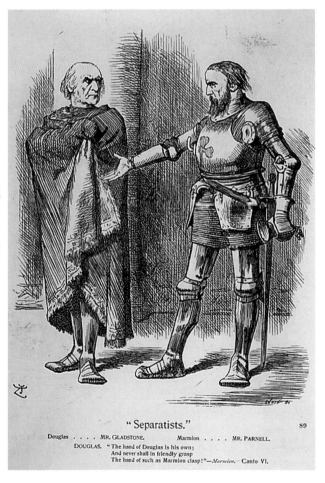

"Separatists." 89

Douglas . . . . MR. GLADSTONE.   Marmion . . . . MR. PARNELL.
DOUGLAS. "The hand of Douglas is his own;
And never shall in friendly grasp
The hand of such as Marmion clasp!"—*Marmion*, Canto VI.

ABOVE: Gladstone broke with Parnell after the infamous O'Shea case.

O'SULLIVAN BEARE, DONAL (1560–1618)

Chief of the O'Sullivans of Beare, County Cork. During the Tyrone rebellion, O'Sullivan held Dunboy Castle against Sir George Carew in 1602. After it fell, he retreated back on Ulster, from where he fled to Spain. Philip III of Spain awarded him a title but he was killed in Madrid.

)))» *George Carew*

O'TOOLE, ST LAURENCE (d. 1180)

Lorcán Ua Tuathail, Prelate and saint. The abbot of Glendalough before he became archbishop of Dublin in 1162, O'Toole showed real skill, for all his saintliness, in worldly politics. Having first lobbied successfully for the high kingship of Ruairi Ó Conchubhair (Rory O'Connor) of Connacht in 1167, he served his royal master on vital missions to Henry II of England. He also played an important part in the Church reform of the late twelfth century.

)))» *Glendalough, Ruairi Ó Conchubhair*

PAGANISM

Religious traditions of Ireland prior to Christianization. One of the few things we seem to know for certain about Celtic religion is that it completely prohibited the use of written script – which means that we must rely wholly on foreign witnesses for all our 'evidence'. The writings of Roman commentators in continental Europe, like those of the early Christians in Ireland, may not in fact be much more reliable than the romanticizing pseudo-scholarship of recent centuries. For what it is worth, Roman visitors to Gaul, from Diodorus Siculus and Posidonius to Julius Caesar, seem agreed on the authority of the Celtic druids. Beyond that little is known for sure – Caesar in particular appearing to see Celtic paganism very much through a Roman theological filter. Ireland's celebrated fairy folk may represent Celtic deities as they have come down in the folk-memory through Christian times – equally well, however, they could represent the dimmed and distorted figures of departed ancestors, or (something along the lines of the Tuatha Dé Danann) the pre-Celtic inhabitants of Ireland. The eternal round of the season and the changeless rhythms of the agricultural year appear to have helped preserve versions of the old pagan festivals right down into modern times. On May Day, or Bealtaine, the first day of summer, cattle were traditionally purified by being driven between two fires; Lughnasa, 1 August, was a harvest festival, at which thanks were offered for the ripening of the corn. As the first day of winter, Samhain, was celebrated on 1 November: as such it corresponded with the Christian feast of All Souls', as the annual festival of the dead.

)))» *Druids, Tuatha*

PAISLEY, IAN (b. 1926)

Northern Irish clergyman and politician, founder of Free Presbyterian Church of Ulster and co-founder of the Democratic Unionist Party. The Reverend Ian Paisley's stentorian tones are known the world over as the voice of Ulster loyalism, austere and uncompromising: for more than 30 years he has stood firm in his resistance to change. Ever since Northern Ireland's Unionist prime minister, Terence O'Neill, showed signs of a more conciliatory approach to cross-border co-operation in 1965, Paisley has shown his genius for mobilizing Ulster's working-class Protestants in their tens of thousands. Opposing the Sunningdale Conference of 1973, the Anglo-Irish Agreement of 1985, and the peace process of the present time, he has driven home the unmistakeable message that 'Ulster Says No'. A hate-figure to some, a comic Quixote to others, Paisley has beyond any doubt been a dominant figure in Northern Ireland politics. Yet he would himself point out that, whatever the force of his personality, he has at all times been articulating the feelings of a large – and angry – section of the Unionist community.

)))» *Democratic Unionists, Terence O'Neill, Sunningdale Conference*

RIGHT: Ian Paisley.

PALE, THE (14TH CENTURY)

Area of early English rule in the east of Ireland. Though nominally the masters of all Ireland, the English in fact felt very much on the defensive through much of the medieval period: only in Dublin and its immediate hinterland did they feel really secure. Poynings' Parliament of 1495 initiated a policy of marking out this area with defensive earthworks: the word 'pale' (like the modern 'paling') derives ultimately from the Latin *palus* or 'stake' and means a 'fence' or a 'railed enclosure'. It ringed the counties of Dublin, Meath, Louth and Kildare (medieval boundaries). Not until Tudor times would the English feel strong enough to dispense with the idea of the Pale, an aggressive programme of colonization extending their rule throughout the whole of Ireland.

))))➤ *Elizabeth I of England, Poynings' Laws*

PAPAL VISIT (1979)

Visit to Ireland by Pope John Paul II. Received by rapturous crowds in Ireland, His Holiness was almost as eagerly acclaimed by the British Press, reporting the

impassioned plea for peace he made to a 250,000-strong crowd at Drogheda: 'On my knees I beg of you to turn away from the paths of violence and to return to the ways of peace.' Nationalists preferred to point to what might be called the 'small print' of his message, his insistence that, without 'justice' peace would be impossible.

PARNELL, CHARLES STEWART (1846–91)

Politician. Elected to parliament in 1875 on a Home Rule ticket, Parnell soon began attracting attention for his obstructionist tactics in the House, holding up proceedings with filibustering speeches and innumerable points of order. This delighted his supporters in Ireland as much as it exasperated the government, but Parnell would soon take his campaign on to a far more positive footing. Appointed president of Michael Davitt's Land League, he proved an enormously charismatic leader – and adept at walking the narrow line between nationalist passion and dangerous sedition. Although he was arrested in 1881, he was able to reach agreement with William Gladstone – the Kilmainham Treaty – and continue a campaign which had soon attained such obvious popular support it could scarcely be disregarded. Apparently about to enter the promised land, Parnell's meteoric star began to fall: first in 1887 he was accused of having expressed sympathy with those who had carried out the Phoenix Park Murders. Though this was assumed by his supporters to be a crude smear (and eventually exposed as such), the news had meanwhile broken of his affair with a married woman, Katherine ('Kitty') O'Shea. In Catholic Ireland, in 1889, this was enough to destroy any political career: a thoroughly marginalized figure, he died in England shortly afterwards.

))))➤ *Kilmainham Treaty, Land League, Kitty O'Shea, Phoenix Park Murders*

LEFT: The pope in Ireland, 1979.
ABOVE: Charles Stewart Parnell.

PARTITION

Idea that Ireland might be divided into a Northern British sector and a southern Irish state; the introduction of such a division by the 1921 Anglo-Irish Treaty. Part of the political language since the eighteenth century (which had seen the partition of Poland), the notion of partition in Ireland began to be raised more frequently in the North. The closer Home Rule seemed to come as a reality, the more angry and resolute the opposition among Northern Protestants and their friends in the British parliament. Gladstone's attempts to introduce Home Rule both foundered on the rocks of Ulster loyalism, and though Lloyd George's nonconformist sympathies are said to have biased him in the Northern Protestants' favour, it is hard to see how any British prime minister could have turned the province loose in the aftermath of World War I. Although clearly not a neat solution, some form of partition was surely inevitable given the deep-rooted identities and enmities involved.

)))➤ *Anglo-Irish Treaty, Boundary Commission, William Gladstone, Home Rule, David Lloyd George*

Legend:
- ☐ NORTHERN IRELAND
- ☐ REPUBLIC OF IRELAND

PATRICK, ST (c. AD 389–461)

Patron saint of Ireland. Thought to have been Romano-British by birth, though hardly the 'patrician' his Latin name 'Patricius' would suggest, Patrick's biography is inevitably sketchy. Though various documents purport to narrate his life, most date from some time afterwards.

Patrick's own *Confessio*, though apparently genuine, is unforthcoming. More a polemical defence of his Irish mission than the personal testimony its title might imply to a modern reader, this text does reveal that Patrick first saw Ireland after he was snatched away from his British home by raiders and sold into slavery there, where he had to work as a shepherd. It was during this period that he first realized he had a religious vocation: after six years, a vision led him to freedom and he escaped to Britain. Training as a priest and rising to the rank of bishop, he felt impelled to return to his place of enslavement as a 'slave to Christ'. In the space of 30 years he converted much of Ireland to Christianity, founded the See of Armagh, banished the snakes and interpreted the shamrock.

)))➤ *Confessio, Shamrock*

LEFT: Map showing the boundaries between Northern Ireland and the Republic of Ireland.
ABOVE: St Patrick's day parade, Dublin.

PEARSE, PÁDRAIG (1879–1916)

Revolutionary. From 1896 prominent in the Gaelic League campaigning for national rebirth through promotion of the Irish language, Pádraig Pearse was a founder member of the Irish Volunteers. A poet and playwright, his oft-articulated concern for patriotic sacrifice seems rather unhealthy now, but wasn't really so different from that to be found in the work of English poets of the time like Rupert Brooke. When, in 1914, John Edward Redmond asked volunteers to support the British war effort, Pearse was a leader of the group that refused to heed his call. A member of the IRB and, by 1915, its director of military operations, his strongest weapon remained his use of language, notably his rousing speech at the graveside of O'Donovan Rossa. In retrospect that oration can be seen to have provided the rhetorical frame through which the military failure of 1916 would be viewed as victory.

)))■ *Easter Rising, Gaelic League, General Post Office, Irish Volunteers*

PEEL, ROBERT (1788–1850)

English politician who played a major role in Irish affairs in the first half of the nineteenth century. Peel first came to prominence as chief secretary for Ireland (1812–18), during which time he was responsible for the introduction of the Peace Preservation Force in 1814;

a police force that could be moved to any area where there was trouble. The Peace Preservation Force were nicknamed the 'Peelers', a name sometimes still used for the police in Ireland. Peel was a strong opponent of Catholic emancipation and mutual animosity between him and Daniel O'Connell almost led to a duel in 1814. As British prime minister (1841–46) he introduced a number of significant measures which were partly aimed at reducing moderate Catholic support for the repeal campaign. These included the three-fold increase in the government grant to Maynooth College; the setting up of universities (Queen's colleges) in Belfast, Cork and Galway; and the repeal of the Corn Laws.

)))■ *Great Famine*

PEEP O' DAY BOYS

Group of Protestant terrorists. In County Armagh in the 1780s the Peep o' Day Boys were the primary instigators of sectarian strife and are regarded as the forerunners of the Orange Order, which came into being after a murderous confrontation between the Peep o' Day Boys and the Defenders at the Battle of the Diamond. Their main activity was the raiding of Catholic houses at dawn, ostensibly in search of illegal weapons, but in reality to terrorize the inhabitants, several thousand of whom were driven from their homes and forced to take refuge in the west of Ireland.

)))■ *Battle of the Diamond, Defenders*

PENAL LAWS

Laws restricting liberties and entitlements of Catholics (and of nonconformist Protestants). The privileges of the established Church were guarded jealously throughout early modern Europe: in Spain and France, for example, there were restrictions on the rights of Protestants and Jews. In England the Anglican ascendancy was protected by rules on the ownership of land, neither Catholics nor nonconformists being allowed to own land outright (as opposed to leasing for limited periods) or to bequeath it in single large parcels (by the system of primogeniture); instead, it had to be divided into ever-smaller units among a growing body of progressively impoverished descendants. The system thus

LEFT: Robert Peel.

hindered the continuation of any sort of Catholic gentry; as did prohibitions on Catholics or dissenters holding public office (as MPs, judges, magistrates, etc). This was hardly an issue in England, where Puritans were a minority and Catholicism all but extirpated: in Ireland, though, it would oppress large sections of the population. Catholics were in the vast majority across much of the country – and where they weren't, in the Plantations of the North, there was a large number of dissenting Presbyterians. Successive governments had seen the introduction of Penal Laws here as likely to be counterproductive. With William III's victories, however, came a determination to smash Ireland's Catholic aristocracy, not only by rules on ownership and inheritance of land and property, but also by restrictions on education, travel and the possession of weapons. The Flight of the Wild Geese in 1691 followed a recognition by Ireland's Catholic aristocracy that its days were numbered; yet the Presbyterian farmers of Ulster were soon emigrating in large numbers too, their growing presence in America an important factor in that colony's restiveness under British rule.

)))))▶ *Presbyterianism, Patrick Sarsfield*

PETRIE, GEORGE (1790–1866)

Antiquarian and scholar. George Petrie was one of the influential group of people interested in Irish history and topography who came together to work with the Ordnance Survey. Originally an illustrator, he published many important archeological papers, including a ground-breaking study of round towers. He also secured a manuscript of the *Annals of the Four Masters* for the Royal Irish Academy and arranged the purchase of such national treasures as the Cross of Cong, the Ardagh Chalice and the Tara Brooch.

)))))▶ **Annals of the Four Masters,** *Ardagh Chalice, Cross of Cong, Ordnance Survey, Tara Brooch*

PHOENIX PARK MURDERS (1882)

Political assassinations of 6 May 1882. When men wielding surgical knives attacked and murdered the Irish chief secretary Lord Frederick Cavendish and his undersecretary T. H. Burke in Phoenix Park, a profound shockwave ran through the British establishment and public opinion. Although the Fenian 'Invincibles' responsible had in fact been following their own very different agenda, the outrage came at a delicate point in the campaign of of the Land League – attempts were indeed made in the British media to associate Parnell with the crimes. Gladstone, inclined to be conciliatory, felt he had no alternative but to be seen to make a stand: the murders thus arguably set progress back several years.

)))))▶ *Invincibles, Charles Stewart Parnell*

LEFT: Detail of the Ardagh Chalice; the purchase of this Irish national treasure was arranged by George Petrie.

PIGGOTT, RICHARD (c. 1828–89)

Journalist and fraud. In 1879, Piggott sold his paper, the *Irishman*, to the Land League, making his living thereafter through political blackmail and intrigue. From 1886 he leaked damaging information about pro-Home Rule politicians to the *London Times*. An official investigation exposed his falsehoods. He fled to Spain where he committed suicide.

))))➤ *Land League*

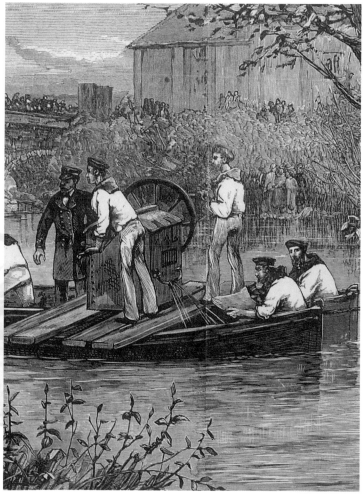

PLUNKETT, JOSEPH MARY (1887–1916)

Poet and revolutionary. The writer of a number of volumes of verse and a co-founder of the Irish Theatre in 1914, Joseph Plunkett was one of the secret council of the IRB that conceived and planned the Easter Rising. He was also one of those executed in its aftermath.

))))➤ *Easter Rising*

PLUNKETT, ST OLIVER (1629–81)

Prelate and saint. Born into an 'Old English' family, Oliver Plunkett was educated at seminaries in Rome and taught there himself until 1669, when he was sent back as Archbishop of Armagh. At first his position was relatively comfortable, the restored Stuart monarchy of Charles II not being characterized by Protestant zeal, but to his cost he would be caught up in the violent backlash. When, in 1679, alarmed at his government's easy-going attitude, Titus Oates cooked up an imaginary 'Popish Plot' to assassinate the king, Plunkett was one of over 20 leading Catholics 'tried' and executed. Although tolerant towards Catholicism, Charles was never actually going to take its side: he refused to pardon Plunkett, despite the utter discrediting of Oates and the other witnesses.

POOR LAW

The Irish Poor Law was enacted in 1838 and for the first time created a nationwide system for tackling poverty. Previously, the welfare of the poor had been the responsibilty of individual parishes. The country was divided into 130 'unions' and each was to have its own workhouse. The system had not been fully developed by the time of the Famine and many of the workhouses were overwhelmed by the number of paupers seeking relief. The workhouses were grim, unpopular places in which families were split up, food was basic and discipline severe. Although they were abolished by the Free State, they continued in existence in Northern Ireland until 1946.

))))➤ *Great Famine, Workhouses*

POTATOES

One of the staple crops grown in Ireland and the one on which the peasantry depended for survival. Harvest failures were common, for example in 1817, 1822 and 1842. Between 1845–49, potato blight (*Phytophthora infestans*) destroyed the crop several years running, causing

a catastrophic famine and outbreaks of typhus. Prices leapt beyond peasant incomes and relief measures were unable to cope with mass starvation. By 1846 mass emigration to the USA had begun.

))))▶ *Emigration, Great Famine*

POYNINGS, SIR EDWARD (1459–1521)

Lord deputy of Ireland (1494–95). Technically subordinate to Prince Henry – later Henry VIII – who, although only three, was still Ireland's viceroy, Sir Edward Poynings was sent to Ireland with 1,000 men by Henry VII to re-establish his authority. This show of military strength, and the ensuing introduction of 'Poynings' Law', helped bring what had been a wayward Irish administration back to heel.

))))▶ *Poynings' Law*

ABOVE: Peasants lament the failure of the potato harvest.

POYNINGS' LAW (1494)

Strictly speaking the Statutes of Drogheda; restriction on powers of lord deputy of Ireland and his council, introduced in 1494. So-called because it was brought in by Sir Edward Poynings, Poynings' Law stipulated that any bills decided upon by the Irish parliament (or indeed the actual summoning of that parliament) had first to be approved by the king and his Privy Council. Intended first and foremost as a curb on the power of the lord deputy, in the light of the political manoeuvring the Earl of Kildare had got up to in that role, Poynings' Law came to be exploited by interests within Ireland as a means of delaying lord deputies' measures and, in the decades before it was rendered obsolete by the Act of Union, to be seen as an oppression of Irish freedom by 'patriot' MPs.

))))▶ *Edward Poynings*

PRESBYTERIANISM

Religious denomination. Originating in Scotland – whence it was brought by settlers participating in the Ulster Plantation of the seventeenth century – Presbyterianism is characterized by its rejection of the hierarchical structures of the Anglican (or Episcopalian Church). That, in charismatic preachers like John Knox (*c.* 1513–72) and others this tended to go along with a more Calvinistic approach to Protestant doctrine, was not in itself the problem in the eyes of the English Crown. But with its intense emphasis on individual piety, its view that the soul was to be saved by God's predestined will rather than any action of the Church, Calvinism had a way of issuing politically in a contempt for the earthly authorities of Church and State: to the absolutist Stuarts, Presbyterianism was a rebellion waiting to happen. Hence the attempts of James VI of Scotland (James I of England) to insist upon the acceptance of bishops and other 'popish' trappings, and those of his successor Charles I to impose an essentially Anglican prayerbook. Thousands signed the National Covenant of 1638 affirming their loyalty to their Church and their defiance of Charles's efforts to establish Episcopalian conformity. In such a hostile climate, many Presbyterians participated in the Ulster Plantation in hopes of finding religious freedom, the Church grew in confidence with the triumph of Puritan rule in Cromwell's England. The Restoration of the Stuarts might have been a calamity –

having thrown in their lot with the revolutionaries, Presbyterians could expect little favour, and several years of bloody persecution were indeed the consequence in Scotland. By now, though, Presbyterianism was too influential within the Plantation to be challenged, and its followers accordingly got off comparatively lightly. They were, on the other hand, to be deeply disappointed by the rule of William III, the hammer of Catholicism seemingly content to maintain the penal laws of earlier times. Thus, in the eighteenth century, the great emigration of Ulster Presbyterians to the American colonies; and what has often seemed in English eyes the peculiar ambivalence of their British 'loyalism'.

PROTESTANT ASCENDANCY

Rule of Ireland by Protestants and, by extension, the Protestant ruling class. Since the nineteenth century a common shorthand for Ireland's Protestant landed gentry, the term 'Protestant Ascendancy' originally referred to the *fact* of Protestant rule. Henry VIII's conscious attempts to install a Protestant landowning class with loyalty to England were a logical continuation of his father's efforts to keep the island's aristocracy in line through Poynings' Law, but England's isolation after the break with Rome lent a new urgency to the problem. The Penal Laws were explicitly intended to perpetuate the Protestant Ascendancy; the campaign for Catholic Emancipation implicitly aimed at its overthrow.

)))▶ *Henry VIII of England, Penal Laws, Poynings' Law*

LEFT: *Papists torture Protestants.*
ABOVE: *Henry VIII.*

PROTESTANTISM

Reforming movements of Christianity which, in 'protest' against the authority of the Roman Catholic Church, broke away to form separate denominations in the sixteenth century. The increase in intellectual confidence in the centuries since the Renaissance, the dispersal of learning in general through the medium of print, and in particular the increased availability of scripture in translation, a decline in deference towards a Church hierarchy which was all too obviously corrupt, all these factors had for some time been feeding into what was becoming an increasingly choppy current of discontent with what had previously been the unchallenged authority of the Catholic Church.

Men such as Martin Luther (1483–1546) in Germany and John Calvin (1509–1604) in Switzerland were only the most famous of a new breed of preacher, concerned primarily with the destiny of the individual soul, the responsibilities of the individual conscience. If this meant a much-mocked tendency to gloomy self-abnegation, it also informed a new sense of self-assertion too, since it saw the believer as answerable directly to his God, rather than to the intermediary of his priest or bishop. The new 'Protestant' theology was thus clearly political in its implications – hence the urgency with which both Church and State in sixteenth-century Europe sought to suppress it. England's Reformation – though, unusually, a matter not of doctrinal difference but of Henry VIII's 1531 falling-out with Rome – meant its emergence as the first major Protestant power in opposition to staunchly Catholic France and Spain. Elizabeth I thus smiled upon Scotland's Presbyterianism, despite its being by Anglican standards theologically extreme, and continued her father's attempts to Protestantize Ireland.

There was a geopolitical angle here: Ireland soon came to be seen as a Catholic Achilles' heel, through which Britain, and England itself, might one day be vulnerable. That expeditionary forces from France and Spain did indeed attempt attacks through Ireland as late as 1798 did nothing to ease such anxieties, or decrease the pressure for Protestantization. This despite the fact that Anglicanism as practised in England remained by and large far less radical in its doctrines than the major Protestant churches to be found in Ireland. Even the Church of Ireland, though in theory at least an Irish annexe of the Anglicanism, was from early on a great deal more 'Protestant' than its mother Church. Yet,

while they may have differed greatly in their religious beliefs, and even more in their motivation, establishment England shared with Protestant Ireland a fear of 'popish' power.

➤ **Elizabeth I of England, Henry VIII of England**

PROVISIONAL IRA (1969)

Revolutionary organization. Protestant alarm at apparent gains made by the Civil Rights Movement led eventually to a breakdown in law and order – a breakdown to some extent spearheaded by the forces of law and order themselves. As Catholic communities came under attack, many began to feel that after several decades on the margins, the IRA could at last be seen as having a worthwhile role. The organization's apparent refusal to take up this challenge led to the split of 1969, when the Provisional IRA left behind an 'Official' IRA still committed to political rather than military action. Though Harold Wilson's Labour government in London started sending in troops that August, its hesitation had seemed powerfully

symbolic and now proved profoundly damaging. Its place as protector of the nationalist community established by default, the Provisional IRA was able to inaugurate a wider campaign dedicated to the overthrow of British rule in Ireland through a sustained campaign of bombings and shootings, in Ireland and in Britain. Over the years that followed, the Provisionals successfully resisted all attempts of the authorities to defeat them – yet showed no sign of achieving any sort of military breakthrough. Hence the

ABOVE: An IRA volunteer walks back into the crowd after reading a prepared statement at a Republican rally.
CENTRE RIGHT: Claudius Ptolemaeus.

increasing prominence since the early 1980s of Sinn Féin's political campaign. The ceasefire of 1994 (broken in 1996, but renewed the following year) only underlined a trend already taking place for the movement's military men to withdraw into the background. This process has been strengthened by two recent acts of decommissioning of weapons.

PTOLEMAEUS, CLAUDIUS (PTOLEMY) (c. AD 100–178)

Greek geographer who lived in Alexandria, whose influential and scholarly work *The Outline of Geography* included the first map to show Ireland in any great detail. Although it is unlikely that he visited Ireland himself, many of the features shown on the map can still be identified. This would suggest that Ireland was connected to the rest of the ancient world by trade.

RAILWAYS (19TH CENTURY)

The railway era in Ireland began in 1834 with the opening of the Dublin Kingstown (now Dún Laoghaire) line which connected the capital with the ferry to Holyhead in Wales. The most rapid development took place in the 1840s under Willian Dargan, who became known as the 'Father of the Irish Railways'. Since Ireland did not have a heavy manufacturing industry, the railways never carried the same volume of goods as in England; however, they greatly improved passenger travel. The railways were detrimental to small local businesses because goods could now be brought quickly and cheaply from English cities, so that within the space of 20 years many regional manufacturers of household items and clothing went out of business. Irish agriculture on the other hand, now had greater access to the English market, and the railways also improved the distribution of newspapers and the post.

Railways remained the dominant method of transport until after World War I. The introduction of motorized transport suited Ireland's many small towns and rural communities, and both the Free State government and that of Northern Ireland, favoured the development of the roads network to the detriment of the railways. By the 1950s many lines had been closed and nowadays the network consists mainly of the inter-city lines and suburban networks in Dublin and Belfast.

RALEIGH, SIR WALTER (1554–1618)

English soldier and adventurer. Sir Walter Ralcigh served in the army in Munster, where he participated in the massacre of 600 Italian and Spanish troops at Smerwick. A favourite of Elizabeth I, he received 42,000 acres – the largest grant in the Munster plantation – which he settled with English tenants. He also cut down and exported much of the native woodland, before selling the estate, and continuing his colonial exploits in north and south America. He is sometimes credited with introducing the potato to Ireland, though this is unlikely.

)))➤ *Elizabeth I of England, Plantation of Ulster*

RATHLIN ISLAND

Island off northern coast of County Antrim. Ten km (6 miles) off the Irish coast at Ballycastle, but only some 26 km (16 miles) from the Mull of Kintyre, Rathlin Island for a long time found itself poised historically between Irish and Scottish destinies. Robert Bruce hid out here in 1306 after the final failure of Wallace's Scottish rising. Irish kin of the MacDonalds of the Isles, the MacDonnells, made their base here in 1399 – the assistance of the Campbell family in the English massacre of 1575 eerily anticipated their more central role in the atrocity at Glencoe 117 years later. Although the MacDonnells remained lords here, the island was sold on in the eighteenth century, the population declining through the nineteenth under the usual pressures of famine and emigration. Rathlin earned itself a footnote in technological history in 1898 when Guglielmo Marconi tested out his wireless transmitter with a message to the Antrim shore in 1898. Today the island is treasured for its natural beauty and historical interest.

ABOVE: Sir Walter Raleigh.

RATHLIN ISLAND MASSACRE (1575)

Atrocity of 1575. Installing themselves in the castle built in the fourteenth century by the Scottish rebel Robert Bruce, the MacDonnells made Rathlin their base for fierce resistance to the 'Enterprise of Ulster'. Acting on instructions from the Sir Henry Sidney and the Earl of Essex, Francis Drake and John Norris landed on the island and took the castle by storm. Despite the castle's surrender, they killed all 200 defenders, as well as 400 civilians cowering among the island's crags and caves.

)))➡ *Sorley Boy MacDonnell*

REBELLION OF 1641

Irish Catholic rebellion, sparking off the Confederate War. Suppression of rebellions under Elizabeth I, and ruthless land settlement left Ireland in a state of high tension. Protestant settlements – 'Plantations' – deprived the chieftain class as well as the peasants from the ancient right to live off the land. In the aftermath of the Battle of Kinsale (1601), the Ulster Plantation seized three million acres of land from families associated with the Tyrone rebellion. The Plantation attracted Scottish Presbyterians to Down and Antrim, ejecting Irish Catholics from their land.

The old Anglo-Norman aristocracy was supposed to be exempt, but crooked lawyers helped 'discoverers' identify flaws in land titles, leading to confiscations to the Crown. Thus, Anglo-Normans increasingly shared an interest with peasants in expelling the English. They were also cheated by Charles I, whom they financially supported in his war with Spain in return for a promise (the 'Graces') that land held for 60 years or more would be secure. Charles took the money and reneged on the land question.

Thomas Wentworth, Earl of Strafford, was lord deputy of Ireland from 1632, representing Charles I in Ireland throughout rising discontent. In 1635 he rigged Irish courts so that Connacht be declared all royal property, to enable further settlement. In 1640 he became lord lieutenant of Ireland. His execution in May 1641 for political reasons removed the principal obstacle to revolt in Ireland.

The Rebellion broke out in 1641, led by Sir Phelim O'Neill. Rebels demanded the redress of land grievances and allied themselves with the Crown. This garnered support from royalists and helped polarize the religious component of the English Civil War. The massacre of thousands of civilian Protestants in Ulster confirmed English Protestant suspicions that the rebellion was a Catholic plot hatched by Charles I to help him against parliamentary Presbyterians. Papal intervention dissuaded the rebels from accepting any settlement not restoring Catholicism to its pre-Reformation state. This guaranteed the continuation of the rebellion, and the outbreak of the English Civil War.

)))➡ *Confederate War, Oliver Cromwell, Drogheda, The Graces, Phelim O'Neill*

REBELLION OF 1798

Irish Presbyterian-Catholic Rebellion. The 1700s were known as the Protestant Ascendancy. Catholics, and even Presbyterians, were excluded from power through the Penal Laws. Catholics suffered even more severe strictures, such as being banned from elective office, bearing arms and, from 1727, the vote.

The Anglican-controlled Irish parliament used its powers to increase Anglican influence and control. Catholics were generally impoverished peasants, while the Presbyterians built their own self-contained community in Ulster.

Tension built amongst the Presbyterians, who resented the requirement that they pay tithes to support the Anglican church in Ireland. Meanwhile, the Anglican aristocracy resented that their lands and wealth were exploited by England to fund her imperial colonial wars and support her industry. For example, Irish wool could only be exported to England.

The American Revolution led to more autonomy for the Anglican power-base when one of them, Henry Gratton, secured legislative independence. This did

ABOVE: Henry Grattan.
ABOVE RIGHT: Theobald Wolfe Tone.

REDMOND, JOHN EDWARD (1856–1918)

Politician. After the discrediting and death of Parnell, the keeper of the constitutionalist nationalist flame, John Edward Redmond had succeeded in persuading Herbert Asquith to entertain a third Home Rule Bill by 1912. Though this in its turn was rejected after Ulster opposition, Redmond had not given up hope of gaining a satisfactory outcome in time: when World War I broke out in 1914 he urged all Irishmen to stand by Britain. While many thousands heeded his call, a revolutionary hardcore took no notice. The Easter Rising and its aftermath rendered him an irrelevance in Irish politics. He died in 1918 a broken man.

)))➤ *Home Rule*

BELOW: John Redmond.

nothing for the Catholics or Presbyterians who saw they shared a common interest in wholesale reform. Theobald Wolfe Tone led demands for parliamentary reform, hoping to create a Presbyterian-Catholic alliance. He founded the Society of United Irishmen in 1791. Although Catholics were given the vote in 1793, sectarian violence and polarization of communities increased. By 1796, Wolfe Tone had become convinced that an armed revolution was essential to win reform. He arranged for French assistance but bad weather turned back a force of 14,000 troops in 1796.

The government order to disarm the Presbyterians in 1797 led to rumours that the next stage was a planned massacre of Catholics. Wolfe Tone and his supporters exploited these fears and Catholics swelled the ranks of the United Irishmen. In 1798 the rebellion broke out but was largely ineffectual thanks to the disarming policy. However, in Wexford further harsh disarming measures provoked an outbreak of violence and atrocities as pike-bearing Catholics threw themselves at Protestant government forces until the latter under Lake routed the rebels at Vinegar Hill. Shortly afterwards a further French invasion was routed at Ballinamuck, with Wolfe Tone also being captured. The outcome was the Act of Union (1800), which ended Irish autonomy for over a century.

)))➤ *Battle of Ballinamuck, Protestant Ascendancy,*
Theobald Wolfe Tone, Battle of Vinegar Hill

REPEAL

Cancellation of the 1800 Act of Union. As though in anticipation of Gladstone's supposed complaint that 'Every time the English begin to understand the Irish Question, the Irish change the question', O'Connell greeted Catholic Emancipation by launching a new campaign, this time for 'repeal'. Specifically the withdrawal of the Act of Union, repeal had a way of meaning all things to all nationalists: to O'Connell himself it seems to have meant a system with 'one king, two legislatures' – a devolution of power to Dublin which would, if anything, have the effect of reinforcing Irish ties with England; hence the increasing impatience of other repeal campaigners, such as the Young Irelanders.

))))➤ *Act of Union, Daniel O'Connell*

REPUBLIC OF IRELAND

A Free State fully independent from Britain, and withdrawn from the British Commonwealth, as of an Act of the Dáil passed in 1949. Despite all the tumults that heralded its foundation, it was not with a bang, but with a whimper that the Irish Republic at last began. Its actual existence was proclaimed, not on the steps of the Dublin GPO by Pádraig Pearse, but by the comparatively colourless figure of John Costello at an international summit in Ottawa, in September 1948. Until then the title of 'Republic' had been held in reserve, as it were, for the hallowed day on which it could be bestowed on a single state comprising the entire Irish island. The national psyche in the Free State – in so far at least as the Free State was prepared to see itself as a 'nation' – had seen the recovery of the North as its defining goal, albeit one not necessarily to be pursued with any urgency, or even actively striven for at all. By closing off this option, Costello certainly pulled Fianna Fáil up short – perhaps his intention – yet he seemed to have given Britain a shock too. He in his turn would be taken by surprise when London responded with its own Ireland Act of 1949, strengthening the ties that bound Northern Ireland with Great Britain in general, and in particular insisting that the 'Six Counties' would thenceforth leave the United Kingdom only by consent of the Northern Irish parliament.

If Costello had hoped, by foiling the aspirations of romantic nationalists, to force his country into a more realistic engagement with modernity, all one can say is that, in the event, precisely the opposite actually happened. The independent posture he had struck, being compounded by Britain's own efforts to distance itself from the new republic, played right into the hands of de Valera with his vision of an idealised village Ireland in which time stood still.

BELOW: The Irish Parliament discusses the treaty with Britain, 1922.

Protectionism and political isolation meant that such a system was self-perpetuating: the 1950s were years of stagnation – some would say stultification – for the Irish Free State. Economic autarchy, repressive social attitudes and severe restrictions on intellectual freedom left Ireland in the grip of what came close to being a sort of elective-Francoism. And,

as other developed nations rushed – with whatever misgivings – to embrace the panoply of liberties afforded by what was known as the 'permissive society' in the 1960s, Ireland's dogged refusal to give ground gave a whole new meaning to the old slogan 'Home Rule is Rome Rule'. If northern Loyalists had always been flatly opposed to an end to partition, now moderate middle-class Protestants were crying 'no surrender'. Meanwhile, liberals abroad looked askance at the rebel nation, now apparently revealed as a race of reactionaries.

To committed Catholic nationalists, of course, such reservations were of no concern, yet the increasing economic problems of the Republic could not be ignored indefinitely. By 1957 unemployment had reached a staggering 78,000 and emigrants were streaming out of the country at a higher rate than at any time since the 1880s. Protectionism was affording no protection to Irish jobs or prosperity; the much-vaunted Irish family was finding it impossible to make ends meet. Even more disconcerting, perhaps, was the feeling that the Catholic Church itself was moving on, leaving Ireland

behind: the Second Vatican Council of 1962–65 saw a profound (if short-lived) revolution in official Catholic attitudes. By the time de Valera went into semi-retirement as president of what was very much 'his' country, it was already evident that this romantically rustic Ireland could not be viable in the second half of the twentieth century – though it was far less clear what sort of country could be built that might realistically replace it. Sean Lemass's attempts in the 1960s to create a thrusting, entrepreneurial Ireland, which was to some degree successful, appeared only to increase the discontents – at least in the short term – as a new breed of affluent Irish started to covet the benefits of consumerist society. Their horizons abruptly enlarged, a new generation of Irishmen and women were soon hankering after everything from washing machines and fridges to extra-marital affairs, while their elders shook their heads at the evil of it all. This same essential tension between an 'old' introverted Catholic, agrarian nation and a 'new' outgoing, secular, industrialized state may be traced through the subsequent history of the Irish Republic. The tension might well have proved tragically irresolvable had not Ireland's economic history effectively sidestepped it, European Community (EC) assistance reconstructing Irish agriculture as a modern business, while the emergence of the post-industrial 'Celtic Tiger' economy was arguably

only possible in a country which had never succeeded in industrializing the first time around. In the event Ireland has been able to modernize with few of the anticipated agonies; its younger people, at least, thoroughly at home in the contemporary world.

))))▶ *Cumann na nGaedheal, Government of Ireland Act, Home Rule, Éamon de Valera*

ABOVE LEFT: Polling in the Irish elections of 1932; troops were often present to prevent intimidation.
ABOVE: Garrett Fitzgerald.

REPUBLIC OF IRELAND ACT (1948)

Legislation by which Ireland officially seceded from the British Commonwealth. One of the first acts of John A. Costello as Taoiseach in 1948 was to announce the intention of his coalition government of revoking the 1936 External Relations Act (which, tying the Free State into the British Commonwealth, allowed the king an effective veto on Irish diplomatic appointments) and of going on to declare Ireland a fully-fledged Republic. Given Costello's conservative record, this decision came as an utter bombshell, causing consternation in particular among northern Unionists.
In reaction, Basil Brooke persuaded Labour prime minister Clement Attlee to pass what amounted to a retaliatory 'Ireland Act', guaranteeing that Northern Ireland would never 'cease to be part of His Majesty's dominions and of the United Kingdom without the consent of the parliament of Northern Ireland'.

REPUBLICANISM

Political doctrine. 'When boyhood's fire was in my blood,/I read of ancient freemen…' says the song. It would indeed have been in their Latin textbooks that, for many generations, schoolboys encountered the idea and learned to cherish the ideal of Republican rule. Its classical paradigm the expulsion of the Tarquin kings – Etruscan overlords – by the people of pre-imperial Rome, Republican-ism had found modern expression in the citizen's revolutions by which America (1775) and France (1789) had shaken off monarchical rule. The United Irishmen's insurrection of 1798 was clearly inspired by the ideals of *Liberté, Egalité et Fraternité* – though for most in the nineteenth century the French Revolution would be remembered for the subsequent Reign of Terror. The successes of O'Connell left more radical philosophies high and dry, the Fenian's marginal position politically underscored by their military failure. Yet, as the

case of the Fenians and their successors would clearly show, Republicans could still win sympathy on account of their heroic idealism, and where constitutionalist nationalism was foundering, that sympathy could harden into something like support.

REVIVAL OF 1859

Evangelical religious revival movement in Ulster. By the 1850s, the Church in Ulster was in a state of atrophy. In 1857 news reached Ulster of the revivalist movement in the USA. A series of prayer-meeting groups began to grow up, but in 1859 public displays of repentance and ecstatic rapture transformed the phenomenon into a sensation. In May 1859, the Reverend Frederick Buick reported to the Synod of Ballymena and Coleraine that the movement took off with the conversion of a family at Ahoghill. Revivalist meetings proliferated, sometimes with several in the same street, with the effect that business became neglected. The Maze horse race normally attracted 12,000 gamblers but only 500 turned up. Whisky distilleries and public houses went out of business.

REYNOLDS, ALBERT (b. 1932)

Politician, Fianna Fáil Taoiseach (1992–94). The brevity of Reynolds' tenure as Taoiseach gives no real sense of his importance as one of the main architects of the current Irish peace process. His partnership with British prime minister John Major in the Downing Street Declaration of 1993, and his handshake with John Hume and Gerry Adams after the IRA cessation of violence the following year give a better sense of his crucial role, not only as his own country's representative but as mediator with others.

))))▶ *Fianna Fáil*

RIBBONISM (19TH CENTURY)

Values and activities of the 'Ribbonmen', nineteenth-century Catholic secret societies. In some senses the heirs to the Defenders of the eighteenth century (their activities were certainly concentrated in the same predominantly northern areas), the Ribbonmen also drew

on earlier traditions of agrarian unrest, issuing threats against unpopular landlords, mutilating livestock, making violent attacks. Ribbonism, however, was by no means confined to agricultural workers – nor even to the rural areas – while its cause, though vague, appears to have been explicitly sectarian. In the north, like the Defenders, they came into frequent conflict with the Orange Lodges – whose traditions of ceremonial with violence they can be seen as mirroring. Ribbonism was also rumoured to be rife in communities of Irish emigrants abroad.

))))▶ *Agrarian Unrest, Ancient Order of Hibernians, Defenders*

LEFT: The French Revolution's cry of 'liberty, equality and brotherhood' was taken up by the United Irishmen in the nineteenth century.
RIGHT: Albert Reynolds.

RICHARD II OF ENGLAND (1367–1400)

King of England (1377–99). Like most of the English kings of the period, Richard found that controlling the Irish beyond the Pale was almost impossible. Roger Mortimer, 4th Earl of March, went to Ireland with the king in 1394, becoming lieutenant of Ulster, Connacht and Meath (1395) and all Ireland (1397). Constant warfare

years later. A campaigner for the rights of women, single parents and homosexuals, she perhaps did more than anyone else to bury the stereotype of a sexually repressive, reactionary Ireland, before stepping down in 1997 to take up a new position as United Nations high commissioner for human rights.

)))➤ *Anglo-Irish Agreement, Labour Party*

against rebellious chiefs like Art Mac Murchadha produced no results until March was killed at Kells in 1398. Richard returned in 1399 to avenge him but was forced to return to England to face a challenge to his crown.

)))➤ *Art mac Murchadha*

ROBINSON, MARY (b. 1944)

Politician, president of the Irish Republic (1990–97). Born Mary Bourke in Ballina, County Mayo, Mary Robinson was named Professor of Law at Trinity College Dublin at the age of 25. She was elected to Ireland's Senate that same year. A member of the Labour Party, she resigned in 1985 in protest against the party's attitude to the Anglo-Irish Agreement, but was their nomination for president five

ROUND TOWERS (AD 795)

Defensive belfries built at monasteries. Viking assaults began in AD 795 on Lambay Island off Dublin and continued for decades. Round towers were installed at monasteries to act as belfries and places of safety. When an attacking force was spotted the bells were rung. Refugees raced to the tower, climbing the ladder to the high entrance. Behind them the ladder was pulled up, offering security while the Vikings sacked the monastery below. The

ABOVE: Ships bringing provisions to the English from Richard II during his campaign in Ireland.
RIGHT: Twelfth century round tower at Ardmore.

Monasterboice tower in County Louth survives to a height of over 30 m (100 ft), with a door around two metres above ground level. Inside, five storeys were connected by ladders.

 Monasteries

ROYAL IRISH CONSTABULARY (1836)

Police force, founded as the Irish Constabulary (IC) in 1836. The 'Royal' prefix was added 1867. As much an army as a police force, the Irish Constabulary was founded to maintain order in an overwhelmingly rural society (Dublin had its own Metropolitan Police), with little conventional 'crime' but any amount of agrarian unrest and associated violence and intimidation. After the Great Famine, however, conditions in the countryside eased: the population had fallen sharply for one thing, but constitutional nationalism seemed to be making progress for another. The old paramilitary force changed over time, taking on a far more civilian role: an ever-increasing proportion of its membership was Catholic. The resulting organization was ill-equipped to deal with the disintegration of order after 1916, its members unable – when they were really willing – to meet the challenge of the IRA.

ROYAL ULSTER CONSTABULARY (1922–2001)

Police force of Northern Ireland. Based on the existing structures of the RIC, the RUC was brought into being to police the new state of Northern Ireland in 1922, and was from the first regarded by many nationalists as the long arm of the Orange Law. The RUC's nakedly hostile response to the Civil Rights Movement brought it into international dispute but, the

battlelines once drawn, it proved hard for the RUC to transcend them. Moves to make the force less paramilitary came up against the need for its officers to defend themselves against the very real threat of violence, while Catholics refused to join a constabulary whose culture was felt to be fundamentally hostile. Persistent rumours of RUC collusion with Loyalist paramilitaries have in some cases been backed by evidence. Despite the force's having won credit in recent years for its firm policing of potentially volatile loyalist demonstrations, nationalists remain profoundly sceptical as to its ability to reform itself. A review of policing in the province was conducted by the British Conservative politician Chris Patton under the terms of the Good Friday Agreement, and although his plans for a new and consciously non-sectarian 'Police Service of Northern Ireland' have been angrily rejected by Unionists of all complexions, some change has taken place, starting with the name recommended by Patton.

RUSSELL, THOMAS (1767–1803)

Known as 'the man from God-knows where' Russell was a radical who played a major role in the organization of the United Irishmen in the northern half of the country. He became a close acquaintance of Theobald Wolfe Tone around 1790 and was also librarian of the Linenhall Library in Belfast from 1794. He was not directly involved in the actions of 1798 as he had been arrested in 1796 and was held until 1801. In 1803 he sought support in Belfast and northern counties for Emmet's planned uprising but after its failure he was arrested again, tried and hanged in Downpatrick.

ST CANICE'S CATHEDRAL, KILKENNY (1251)

Church of Ireland cathedral. Built on the site of St Canice's original monastery, the cathedral in Kilkenny's Irishtown is one of Ireland's most beautiful and best-preserved medieval churches. Started in 1251 and added to in the course of the fourteenth and fifteenth centuries, it stands as a fine example of the Gothic decorated style. The adjacent library contains a number of rare books, including the important psalter, the 'Red Book of Ossory'.

LEFT: Royal Ulster Constabulary supporter William Montgomery handcuffed to the gates outside Downing Street in protest at the disbanding of the RUC.

ST MARY'S CATHEDRAL, LIMERICK (1180)

Church of Ireland cathedral. Limerick's cathedral, in what is now known as Englishtown, was begun around 1180 by one of the O'Brien kings, who had made the city their capital in the course of the tenth century. Of that first construction only the nave and west portal survive, in addition to parts of the side-aisles and transepts: the remainder was added through the fourteenth and fifteenth centuries and subsequently restored.

ST PATRICK'S CATHEDRAL, DUBLIN (1192)

Church of Ireland cathedral. Dublin has two Church of Ireland cathedrals (not to mention a Roman Catholic pro-cathedral), a fact which can cause confusion – and has in its time caused acrimony. In fact St Patrick's, completed in 1192 but built on the site of a much earlier church from the Viking period, was from 1213 promoted by a clerical faction as a rival to Christ Church. In 1300 the festering dispute was resolved by the direct intervention of the pope, who awarded the pre-eminence to Christ Church: St Patrick's was left to languish, a mere parish church. In more modern times a new role would be found for it as the 'national' cathedral for a Protestant Ireland: the writer Jonathan Swift was dean here from 1713–45.

)))▶ *Christ Church Cathedral, Jonathan Swift, Vikings*

SANDS, BOBBY (1954–81)

Revolutionary and hunger-striker. Leader of IRA inmates in Northern Ireland's Long Kesh prison, Robert 'Bobby' Sands was leader – and first casualty – of the hunger strikes of 1981. The culmination of a lengthy campaign to compel the authorities to concede 'political', prisoner-of-war status, the action did not, to begin with, have the backing of the IRA hierarchy, who feared its humiliating collapse. In the event, Sinn Féin would succeed in turning the episode brilliantly to political account: Sands was put forward as parliamentary candidate for the Fermanagh and South Tyrone by-election – and elected amid massive worldwide publicity. The hunger strikes taking their course,

ABOVE: Ken Livingstone speaking at a rally at County Hall to commemorate the first anniversary of the death of hunger-striker Bobby Sands in 1982. RIGHT: Patrick Sarsfield.

meanwhile, the resolution of British prime minister Mrs Thatcher was matched by the resolve of the men: Sands died, and nine fellow protestors followed in succession.

)))▶ *Hunger Strikes, Irish Republican Army*

SARSFIELD, PATRICK (d. 1693)

Earl of Lucan and soldier under James II. He commanded Irish troops in England and fled with the deposed James II to France in 1688. He accompanied James to Ireland to prosecute his campaign to recover the Crown, and was appointed a privy councillor and colonel of horse. He was active at the Battle of the Boyne in 1690 and remained in Ireland after James fled once more to France. Created Earl of Aughrim in 1691 he commanded part of the remaining Jacobite forces at Aughrim, where he was decisively defeated by William III's army. After the Treaty of Limerick he followed James to France where he remained loyal to the deposed monarch, fighting against William III at Landen in 1692, where he was fatally wounded.

)))⯈ *Battle of the Boyne, James II of England, Siege of Limerick*

SAYERS, PEIG (1873–1958)

Irish-language writer and storyteller. Peig Sayers was from Dún Caoin in the Kerry Gaeltacht. She married a man from the Blasket Islands and went to live there. Her autobiography *Peig* (1936) and her *Machnamh Seanamhná* (1939), published in English as *An Old Woman's Reflections*, are regarded as classics of folk literature and are still widely read because of the insight they give into life on the now – abandoned Blasket islands and because of the richness of her language.

)))⯈ *Blasket Islands*

SCOTUS, JOHANNES DUNS (c. 1266–1308)

Irish-born Franciscan who became professor of divinity at Oxford in 1301. Regarded as a genius, his lectures on philosophy and theology attracted large numbers and he was soon transferred to Paris, the major intellectual centre in Europe at that time. Later he moved to Cologne, where he died in 1308. In the sixteenth century when some of his teachings fell out of favour, his followers were labelled 'dunce', meaning slow of learning. It appears to have originally meant 'from County Down.'

SHACKLETON, SIR ERNEST (1874–1922)

Explorer, born in County Kildare. Shackleton accompanied Scott's Antarctic expedition of 1901–04 but was invalided out in 1903. He led the British Antarctic expedition of 1907–09, nearly reaching the South Pole. Next he led the British Imperial Trans-Antarctic expedition of 1914–16, remembered for Shackleton's epic mission to seek help from South Georgia after the expedition ship, *Endurance*, became stuck in ice.

SHAMROCK

A three-leaved, clover-type plant recognized internationally as a symbol of Ireland. Legend has it that St Patrick explained the concept of the Trinity to a disbeliever by showing him a plant with three leaves on one stem. It is worn in the lapel by the Irish and by people of Irish descent at home and abroad on St Patrick's day (17 March), and has been adopted as a symbol by Ireland's national airline Aer Lingus and other companies wishing to emphasize their Irishness. Nowadays, it is a cultural rather than a religious symbol.

)))⯈ *St Patrick*

SHANNON, RIVER

River in the west of Ireland. The Shannon is Ireland's largest river, rising in Leitrim and flowing more or less due south, before heading west to flow into the Atlantic Ocean just beyond Limerick. In the medieval period the Shannon was an artery of communication in what was still a largely roadless region – hence, for example, the siting on its banks of the monastic centre Clonmacnoise.

)))⯈ *Clonmacnoise*

BELOW: Ernest Shackleton.

SHAW, GEORGE BERNARD (1856–1950)

Dublin-born playwright who won the Nobel Prize for Literature in 1925. Shaw spent most of his adult life in England where, after a slow start, he became the most successful dramatist of his day. His plays include *Pygmalion, Saint Joan, Arms and the Man* and *John Bull's Other Island*. He was also a noted critic of music and drama and was widely recognized as being independent and outspoken in his views. As a socialist and a pacifist his views were often regarded as controversial, especially during World War I. He attributed his longevity to his vegetarian diet and he died after breaking his hip in a fall from a tree.

SHEARES, HENRY (1753–98) AND JOHN (1766–98)

Brothers and members of the United Irishmen. Both were lawyers. John Sheares travelled to France and was highly influenced by the events of the French Revolution, and persuaded his brother to share in the cause of revolutionary reform in Ireland. John wrote for the *The Press*, an anti-government newspaper. Both men took part in organizing the 1798 Rebellion but were captured and executed.

))))**➤ Rebellion of 1798, United Irishmen**

SILKEN THOMAS (LORD OFFALY, THOMAS FITZGERALD, 10TH EARL OF KILDARE) (1513–37)

Son of Gearóid Óg, the 9th Earl, Silken Thomas led a rebellion against English rule while his father was being held in the Tower of London. One hundred and forty horsemen with silk fringes on their helments rode to Dublin and publicly renounced Silken Thomas's allegience to the king. Later, he unsuccessfully attacked Dublin Castle and was forced to withdraw to his stronghold at Maynooth. When this garrison surrendered six months later, they were all executed in the infamous 'Pardon of Maynooth'. Silken Thomas, who had been absent, later surrendered to Grey, the new marshall of Ireland, as his personal safety was guaranteed. In October 1535, he was sent to the Tower of London and in 1537, he and his five uncles were hanged, drawn and quartered at Tyburn.

SIMNEL, LAMBERT (1475–1535)

False claimant to the English throne. Simnel apparently bore some resemblance to the English King Edward IV. When it was rumoured that Edward's sons, the 'Princes in the Tower' were alive, an Oxford priest, Richard Symonds, took Simnel to Ireland and passed him off as the English heir. He was crowned as Edward V in Dublin in 1487, but was taken prisoner during the Battle of Stoke the same year and Henry VII employed him in his kitchens until his death.

))))**➤ Henry VIII of England**

SINN FÉIN (1905)

Republican political party. Sinn Féin (the name means 'we ourselves') was founded in 1905 by Arthur Griffith and Bulmer Hobson. At the outset it was not so much a party as an umbrella organization intended to co-ordinate the work of other, smaller nationalist groupings; nor was it to begin with so much more radical in its aims than the other Home Rule parties: though Sinn Féin aspired to an independent Irish parliament – and called on nationalist MPs to withdraw from Westminster until it was granted – it was

ABOVE LEFT: George Bernard Shaw.
ABOVE: Sinn Féin conference, 2001
RIGHT: The monastery on Skellig Michael.

content for such an assembly to exist under the authority of the British Crown in a system of 'dual monarchy'. The party's identification with violent republicanism seems originally to have been no more than a British media smear – but then, with armed struggle on the increase after 1916, the actuality caught up with the stereotype. Sinn Féin's failure to create a new nationalist middle ground, radical yet non-violent, was a disappointment to Griffith. Ever since the 1920s, though, it has been the political arm of Irish republicanism.

))))➤ *Arthur Griffith*

SITRIC SILKENBEARD (d. 1042)

King of the Vikings at Dublin (also known as Sigtryggr). His widowed mother Gormfhlaith married Mael Seachnaill II, who ousted her. She drew Sitric into Ireland's chieftain wars by persuading him to fight with her brother Mael Mordha against Mael Seachnaill II and Brian Bóroimhe. Sitric was defeated by Brian at Glen Mama, but reinstated at Dublin by Brian, whose daughter he married. A further attempt against Brian ended in defeat at Clontarf in 1014. Sitric's ambitions suffered further setbacks with defeats by the Leinster forces in 1020 and by Niall of Ulster in 1022. Sitric became a Christian, travelled to Rome, en-couraged poetry and is attributed with having founded Christ Church Cathedral in Dublin.

))))➤ *Brian Bóroimhe, Battle of Clontarf, Gormfhlaith,*
Mael Sechlainn II

SKEFFINGTON, WILLIAM (d. 1535)

Sir William Skeffington, 'the Gunner', appointed lord-deputy of Ireland in 1529 until 1532, when the Earl of Kildare persuaded Henry VIII that he should be restored to the position. Skeffington was reinstated in 1534 over doubts of Kildare neutrality regarding the royal divorce. Kildare's recall to England led to the rebellion led by his son, Silken Thomas. Skeffington orchestrated the campaign against Silken Thomas, defeating him in 1535 at Maynooth.

))))➤ *Silken Thomas*

SKELLIGS, THE

Island group in the Atlantic Ocean, 13 km (8 miles) off the western coast of County Kerry. Although signs have been discovered of occupation since prehistoric times,

the Skelligs came into their own in the medieval period, when this rugged, rock-bound island group became a remarkable monastic centre. A cluster of beehive-shaped stone huts (*clochans*), a couple of small chapels, a church and two holy wells, 670 giddying steps above the shoreline on the largest island, Skellig Michael, St Fionan's monastery was a functioning religious community well into the fourteenth century. At times of persecution under the Penal Laws, Catholics on the run would find a haven in here, while in a more peaceful age it has been an inspiring place of pilgrimage.

))))➤ *Penal Laws*

SMITH O'BRIEN, WILLIAM (1803–64)

Politician. Although he allied himself with the cause of the Catholic Association from his very first parliamentary speech in 1828, and went on to support repeal, William Smith O'Brien – himself a Protestant – could never quite resolve the contradictions of his relationship with nationalism. Uncomfortable with the radicalism of Daniel O'Connell's aims to begin with, he was unhappy, too, at the Liberator's apparent willingness to compromise them after Clontarf; co-founding a new nationalist alliance, the Irish Confederation, he found himself ill at ease with more hot-blooded members such as James Fintan Lalor and John Mitchel. Caught up against his nature in a revolutionary uprising, he ended up the ignominious anti-hero of the Battle of the Widow McCormick's Cabbage Patch. His condemnation to death commuted to transportation, and finally to a full pardon, he retired thereafter into political obscurity.

))))➤ *Catholic Association, Irish Confederation,*
John Mitchel

SOCIAL DEMOCRATIC AND LABOUR PARTY (1970)

Political party in Northern Ireland. Founded in 1970 with the merger of several opposition parties, the SDLP quickly established itself as the main voice of constitutionalist nationalism in the North of Ireland. Though it had the long-term aspiration of a united Ireland, it was committed to achieving that outcome only through consent, and was more immediately concerned to build on the achievements of the Civil Rights Movement. Until 1979 the party was led by the West Belfast MP Gerry Fitt; after that its leader would be John Hume, MP for Foyle (Derry).

⫸ *Civil Rights Movement*

SOLEMN LEAGUE AND COVENANT (1912)

Pledge of commitment to resist Home Rule, signed by Ulster Protestants in 1912. Its title a conscious echo of that of the 'National Covenant' by which, in 1637–38, thousands of Scots promised to stand by the principles of their Presbyterian Church, the Solemn League and Covenant pledged Protestant Ulstermen to hold out against moves being made in parliament towards Home Rule. Almost half a million signatories swore to defend themselves and their children 'using all means which may be found necessary' against what the Covenant described as a 'subversive … destructive … perilous … conspiracy'.

⫸ *Ulster Volunteer Force*

SPANISH ARMADA (1588)

Fleet sent to attack England by Philip II of Spain. Supported by the pope, Philip's ambition was to restore Catholicism in England. In 1587 the execution of his aunt, Mary, Queen of Scots, a prominent Catholic, outraged the Spanish king, and he feared for his lands in the Netherlands.

The Armada was attacked in harbour at Cadiz by Sir Francis Drake in 1587. A new fleet of 130 ships was prepared by July 1588, carrying a force of around 19,000 troops. The more manoeuvrable

English ships under Lord Howard of Effingham drove the Armada up the Channel and attacked them off Calais and Flanders. The remaining Armada escaped into the North Sea but storms wrecked dozens of them on the Scottish and Irish coasts. Surviving Spaniards were frequently attacked and killed by English soldiers in Ireland, though some received protection from rebels like Tiernan O'Rourke. The episode destroyed Philip's ambitions.

⫸ *Elizabeth I of England*

STEELBOYS (1769–72)

Ulster-based protesters, known as 'Hearts of Steel'. The Steelboy disturbances were triggered off by increased rents, higher rates of taxation and the eviction of tenants from farms. Their activities focused on Antrim, Down, Armagh, Derry and Tyrone. They used night raids and threatening letters to object to the situation.

STEPHENS, JAMES (1825–1901)

Revolutionary. As aide-de-camp to William Smith O'Brien, engineer James Stephens took part in the abortive uprising of 1848, fleeing in its aftermath to Paris, the scene of a rather more successful revolution that same year. Persuaded that revolutionary activity really could stand some chance, in 1858 he became a co-founder of the Fenian Brotherhood, but was arrested in the official clampdown of 1865. Escaping from prison the following year, he returned to Ireland in triumph in 1867, but was blamed for leaving that year's attempted rising in the lurch.

⫸ *Fenian Brotherhood, William Smith O'Brien*

STOKER, BRAM (1847–1912)

Dublin-born novelist. Stoker is best known for his vampire novel, *Dracula,* first published in 1897. He began his career as a civil servant in Dublin but moved to London in 1878 as agent for actor Henry Irving, whose performances he had reviewed favourably when he played in Dublin. He wrote about half a dozen other novels and many short stories but none had the same enduring success as *Dracula.*

STORMONT (1932)

Parliament building of Northern Ireland. An impressive neo-classical pile on the eastern outskirts of Belfast, Stormont was purpose-built as the home of the Northern Ireland parliament, and opened in 1932. But 'Stormont' was always more than a building, the name becoming synonymous with the unchallengeable authority of the Orange State. With the introduction of Direct Rule from Westminster in 1972 it became home to the civil servants of the Northern Ireland Office. 'Stormont Castle', the nineteenth-century house in whose grounds the parliament building was sited was the official residence first for the prime ministers of Northern Ireland, and latterly for London-appointed Northern Ireland ministers.

))))➤ *Westminster Direct Rule*

STRUGGLE FOR INDEPENDENCE (1916–94)

War fought in pursuit of an independent Irish state after the suspension of Home Rule in 1914. Following the political manoeuvring after the election of 1910, the Ulster Volunteers were founded to fight in case Home Rule went through, and the IRB now founded the Irish Volunteers (forerunners of the IRA). Sectarianism was now organizing into paramilitary groups. Home Rule was passed but postponed in 1914 when war with Germany broke out.

The Irish Volunteers sought German support for the Easter Rising of 1916. Although unpopular amongst many Irish, intellectuals saw it as part of the centuries-old war with England for independence. Executed rebels became martyrs and in the General Election of 1918, Sinn Féin triumphed with 73 seats.

In Dublin in 1919, the Sinn Féin candidates declared themselves the Dáil Éirann (Irish parliament) in a declaration of independence, with supreme legislative powers in Ireland, and demanded expulsion of all British institutions, forces and offices. The Irish Volunteers became the new government's army, renamed the Irish Republican Army (IRA). Although political power lay with the Sinn Féin elected members, real power lay with the 15,000 active members of the IRA.

Guerrilla warfare now broke out between the IRA and the British forces of 'Black and Tans' and Auxiliaries. Both sides committed atrocities. The Government of Ireland Act (1920) attempted to set up separate Ulster and Irish parliaments. Accepted in Ulster, where Catholics were now set upon, the war continued until 1921 when the peace treaty established the Irish Free State in the south, enjoying substantial independence from Britain, while Northern Ireland remained part of the UK.

Civil war now broke out in Ireland between the pro- and anti-Treaty factions, the latter being led by the president of Sinn Féin, Éamon de Valera. The war was over by 1923 and 1927 de Valera led the anti-Treaty faction into the Irish parliament in his Fianna Fáil party. This reduced the IRA and Sinn Féin to dissident groups. In 1937 de Valera renamed the republican state Éire and a republic was declared in 1948. In the 1970s violence resumed in Ulster over Protestant persecution of Catholics, exploited by the IRA in their goal of a wholly independent Ireland, encompassing all 32 counties. Violence lasted until 1994 when political negotiations for a peaceful settlement began. Since then, however, splinter groups have continued to pursue violent options, and violence remains a part of Catholic-Protestant life in Northern Ireland.

))))➤ *Irish Republican Army, Irish Volunteers, Sinn Féin*

SULCOIT, BATTLE OF (AD 968)

Battle seizing Cashel for the kings of Munster. The background to the battle lay in the long-running warfare with the Vikings. By the mid-tenth century, the Dalcassians had been expelled from Munster by the Eóganacht into County Clare, and pushed further back by the Vikings. Brian Bóroimhe, a Dalcassian leader, wanted to fight, but his brother Mathghamhan wanted to negotiate. When the Eóganacht king Donnchadh died in AD 963, Mathghamhan claimed the kingship of Cashel. The weakened Eóganacht sought assistance from the Vikings in Ireland. Brian and Mathghamhan defeated the combined force of Eoghanacht and Vikings under Ivar at Sulcoit, giving them the momentum to go on to seize Limerick where Brian killed thousands of Vikings when he found Irish children enslaved there.

))))➤ *Brian Bóroimhe, Rock of Cashel, Munster*

FAR LEFT: Map of the British Isles showing the route of the Armada.
LEFT: Bram Stoker.
ABOVE: Stormont, Belfast.

SUNNINGDALE AGREEMENT (1973)

In May 1973 the Northern Ireland Assembly Bill became law, with elections following on 28 June. The Assembly proceeded to draw up details of the power-sharing executive. At Sunningdale, England, in December a conference met to resolve final differences. This was the first occasion the UK prime minister, the Irish Taoiseach and a Northern Ireland government had met to discuss Northern Ireland since 1925. On 9 December it produced an Agreement under which a Council of Ireland made up of a Council of Ministers, and a Consultative Assembly drawn from the Northern Ireland executive and Eire government to oversee shared interests, the 'Irish Dimension'.

SWIFT, JONATHAN (1667–1745)

Dublin-born Anglican clergyman, polemicist and novelist. Dean Swift's most famous work is *Gulliver's Travels* (1726). An earlier work, *A Tale of a Tub* (1704), an attack on religious zealots, resulted from his first posting as a clergyman to the predominantly Presbyterian parish of Kilroot in County Antrim. He later moved to London, where he edited the Tory paper *The Examiner* and became friendly with many of the leading literary figures of the time. In 1714 he was appointed Dean of St Patrick's Cathedral in Dublin, a post he held until shortly before his death. He wrote over 60 pamphlets on Irish affairs and helped to develop a distinctive Irish Protestant literary mentality.

))))➤ *St Patrick's Cathedral*

SYNGE, JOHN MILLINGTON (1871–1909)

Dublin-born playwright. Synge studied music and literature in Ireland and on the Continent before travelling to the Aran Islands to learn Irish. *The Aran Islands* (1907) is an account of the islands and their people as observed over several summers. These visits also provided the inspiration for several of his most famous plays, including *Riders to the Sea* and *The Playboy of the Western World,* which were produced by the Abbey Theatre. An associate of W. B. Yeats and Lady Gregory he became managing director of the theatre in 1908 and continued to write up to his early death from Hodgkin's disease in 1909.

))))➤ *Abbey Theatre, Lady Augusta Gregory, W. B. Yeats*

TÁIN

Type of epic tale found in the early Irish tradition of which the *Táin Bó Cuaigne*, the *Cattle Raid of Cooley* is the most famous. Another example is the *Táin Bó Fraich, Fraech's Cattle Raid*, which is also set against the background of the tensions between the ancient kingdoms of Ulster and Connacht.

))))➤ **Cattle Raid of Cooley**

TALBOT, MATT (1856–1925)

Reformed juvenile alcoholic, and ascetic. Born into Dublin poverty, Talbot began drinking at the age of 12. With a priest's help he started rehabilitation at 16. He modelled his adult life on early Christian monks, giving away most of his wages, and committed himself to the Irish Transport and General Workers Union. The Catholic Church declared him 'Venerable' in 1973 and a campaign now seeks his canonization as a saint.

TALBOT, RICHARD, EARL OF TYRCONNELL (1630–91)

Richard Talbot, Earl of Tyrconnell from 1685, fought in the Royalist army at Drogheda. He remained loyal to James, Duke of York (afterwards James II), and represented Irish Catholic interests at court. He was implicated in the Popish Plot of 1678. Under James II he began reinstatement of Catholicism in Ireland and organized Irish Catholic troops. He led James's forces at the Boyne, and at Aughrim, dying soon afterwards in a fit of rage.

))))➤ *Battle of Aughrim, Battle of the Boyne, James II of England*

TANDY, JAMES NAPPER (c. 1740–1803)

Revolutionary. The son of a city tradesman, James Napper Tandy came to prominence as campaigner for the patriots – Protestant Irishmen committed to a separate status for Ireland under the British Crown. In the 1790s, a friend of Wolfe Tone and Russell, he became a co-founder of

FAR LEFT: *John Millington Synge.*
LEFT: *James Napper Tandy.*
BELOW: *Statue of St Patrick in Tara, County Neath.*

the United Irishmen. Fleeing the country in 1793, his contacts with the Defenders having been adjudged treasonous, he returned five years later to bring a body of French troops ashore on Rutland Island, Donegal. His part in the insurrection of 1798, although enthusiastic, appears to have been all but completely unavailing: hardly had he landed

than, hearing of Humbert's surrender, he withdrew. Captured subsequently in Hamburg, his arrest sparked a diplomatic incident; though brought back to Ireland, he was released after representations from Napoleon.
))) **Society United Irishmen**

TARA

Prehistoric complex and semi-mythical seat of the Irish High Kings in County Meath. A burial site since the second millennium BC, Tara is rich in relics from the prehistoric period, with earthworks and foundations too from the Celtic period. The archaeological evidence stops some way short of confirming Tara's traditional status as seat of the Kings of Ireland: historians are deeply sceptical, indeed, that Ireland was ever a single kingdom. If the kings of Tara do appear to have enjoyed unusual esteem in Ireland as a whole, this was very likely because the place was hallowed in still older religious traditions. The warrior-queen of Connacht, Méadhba (Maeve), was widely worshipped as a goddess, and Tara, as her legendary birthplace, was her greatest shrine.
))) **Meath**

TARA, BATTLE OF (AD 980)

One of the battles marking the decline of Viking power in Ireland. The emergent king of Meath, Mael Seachnaill, decisively defeated the Dublin Vikings at Tara, thereby securing a powerful psychological victory, given Tara's potent symbolic importance as the ancient religious and cultural capital of Ireland. The Vikings were now effectively part of Mael Seachnaill II's power base, and he installed his Viking stepson, Sitric, as king of Dublin.

))))➤ *Mael Seachnaill II*

TARA BROOCH

White bronze Celtic ring brooch. Now held in the National Museum of Ireland, the brooch, dating from eighth century, was found at Bettystown, south of Drogheda. The very long brooch is made up of sunken panels of delicate filigree work and presumably would have been worn on the shoulder.

))))➤ *Celts*

TÍR NA NÓG

'Land of eternal youth'; mythical Celtic paradise which appears in early myths and traditional folklore. In one story Oisín, son of Fionn mac Cumhail goes off on horseback to Tír na nÓg with a beautiful girl, Niamh Cinn Óir (Golden-haired Niamh). Eventually feeling homesick he asks for permission to return to Ireland. He is oblivious to the fact that several centuries have gone by, and that Ireland has been Christianized. When he accidentally touches the ground he ages rapidly, and only has time for a theological discussion with St Patrick before he dies.

))))➤ *Fion mac Cumhail, Oisín*

TITANIC (1912)

When built by Belfast ship-builders Harland and Wolff in 1912, the *Titanic* was the world's largest ocean-going liner. Attempting to set a record for the trans-Atlantic crossing, it struck an iceberg off Newfoundland and sank within a few hours with the loss of 1,490 lives. As well

as being a major human tragedy the disaster also had a serious psychological effect on both sides of the Atlantic, showing that despite great scientific progress, man was still at the mercy of the elements.

TITHE WAR (1830–38)

Not a war, but a campaign in rural Ireland against the hated system of the tithes, wherein farmers had to pay a tax equivalent to one-tenth of their agricultural produce to the Established Church, no matter what their own religion was. There had been earlier protests against tithes by the Whiteboys, Oakboys and Hearts of Steel, but it was after the success of the campaign for Catholic emancipation, which had been granted in 1829, that the matter came to a head, following a confrontation in Graiguenamanagh in County Kilkenny in 1830. Unlike the earlier protests, this new campaign had the support of larger farmers and the Catholic clergy. Attempts by the authorities to enforce the collection of tithes with the assistance of the police and yeomanry, brought bloody confrontation to a campaign that was otherwise one of passive resistance. There were fatalities on both sides and in some areas the amounts collected were more than halved. The Tithe Rentcharge Act of 1838, which meant that tax was collected as part of the tenant's rent, made the issue less contentios, though it was still collected until the disestablishment of the Church of Ireland in 1869.

)))) *Catholic Relief Act*

TONE, THEOBALD WOLFE (1763–98)

Revolutionary. Born into a Protestant family and trained as a lawyer at Trinity College Dublin, Tone shared with other 'patriots' of the day a belief that Irishmen of every creed stood to gain from their country's increased autonomy from England. The author of the influential *Argument on Behalf of the Catholics of Ireland* (1791), he became secretary of the Catholic Committee and organized the Back Lane Parliament the following year. A co-founder of the United Irish Society, he was becoming more ambitious in his goals as time went on, increasingly unconvinced by the assumptions of his position as 'patriot'. Convinced that

the autonomy the patriots sought could not be attained whilst Ireland remained under the rule of the British Crown, the radical was fast becoming a revolutionary. So the British would conclude, at any rate, when his views were unwittingly betrayed by the Reverend William Jackson in 1795: Tone was forced into exile, first in America and then in France. There he persuaded the government to assist in an Irish insurrection. Captured before he could play any real part in the United Irishmen's insurrection of 1798, he committed suicide while waiting under sentence of death.

)))) *Back Lane Parliament, United Irishmen*

TORY

Although nowadays used to describe a member of the British Conservative party, the Irish word *tórai* originally referred to an outlaw or rapparee. Historically the word referred to dispossessed Irish Catholics who waged a guerilla war on the government in the seventeenth century, and by association it was applied by the Whigs in the 1680s to English supporters of King James II. Later it was applied to the party which opposed the Whigs, who became the Conservatives.

TORY ISLAND

Tory (Irish *Toraigh*, meaning 'Towery') is 4 km (2.5 miles) long and lies 14 km (9 m) from the coast of County Donegal, its craggy profile resembling castle towers along its skyline. Its rocky shore and wild climate made it the centre of an ancient myth about a Cyclops. Tory Island was a traditional centre of religion and learning, centred around the monastery founded by St Colm Cille in the sixth century, until it decayed into disuse under Elizabeth I. It remains inhabited with fishing communities living alongside the antiquities and nature reserves.

)))) *St Colm Cille*

LEFT: The Titanic.
RIGHT: Theobald Wolfe Tone.

TRADE UNIONISM

By 1925 trade union membership in Ireland stood at 123,000. From the 1930s to 1980 there was a continual growth. Membership reached a peak in 1980 with over half a million members. Many reasons have been put forward to suggest why membership has since dropped but it is really a combination of factors such as the growth in part-time and contract work, new sectors of the economy and a hardening of employers' attitudes towards trade unionism. The Irish Trade Union Congress was formed in 1894 and the first general union, The Irish Transport and General Workers Union was established in 1909. Trade unions legal status is regulated by a number of statues, including the Trade Union Acts of 1871, 1913, 1941 and 1975 as well as the Industrial Relations Act 1990. The largest union is the Services, Industrial, Professional and Technical Union with 190,500 members.

TRANSPORTATION (1789–1868)

Transportation of convicted criminals to prisons in Australia from 1789–1868, used as a means of disposing of Irish dissidents from 1795 when United Irishmen and Defenders were sent there in the convict ship *Marquis Cornwallis*. The 1798 Rebellion increased the numbers between 1800 and 1805. Some were tried while others, such as Joseph Holt, leader of the County Wicklow 1798 rising, agreed to be transported. Many more were summarily transported with neither trial nor agreement. In Australia the Irish were regarded as Jacobite traitors and singled out for special oppression, fearing in particular the educated dissidents, known as the 'Specials'.

)))⏵ *Defenders, United Irishmen*

TREATY PORTS

Free-State ports in which Britain retained special rights of use. Under the terms of the Anglo-Irish Treaty of 1921, the British were to be allowed certain port facilities at Berehaven, Cobh and Haulbowline (all in County Cork) and at Lough Swilly and Rathmullen

ABOVE RIGHT: David Trimble.
FAR RIGHT: Trinity College.

(Donegal). A galling reminder of the incompleteness of Ireland's independence, the agreement was resented by successive Free State governments, without satisfying the British Admiralty, who thought the arrangement impracticable and the facilities expensive to maintain. In 1938, the ports were returned as part of the agreement that brought to an end the 'economic war' – though many in Britain, notably Churchill, were furious at this climb-down.

)))⏵ *Anglo-Irish Treaty*

TRIMBLE, DAVID (b. 1944)

Ulster Unionist politician. Trimble's early career was uncompromisingly Unionist. As a Vanguard Unionist he opposed the Sunningdale Agreement (1973), demanded independence for Ulster and helped topple the power-sharing executive in 1974. After 1978, Trimble joined the Ulster Unionists but disappeared from public while working as a university law lecturer. In 1990 he was elected MP for Upper Bann, remaining hostile to compromise with Republicans. Trimble became party leader after Sir James Molyneux's retirement, re-emerging as a moderate. In 1998 Trimble compromised with the Republicans, making the 1998 Good Friday peace agreement viable, winning the Nobel Peace Prize. His position as the Northern Ireland executive's first minister has remained under constant threat from more extreme elements opposing compromise. He resigned temporarily on 1 July 2001 over the IRA's failure to disarm.

)))⏵ *Good Friday Agreement, Sunningdale Agreement, Ulster Unionists*

TRINITY COLLEGE DUBLIN (1592)

Opened in 1592, Trinity College was from the outset a Protestant institution, attended largely by the English of the Pale, and later by the Anglo-Irish. Modelled on a Cambridge college, it was very English-orientated and

one of its primary functions was to educate ministers for the Protestant Church in Ireland. In the eighteenth century it was a key element in the Protestant Ascendancy, although a number of radical thinkers among staff and students, and the relaxation of Penal Laws in 1795, which allowed Catholics to be admitted, ensured greater intellectual freedom. Trinity College was particularly noted for its legal and medical schools as well as for its divinty faculty. The first half of the twentieth century saw the

university stagnate as its Anglo-Irish ethos was out of favour with the mood of the Free State, but in recent years, the university, where the majority of the students are now Catholic, is regarded as a bastion of liberalist and pluralist ideas.

Situated in the heart of Dublin, with its fine architecture and the treasure of its library, including the *Book of Kells* it attracts large numbers of visitors.

))))➤ *Elizabeth I of England, Book of Kells*

TROUBLES, THE (1960s–94)

Period of sectarian warfare which broke out in Northern Ireland in the late 1960s, continuing until the ceasefire of 1994, and intermittently thereafter. The origins of the Troubles lay deep in the sectarian divisions of Ulster, stretching back to the Plantation of 1610 and beyond. However, the appointment of the moderate Unionist Terence O'Neill as prime minister of Northern Ireland in 1963 brought a new tone to Ulster politics when he organized the first meeting with the Taoiseach. This apparently innocuous move was a trigger for Protestant sensibilities,

British brutality, summary searches and arbitrary policing soon turned the wider Catholic population against British security forces and government. The IRA found it easy to convert this into patriotic support for their cause, leaving the Civil Rights Movement and its socialist-radical leadership foundering. From here it was simple for the IRA to start organizing the rioting by directing attacks on security forces and providing arms like grenades to supplement the home-made petrol bombs. The riots had been redrawn as a war by the IRA and terrorism by the Northern Ireland and British governments. There was a rapid decline into murderous violence. From 1970 RUC officers were killed wherever and whenever it was possible to do so, regardless of whether they were unarmed, off-duty, with their families or relaxing. To these were soon added young British soldiers

In August 1971 Brian Faulkner, prime minister of Northern Ireland, announced that dealing with the IRA was impossible within the normal course of the law. Internment without trial was introduced, justifying this as an acceptable sacrifice of democracy during a war. Arbitrary arrests and releases followed as authorities fumbled after the right targets, but hundreds ended up behind bars, provoking a vast increase in recruitment to the IRA. By calling it a war, Faulkner had given the IRA precisely the credibility it desired by linking it to the greater historical tradition of the Easter Rising and the War of Independence, while wasting the chance to exploit the reluctance of many Catholics to condone IRA actions.

seeing it as blatant betrayal. Confrontation developed when the republican Civil Rights Movement in Ulster led a march in Derry in October 1968. It was brutally broken up by the RUC. A further march was attacked by a Protestant mob in January 1969, with the RUC arresting numerous marchers.

During the rest of 1969 Catholic nationalist riots broke out in Dungannon (April) and Derry and Belfast (August). The RUC responded with machine guns and tear gas, resulting in a few deaths and hundreds injured. By mid-August British troops were on the streets, causing fury in the Republic of Ireland. To begin with the IRA was entirely marginalized from events, thanks to the failure of the 1956–62 campaign which had discredited them.

LEFT: IRA marching, Northern Ireland, 1977.
ABOVE: Political graffiti in Londonderry.

Bloody Sunday on 30 January 1972 proved a decisive event, when British soldiers shot dead 13 unarmed civilians in Derry, illustrating the hopeless consequences of pursuing a military solution to the problem. In March the British government resumed direct government of Northern Ireland with the intention of resolving Northern Ireland permanently.

The fundamental opposition to anything remotely resembling a united Ireland came from the Unionists. Unionist positions became more deeply entrenched in a determination not to sacrifice any aspect of their power and autonomy. Men such as David Trimble and Ian Paisley

adhered rigidly to Loyaland tradition, while symbols of the Protestant past such as William III, the Boyne, and Apprentice Boys' marches, became totemic focal points of Protestant sensibilities and cultural identity. Loyalist paramilitary groups, for example the UDA, provided a terrorist answer to the IRA. Violence proceeded apace. By autumn 1972, 100 British soldiers had been killed, while the IRA also used car bombs to kill innocent civilians indiscriminately. Unionists retaliated with bombs in Eire.

It was Unionist entrenchment which cause the foundering of the Northern Ireland Assembly formed out of the Sunningdale Agreement. Province-wide strikes brought Northern Ireland to a standstill. Direct rule returned in May 1974, leaving a stalemate in which the IRA would accept nothing less than a united Ireland, and a Unionist majority in Ireland which rejected any such suggestion.

BELOW LEFT: A soldier of the British paratroop regiment arrests a rioter in Londonderry.
BELOW: Terence O'Neill, Northern Ireland prime minister, during the Troubles.

The Troubles continued unabated until 1994, by which time more than 3,000 people had been killed. Victims included 21 customers in Birmingham pubs (21 November 1974), 18 soldiers at Warrenpoint, County Down, and on a boat, Lord Mountbatten of Burma and some of his family (27 August 1979), Conservative Party members at Brighton (12 October 1984), 11 civilians killed and 63 injured at Enniskillen (8 November 1987), and two small boys at Warrington (20 March 1993), while Loyalist paramilitaries also killed innocent Catholics north and south of the border. 'Martyrs' on both sides, such as the IRA hunger strikers of 1981, motivated and polarized sectarian feelings further.

Further initiatives, such as the Northern Ireland Assembly of 1982–86, foundered once more on a total refusal by all parties to compromise. The Anglo-Irish Agreement of 1985 involved the Irish Republic in Northern Irish affairs but led to Unionists strikes, rioting and assaults on the RUC. But the Agreement's production of an Intergovernmental Conference left the Unionists with no choice but to negotiate, while the British government began to acknowledge that military activity would never defeat the IRA, while equally parts of the IRA and their associates in Sinn Féin began to see that violence would not achieve Irish unity. The Downing Street Declaration (1993) and the IRA ceasefire of 1994 opened a new chapter in Irish history, though paramilitary splinter groups remain active and full disarmament remains to be achieved.

⫸ *Anglo-Irish Agreement, Bloody Sunday, Home Rule, Irish Republican Army, Terence O'Neill, Sinn Féin, Plantation of Ulster, Westminster Direct Rule*

TUATHA (c. 700 BC)

Irish word meaning 'people' or 'community', and referring in Celtic and early Gaelic Ireland to the groups of people who made up the population before there were parishes or towns. Ideally these groupings were self-sufficient and held their land communally, but they also formed alliances with neighbouring communities, so that by the time Christianity arrived, Ireland could be seen to have five provinces: Ulster, Munster, Leinster, Connacht and Meath. The latter is now represented by the counties of Meath and Westmeath, but the Irish word for province, *cúige*, meaning 'a fifth', retains this tradition even thought there have been only four provinces for centuries.

TUATHA DÉ DANANN

Race in Celtic mythology that inhabited Ireland. Said to have arrived in Ireland on a cloud of mist after they were banished from heaven, this race had magical skills. They are reputed to have been overcome by the Milesians and are now associated with the legendary Irish fairies.

))))➤ *Milesians*

TYRONE

County in Ireland. The ancestral home of the O'Neills, once the central region of the kingdom of Ulster, now lies in the west of 'Northern Ireland', a border

ABOVE: Beaghmore stone circles, near Cookstown, County Tyrone.
CENTRE: The Joshua Tree album by U2.
FAR RIGHT: Whitepark Bay on the north Antrim coast, Ulster.

county. Following the Flight of the Earls in 1607, lands here which had hitherto been spared were opened up to English settlers for plantation. The rising of 1641, while immediately delaying colonization, arguably only made it more ruthless in the long term. Yet Tyrone would never be settled as systematically as Ulster's more easterly counties: although marginalized, its native population would remain an important presence.

))))➤ *Flight of the Earls, O'Neill Dynasty*

U2

Ireland's most successful rock group formed in Dublin in 1977. The four-piece group fronted by Bono (Paul Hewson) has had major international success for more than 20 years by virtue of the fact that the band has changed and revitalized its music every few years. They have also demonstrated a political and social awareness which has led both fans and critics to take the band seriously.

ULIDIA

Medieval kingdom. With a capital at Eamhain Macha (Armagh) and territories extending as far south as the Boyne and westwards into Leitrim, the chiefs of the Ulaid were for several centuries the dominant dynastic force in eastern Ulster. The later name of the province was indeed derived from them, the 'Ulstermen' who fight the Connachta in the Táin. In fact, 'Ulidia' does not seem at any point to have included large parts of the western counties of the province as understood since the seventeenth century. Even further to the east, the Ulaid were on the retreat by the fifth century: they were conquered completely by the Anglo-Norman earl John de Courcy in 1177.

))))➤ *John de Courcy*

ULSTER

Province of Ireland. Although the name 'Ulster' is often used as though it were interchangeable with that of 'Northern Ireland', the modern (British) province does not correspond exactly with the historical Irish one. Counties Monaghan and Cavan both belong to Ulster but not to 'Northern Ireland' – as, for that matter, does Ireland's most northerly county, Donegal. That 'Ulster is British' would certainly have surprised those ancient heroes who slugged it out with the Connachtmen in the ancient legends, while even in late-medieval times the province was considered to lie well 'beyond the Pale'. The Scottish connection was established early on, however, the kingdom of Dál Riada only giving territorial definition to what had long been established as a cultural and commercial continuity linking northeastern Ireland with the west of Scotland and its isles.

The first serious moves to make Ulster a part of Britain would indeed come across that same strait, although it would for the most part be from the central Lowlands that the great wave of Scottish settlers came in the seventeenth century. Although the Anglo-Norman adventurer John de Courcy had conquered Ulster as early as the late twelfth century, little effort was made to consolidate the colonizations he had set in motion. Even through the Tudor period, when English rule was being extended in earnest further south, English policy was aimed by and large at manipulating the native chieftains diplomatically rather than subjecting or replacing them. Not until the seventeenth century were serious attempts made to take possession of Ulster by force and to hold it by establishing a Protestant population which would owe its allegiance to the English Crown. The 'Scots-Irish', as they have been called, have in fact felt a complex if not confusing mesh of loyalties, their identity perhaps even less comprehensible to the English than it has been to Irish nationalists. Ulster's history has for the last two centuries been dominated by the struggle of its Protestant people to resist Home Rule in its various forms, to stand out against their absorption into the greater Irish nation. Despite the peace process, there is no reason to suppose that struggle is over.

)))➤ *John de Courcy, Home Rule, Northern Ireland*

ULSTER DEFENCE ASSOCIATION (1971)

Loyalist paramilitary group. Set up in 1971 with the ostensible aim of protecting Northern Ireland's Protestant communities, the UDA gathered momentum through 1972 at a time when, with the introduction of Direct Rule, the Stormont state was being shut down. Nationalists saw its real function as being intimidatory, though, and what seems to have been at the very most a semi-detached splinter group, the Ulster Freedom Fighters (UFF), was responsible for a series of sectarian murders from the mid-seventies until its 1994 ceasefire. Despite its murderous record, however, the UDA has arguably on occasion shown itself more open-minded in its approach to the search for peace than that of official unionism.

ULSTER, PLANTATION OF (1610)

Part of the process of evicting Irish Catholic farming communities from their land in Ulster, and imposing the settlement of English Protestant or Scottish Presbyterian landowners. The Ulster Plantation took place in 1610, and was followed by the Cromwellian Plantation (1652) and the Williamite Plantation (1693). By the end, more than 80 per cent of Ireland's productive land had been transferred to ethnically and religiously distinct communities. Moreover, the vast bulk of Ireland's agrarian wealth had been transferred to non-native landlords, causing catastrophic poverty amongst the indigenous population. The Plantations are sometimes regarded as the seventeenth century's version of 'ethnic cleansing'.

ABOVE: The kingdom of Ireland in 1616.
ABOVE RIGHT: Silver coin showing Oliver Cromwell, 1658.
RIGHT: Elizabeth I of England.

The consequences of the Ulster Plantation were to help provoke the 1641 Rebellion, establish the Ulster Presbyterian communities, and contribute to the polarization of religious tribalism in Ireland and ultimately the sectarianism which has characterized Irish politics to this day. It has been described as England's only successful Irish colony.

Although the arrival of the Anglo-Normans in the twelfth century established Irish land ownership from England, the deliberate policy of planting settlers did not arise until the reign of Henry VIII. With the Wars of the Roses over, and English politics comparatively settled, Henry turned his attention to re-establishing the Crown's hold on Ireland. Irish peers were becoming increasingly autonomous and 'Irish' in habits and sympathies. Henry was also concerned at Ireland's strategic potential as a base for a Catholic foreign power.

In 1519, Henry investigated the possibility of a plantation of loyal English colonists who would act as a reliable garrison. However, in a prophetic conclusion he recognized that such a plantation would require colossal expenditure on soldiers. Instead, he opted for a coercive policy of anglicization. Patchy attempts at plantations between the 1550s and 1580s failed to reap any benefits to the crown, largely because a lack of support, a failure of investment and rebellions of the dispossessed.

Elizabeth I's ruthless policy in Ireland forced Irish chiefs to surrender their lands and submit themselves to the Crown, in return for which these lands were re-granted, usually with an English title. The outbreak of three rebellions (Shane O'Neill, Desmond, and O'Neill (Tyrone)-O'Donnell) were ruthlessly suppressed in scorched-earth actions of land confiscations, evictions and religious oppression. At the Battle of Kinsale (1601) the English Crown essentially destroyed the old Gaelic order in Ireland.

The 1610 Plantation was properly organized to take land, and therefore power, from dissident Irish chiefs. It would also establish a minority class which owed its land and wealth to the Crown, guaranteeing its loyalty in the event of further rebellions. The Plantation was also supposed to expel peasants to the harmless remoteness of Connacht.

The Ulster Plantation seized about 1.2 million hectares (3 million acres) in the six counties of Ulster, mainly from the Irish nobles and their supporters who had been defeated at Kinsale (principally O'Neill, O'Donnell, O'Reilly, O'Hanlon, and O'Doherty).

The Plantation of Derry, both city and county, for example, was awarded to the City of London as if it was a new colony. The City companies divided up the land amongst English and Scottish settlers, with around five per cent going to military veterans. Irish tenants and labour were excluded from almost all of this but here, as elsewhere, the need for labour meant they were kept back – on miserable wages and extortionate rents. Their continued presence frustrated plans at the 'purity' of the colony and their proximity to what they had lost, together with their merciless exploitation, generated the resentment which would lie behind the demands for land reform in the 1700s and 1800s. Meanwhile, the Protestant settlers only felt more insecure.

Scottish Presbyterians were allowed to settle in counties Down and Antrim, though they received no financial assistance to do so, evicting native Catholic communities as they went. Highly successful immigrants, arriving as individuals and in groups, they had started to arrive under a private deal in 1606. They benefited from the Plantation, expanding into gaps in the main process. The new arrivals formed the basis of the Ulster Presbyterian communities, whose descendants have continued to dominate Ulster politics, its economy and society, to this day.

The descendants of the Anglo-Norman lords were largely immune from the confiscation of the Ulster Plantation but faced a different threat. Corrupt lawyers and opportunists ransacked legal records to identify defects in titles to land and estates. Any such fault meant automatic forfeiture to the Crown, and a percentage to the 'discoverer'.

Charles I's lord deputy, the Earl of Strafford, extended the land seizures to include Connacht, planning further English land settlement. Charles promised reforms ('The Graces') to the Anglo-Irish nobles, known as the 'Old English', including a law which would confirm the title to land in anyone who had held it for more than 60 years in return for a substantial contribution to his war with Spain. Thanks to Charles's pro-Catholic sympathies, this automatically began to identify the royalists with Catholicism and the old landowner interests in Ireland. Charles reneged on 'The Graces' under pressure from parliament.

When the Rebellion of 1641 broke out the demands were for reform of land grievances, but the immediate target was the Protestant community in Ulster. Thousands were murdered with rumours of atrocities rife, 'proving' to a paranoid community in England that the rebellion was a royalist Catholic plot. This led to the ruthless suppression of the Irish by Cromwell and the further plantations.

)))➤ *Cromwellian Plantation, Elizabeth I of England, The Graces, Battle of Kinsale, Williamite Plantation*

ULSTER-SCOTS

From the Scottish Presbyterian settlers of the seventeenth century. In the 1600s the English began the Plantation of Ireland and many Scottish people settled in the province of Ulster. The descendants of this Scottish population are referred to as Ulster-Scots or the Scottish-Irish. The term is also used to describe the variety of Scots spoken in the north and north east of Ireland, particularly in the counties of Donegal, Derry, Antrim and Down.

ULSTER UNIONISTS

Political party. From the establishment of Stormont in 1921 to the introduction of Direct Rule from Westminster in 1972, the Ulster Unionists ruled what appeared to be a one-party state. This was to some extent a misleading impression, however, the heirs to generations of opposition to Home Rule in the North actually constituting a wider, more restless coalition than might have been imagined. In addition to an important landed interest, the dominant voice was that of the professional middle class. The views of the urban working class went largely unrepresented. Under the stresses and strains of the civil rights era, this coalition began to break up, a small number of liberals going off to found the moderate Alliance Party and a much larger number of militants following the banner of Ian Paisley's DUP, though the Ulster Unionist Party would remain the 'official' voice of Ulster Unionists.

))))▶ *Anglo-Irish Agreement, James Craig, Westminster Direct Rule*

ULSTER VOLUNTEER FORCE (1913)

Name used by Protestant paramilitary organizations of the Home Rule era and more recent Troubles. Assembled in 1913 by supporters of Sir Edward Carson, the UVF set out to give the threats of the Solemn League and Covenant some real military backing. With some 90,000 members led by retired British Army officers, the organization was quite capable of giving the London government cause for concern. A small, secret UVF was re-formed – allegedly with the support of Stormont – at moments of tension in the 1920s and 30s. In 1965 the name resurfaced on the Shankill Road, Belfast, adopted by a group opposed to the liberalizations of Terence O'Neill, the most violent of the main Protestant paramilitary groups until its 1994 ceasefire.

))))▶ *Sir Edward Carson, Home Rule, The Troubles*

ULSTER WORKERS' COUNCIL AND STRIKE (1974)

Alliance of – and strike by – loyalist workers, 1974. An *ad hoc* alliance of Protestants united by their determination to destroy the Sunningdale Agreement with its proposals for cross-border co-operation with the Republic and for a 'power-sharing' executive to include constitutional nationalist representatives. Backed up with muscle supplied

LEFT: Shankhill Road Mural, Belfast.
ABOVE RIGHT: The Ulster Volunteer Force in 1913.
RIGHT: William Ewart Gladstone.

by the UDA, key workers brought the business of Northern Ireland to a virtual standstill, Harold Wilson's Labour government shrank from sending in the army to end the protest. Not only did the new executive collapse in chaos, but Loyalists were sent an unmistakable signal that they would be able to impose their veto by force on any future settlement.

))))▶ *Sunningdale Agreement*

UNIONISM

Political tradition founded on belief that Ireland – and certainly Ulster – should be part of Britain. Unionism's rise in the nineteenth century mirrored that of nationalism, as exemplified in the Catholic Emancipation and Home Rule movements, to which developments it was a clear reaction. The autonomous Ireland envisaged by the nationalists was evidently to be an overwhelmingly Catholic country, in which Protestants feared losing not only their political privileges but their religious rights. The belief that Home Rule would be 'Rome rule' spoke to the deepest anxieties of an ideologically-charged Protestantism which since the seventeenth century had defined itself by its consuming hatred of 'popery'. Unionism with a capital 'U', as a clearly-delineated political organization, had its origins

in the Home Rule Crisis of 1885–86. That Home Rule had found at the heart of the British Establishment in the person of prime minister William Ewart Gladstone caused widespread anger, and deep suspicion, among Irish Protestants. Repeated attempts to introduce Home Rule only stoked up ever more acrimonious resistance, especially in Ulster, whose Protestants ultimately succeeded in exempting themselves from the 1921 Free State. An establishment all their own in the new political entity of Northern Ireland, Unionists continued to feel threatened by Irish irredentism – especially, paradoxically, after the introduction of Direct Rule from Westminster in 1972. The apparent 'paranoia' of Protestant Ulster, and its hostility towards a Britain with which it is supposed to identify, has been a constant source of puzzlement to liberal opinion in Britain. Yet the explanation is simple enough: the perceived faint-heartedness of Britain over time, its readiness to appease nationalism and its assumed eagerness to shake off a Union which has grown irksome.

))))▶ *Catholic Emancipation, Home Rule, Westminster Direct Rule*

UNIONIST PARTY (1910)

 Political party. The ancestor of the Ulster Unionists, the Irish Unionist Party was formed by Sir Edward Carson in 1910 to bring unionist-minded MPs at Westminster together to present a single, organized front against Home Rule. In principle committed to 'saving' the whole of Ireland from this fate, the party inevitably drew much of its support from the Protestants of Ulster. Some diehards (including Carson) saw the Treaty of 1921 as a defeat, though most would accept a settlement which seemed to guarantee their continued power where it really counted. Under the leadership of James Craig, the Ulster Unionist Party would go on to rule the new statelet of Northern Ireland without interruption from 1921 until the introduction of Direct Rule a half-century later.

))))▶ *Anglo-Irish Treaty, Sir Edward Carson, Ulster Unionists*

UNITED IRELAND PARTY

 Alternative name for Fine Gael. The English title of the Fine Gael Party, and indeed the name by which it was generally known in its early years, the wording reflected the party's coalition origins while maintaining a degree of nationalist credibility. Some would argue indeed, that thanks to their conscious renunciation of irredentist rhetoric, Fine Gael leaders like Garret Fitzgerald and John Bruton have done more to advance the cause of a 'United Ireland' than the fieriest Fianna Fáil patriot.

))))▶ *John Bruton, Fine Gael, Garret Fitzgerald*

UNITED IRISHMEN (1791)

Revolutionary organization responsible for Ireland-wide insurrection in 1798. The Society of United Irishmen held its first meeting in Belfast on 18 October 1791, a gathering summoned by Samuel Neilson (1761–1803), Theobald Wolfe Tone and Thomas Russell. All three of these founders were Protestants (Neilson was the son of a Presbyterian minister), as was James Napper Tandy, who helped host the society's second meeting in Dublin a few weeks later. A spirit of rebellion was in the air at this time. In 1775 the American colonists had successfully rebelled against British rule, while in France the monarchy had been overthrown by the Revolution of 1789. An avowedly radical group, the Society of United Irishmen was clearly inspired by these acts of resistance to monarchical authority: even so, it was only gradually that its members came round to the republican views with which they have since been associated. Not all members thought alike, in any case, Wolfe Tone arguing passionately for universal suffrage, to include Roman Catholics, as a means of presenting a genuinely 'United' Irish front against English domination, whilst other Protestants remained uncomfortable about the idea of mobilizing a mass electorate of papists. Sheer sectarian prejudice played its part, no doubt, but many genuinely radical Protestants would have wondered how progressive politics were to be advanced by an electorate brought up from birth to slavish obedience to its parish priests. For much of the decade, though, such issues were up for debate at the Society's meetings and in the columns of its widely read newspaper, the *Northern Star*.

A series of repressive measures taken by the authorities probably helped catalyze – rather than cause – the society's drift into revolutionary conspiracy. Aimed specifically at the United Irishmen, the Convention Act of 1793 outlawed quasi-parliamentary gatherings (like the previous year's 'Back Lane Parliament'), while the Gunpowder Act prevented the legal import of guns, such legislation, it was subsequently argued, compelled the Society to choose between extinction and plotting in secret. Whether or not this can really be true, there is an unmistakeable sense of things unravelling in the next few years and of the Society's actions being borne along increasingly by events taking place outside it. Would the United Irishmen, in other circumstances, have ended up seeking the assistance of the French? When the radical clergyman-turned-agent William Jackson came to Dublin in 1795 to test the reaction among radicals there to the idea of an invasion on the part of his French revolutionary masters, he little realized that his travelling companion, John Cockayne, was an English spy. Tone seems to have said enough to the unguarded Jackson to convince the authorities that he and his fellow United Irishmen were a real threat.

FAR LEFT: Sir Edward Carson.
LEFT: Garret Fitzgerald.
BELOW: Thomas Russell, the leader of the rebels, is apprehended.

the Society was suppressed and Tone himself was forced into exile. 'I … sought for aid wherever it was to be found,' Tone would eventually tell the military court which tried him, and he may indeed to some extent have been driven by desperation.

Certainly, from the middle of the decade, the Society seems to have had nowhere politically to go but towards armed insurrection: by the middle of 1796 it had completed its reinvention as an oath-bound revolutionary organization. That the planned French invasion of that year was foiled by a 'Protestant wind' which smashed the 33-strong fleet of Admiral Hoche was a considerable setback, but by no means a fatal blow, for the United Irishmen. The near-miss of 1796 seems to have caught the the imagination of the Irish people: by the beginning of 1798, the Society of United Irishmen could boast some 280,000 members. History, however, seldom proceeds as calmly or as logically as it should: profoundly underwhelmed by the levels of popular support evident on the ground in 1796, the French dragged their heels in 1798, sending only a small expeditionary force, and that belatedly

How far the insurrection of 1798 really reflected the values of the Society of United Irishmen is also a matter of dispute: the repressive campaign of General Lake in Ulster and afterwards around Dublin had, to some extent, shattered its organizational structures in those key areas. The famous Wexford uprising in particular was to some extent a 'peasants' revolt' and involved sectarian massacres of which the Society could never have approved, while in Dublin and Kildare, too, the rebellion went ahead in spite of the opposition of important sections of a divided leadership. Volunteers in Ulster also rose spontaneously in support of their fellows in south-east Leinster, exasperated by the caution of their nominal chiefs, while 2,000 rallied to the revolutionary banner of General Humbert in the west (and were afterwards massacred). There remains some doubt, therefore, as to how far the Society actually had possession of the insurrection that bears its name; only in romantic retrospect do the men of '98 really seem 'united'.

⫸ *Back Lane Parliament, Thomas Russell, James Napper Tandy, Theobald Wolfe Tone*

VIKINGS (AD 795)

After the Celts had established themselves in the last centuries BC, Ireland enjoyed freedom from invasion until the late eighth century AD. Compared to the events across the rest of Europe following the collapse of the Roman Empire and the spread of Germanic and Scandinavian peoples,

it was the Irish who had colonized Scotland, Wales and Cornwall. There seems to be doubt as to whether the island monastery of Lambay, off the coast of County Dublin, known as Rechru, or Rechrainn, was the target of the first Viking invasion or whether it was Rathlin Island, off the Antrim coast. In either case this was simply a raid. Inevitably the scale and frequency of Viking attacks on monasteries, in particular, increased. Not only were the Vikings interested in plunder, they were also concerned with collecting food, livestock and people to be sold as slaves. As far as the Vikings were concerned, the softest targets in Ireland were the monasteries.

Their sturdy longboats, with a shallow draught, could be relied upon to undertake long sea voyages. It was possible to beach these ships in shallow waters. This enabled the Vikings to abandon their craft and plunge into the countryside in search of pillage and plunder. During the ninth and tenth centuries a raid occurred approximately every 18 months, but between AD 795 and 820, 26 Viking raiding parties made landings. As a result, many of the smaller monasteries found it difficult to continue as their economic resources disappeared on a Viking longboat. The monastery at Bangor was raided in AD 823 and 824. Bangor was extremely exposed to attack from the sea. After AD 837 Viking activity in Ireland reached a new and intensive level.

Permanent Viking bases had been set up in the country although, unlike across the water in England where the Vikings controlled half the country, these Irish settlements were restricted to a few coastal areas. It was the Celts' in-ability to join together as a coherent group that prevented – at least initially – Viking colonization. The Vikings could range the countryside at will, eliminating or subjugating smaller groups of Irish, but they seemed unable to deal a knockout blow as there was no central structure. The Viking settlers were predominantly Norwegian, with a much longer sea journey to Ireland than the Danes, who had conquered most of England. The Danish attacks involved much larger raiding parties than the Norwegians were able to muster.

Considering Ireland in the wider geographical context, historians have noted that raids and activity in Ireland slackened during Viking periods of concentration in England. Equally, the Norwegians were colonizing Iceland, Greenland and the Faroes. A Viking base was established at Dublin in AD 841 but it seems that the Vikings were keen to encourage alliances between themselves and the Irish. In fact, the first recorded alliance occurred in AD 842. There was no real Irish attempt to drive the invaders back into the sea. At the Battle of Clontarf (1014), although often portrayed as a victory by the Irish over the

Vikings, the Irish king Brian Bóroimhe was, in fact, engaged in a dynastic struggle against his rival Mael Seachnaill. The Battle of Clontarf was, the culmination of a revolt led by the king of Leinster against Brian and it now appears that Vikings fought on both sides. Scandinavians who had settled in Limerick and Waterford fought for Brian and the Vikings of Dublin fought for Mael Seachnaill.

In the AD 850s the Danes and the Norwegians fought for control over their settlement in Dublin. By AD 902 the settlement was abandoned and Viking interest in Ireland ceased for around 40 years. By AD 920, with the Vikings finding themselves checked in other parts of Europe, another series of raids was launched on Ireland, followed by settlement. The Dublin colony was re-established in AD 917 and new settlements sprung up at Wexford, Waterford and Limerick. This period became known as the Second Viking Age. By the mid-tenth century the Vikings were being absorbed and assimilated into Irish society. The Norse language had not survived but the Viking descendants proved valuable traders. A mint was established in Dublin

in AD 997 and the city had become a natural harbour that linked Ireland with Scandinavia, Western France and the Mediterranean. The Vikings used Dublin as a major manufacturing and trading centre that included bronze smiths and leather workers. By the end of the eleventh century Scandinavian art had made a major impact on Irish culture. The Norse trading towns were not politically powerful and were subjected to control by the Irish kings. Nevertheless, they continued to expand trade and communication and brought in valuable sources of wealth to the Irish. Recent archaeological finds have radically changed the view of the Viking contribution to Irish society and culture. Large-scale excavations in Dublin have attested to the Vikings peaceful and productive co-existence with the indigenous population. Notable is the Wood Quay site.

FAR LEFT: St Kevin's Church, Glendalough.
LEFT: Brian Bóroimhe is slain by the Viking Brodir.
ABOVE: Reconstruction of a Viking longhouse.

VINEGAR HILL, BATTLE OF (1798)

Climactic rout of the rebellion of 1798. The Catholic rebels in Wexford defeated the North Cork militia, in fact Catholics themselves, at Oulart. They then seized Enniscorthy and set up camp nearby on Vinegar Hill. However, it was a disparate gathering of would-be rebels, refugees and looters, with little fighting equipment or shelter. Some captured Protestants were imprisoned in a windmill and summarily executed, with others being burned to death in a barn at Scullabogue. The lack of leadership and planning allowed government forces under General Lake to organize, defeating them first at Arklow. The assault on Vinegar Hill on 21 June by Lake was total and ruthless and finished the rebellion, although killings of scattered bands of rebels continued.

))⫸ *General George Lake, Rebellion of 1798*

VOLUNTEERS (18TH CENTURY)

Militia raised in late-eighteenth-century Ireland. The Volunteers were at first an impeccably official part-time militia raised to begin with in 1778–79, a time when the regular army was stretched by its involvement in the American War of Independence. In so far as it had any sort of nationalist significance, it was in offering Ireland's Protestant 'patriots' an opportunity of demonstrating their public-spiritedness and loyalty: Henry Grattan, for example, was a dedicated Volunteer. Only over time did the Volunteers come to be associated with more potentially disruptive brands of patriotism: by the 1790s, though, they were regarded as the armed wing of the United Irishmen.

))⫸ *Henry Grattan*

WADDING, LUKE (1588–1657)

Franciscan priest who studied on the Continent before becoming president of the Irish College in Salamanca in 1617. He later moved to Rome where, as well as setting up other colleges, he played a diplomatic role between the Irish bishops and the Holy See, especially during the troubled 1641 period. He was also a noted

BELOW: The Battle of Vinegar Hill.

LEFT: *Ernest Walton.*
BELOW: *Perkin Warbeck admits his imposture as the supposed heir to the English throne.*

in Cork in 1491, stating that he was going to England to seize his crown from the usurper, Henry VII. He found support not only in Ireland but in Scotland and France, but an invasion attempt of 1495 met with failure. He continued to be an irritant, though, joining in a local rebellion in Munster, where he was again defeated. He was finally arrested by Henry's forces and hanged in Cornwall in 1499.

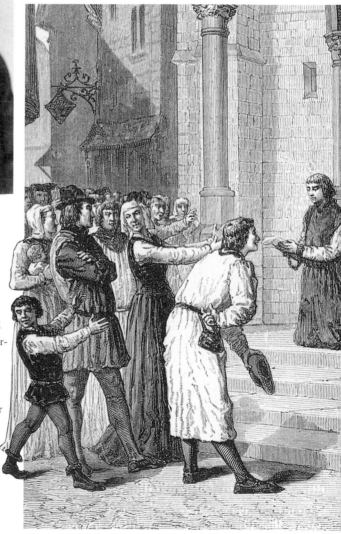

scholar, producing, among other works, an eight-volume history of the Franciscan order and the first critical edition of the entire works of Duns Scottus in 12 volumes.
)))➤ *Johannes Duns Scottus*

WALTON, ERNEST (1903–95)

Nuclear physicist, from Dungarvan, County Waterford. Walton worked under Ernest Rutherford at Cambridge, experimenting in high-energy particle acceleration, successfully transferring to low-energy methods in 1929, when power sources of the time proved inadequate. He worked with John Cockcroft, producing a nuclear reaction from non-radioactive lithium with their accelerator in 1932. In 1951 they shared the Nobel Prize for Physics.

WARBECK, PERKIN (c. 1474–99)

Pretender to the English throne, claiming to be 'Richard IV'. Supposedly one of the 'little princes' until then assumed to have been murdered in the Tower of London by Richard III, Flemish-born Warbeck arrived

WATERLOO, BATTLE OF (1815)

Climax of the Napoleonic Wars, fought 16–18 June 1815. Napoleon, emperor of France from 1804, abdicated in 1814, but made a further bid for power in 1815. Napoleon defeated Britain's Prussian allies at Quatre Bras and Ligny but faced Wellington's army with Blücher's Prussians at Waterloo. Napoleon's failure to follow through an onslaught on the Prussians allowed them to rejoin Wellington. Weight of numbers carried the day and destroyed Napoleon's ambitions.

WELLINGTON, ARTHUR WELLESLEY, 1ST DUKE OF (1769–1852)

Soldier and statesman, British Conservative prime minister (1828–30, 1834). The hero of Waterloo, and indeed pre-eminent British general of the Revolutionary and Napoleonic period, though born in Ireland, made his political career largely in England. A senior figure in the Tory Party through the 1820s, he had vigorously opposed the idea of Catholic Emancipation, but came to view things differently after O'Connell's propaganda triumph in the

Clare by-election of 1828. His unimpeachable British patriotism made him an influential lobbyist for a change of policy.

))))) **Vesey Fitzgerald**

WESTMINSTER DIRECT RULE (1972)

Suspension of the Stormont government and introduction of rule from London, March 1972. The Civil Rights Movement's complaints of a sectarian state having been only too brutally vindicated by the response of the forces of law and order, the Bloody Sunday shootings merely put the finishing touches to what had been a protracted publicity nightmare for the British government. Conservative prime minister Edward Heath, concluding that he could not be seen to support so discredited a system accordingly introduced a system of Direct Rule from Westminster, supplanting Stormont. William Whitelaw thus became the first holder of the office of secretary of state for Northern Ireland.

))))) *Bloody Sunday, Stormont*

WHITEBOYS (1761–c. 1765)

Agrarian protest movement with origins in County Tipperary. Resisting the enclosure of common land and the payment of tithes to the Church, the Whiteboys, dressed in their coarse white linen overshirts, tore down fences, hedges and walls. They also filled ditches and dug up pastureland. The Whiteboy Act (1765) made their activities illegal.

WILDE, OSCAR (1854–1900)

Irish novelist and playwright. Oscar Wilde was born in Dublin but moved to London to pursue a literary career. Well known as an extrovert and a wit, he achieved great success with a number of comedies writtem for the stage including, *Lady Windermere's Fan* (1892), *An Ideal Husband* and *The Importance of Being Ernest*, both produced in 1895. The same year, at the height of his success and fame, he took an unsuccessful libel action against the Marquis of Queensbury. Evidence presented during this case led to a counter-charge and he was convicted of sodomy. After two years in jail, disgraced and bankrupt, he left for the continent and died in poverty in Paris in 1900.

LEFT: The Battle of Waterloo.
BELOW: Oscar Wilde.

WILLIAMITE PLANTATION (1693)

Confiscation of over half a million acres of land following the Battle of the Boyne. The deposed English monarch James II was defeated at the Battle of the Boyne by William of Orange in June 1690. After this William established the Williamite Plantation, which effectively reduced Catholic ownership of the land from 22 to 14 per cent. Now 81 per cent of the productive land was in Protestant hands. The idea behind the Williamite Plantation was the integration of the Irish and British cultures, but in the event the two cultures did not assimilate; instead their differences were even more obvious. The Irish Gaelic speaking landless Catholics amounted to 75 per cent of the population but the affluent, ethnically British Protestants owned the majority of the land. The dividing line between the conquerers and the vanquished had been drawn.

WINDSOR, TREATY OF (1175)

 Agreement signed by Henry II of England and Ruairi Ó Conchubhair of Connacht in 1175. The Norman kings' difficulties in keeping control of their barons were all

too real: Henry II faced particular problems given the scale of Richard de Clare's Irish conquests. In 1171 Henry made an expedition to Ireland to assert his authority, claiming the island's more easterly areas as his own. He granted Ó Conchubhair overlordship of the remainder by treaty three years later. An attempt to rein in an ambitious Norman aristocracy, the treaty failed through the weakness of both kings: Anglo-Norman adventurers ignored both the strictures of their own king and the threats of the Irish.

)))➤ *Richard de Clare, Henry II of England, Ruairi Ó Conchubhair*

WOOD QUAY

Dublin Viking archeological site. The Augustinian friar and medieval historian Francis Xavier Martin (1922–2000) spearheaded the popular campaign between 1977–81 of demonstrations and court action to have the site excavated and preserved, in the face of opposition from civic authorities determined to build new offices. However, although much of the site was excavated, civic offices were built over it. Excavations produced extensive evidence of tenth-century houses, while exceptional conditions of preservation provided evidence of clothing and food. DNA analysis showed that the Dublin Vikings exclusively used indigenous livestock. Wood Quay became notorious in Irish cultural politics and occasioned a sea-change in attitudes to the country's heritage.

WORLD WAR I (1914–18)

European-wide conflict also involving British dominions and America. The unexpectedly protracted nature of the war meant reliance on the Regular and Territorial Armies had to be abandoned. Lord Kitchener built up a volunteer force across the British Isles. Eventually 150,000 Irishmen would volunteer. By the end of 1915 around 1.2 million men had been recruited, amongst which was the 36th (Ulster) Division, popularly known as 'Carson's Army'. Even this was not enough, though, and conscription was introduced in March 1916.

With the conflict at stalemate, the Germans began an offensive in the Battle of Verdun in February 1916. A futile attempt to turn the war in Britain's favour by relieving the beleaguered French at Verdun came with the Battle of the Somme, beginning on 1 July.

The Ulster Division consisted of 10 battalions, each of 730 men, assembled in Thiepval Wood. The Ulstermen advanced quickly towards German positions but machine guns cut many officers down. The soldiers took the Schwaben Redoubt but found themselves trapped by German defence further ahead beyond the reach of supplies and reinforcements. By the end of the day the remainder retreated to their original trenches. Two thousand had been killed, and 2,700 wounded, contributing to the British Army's largest loss in a single day. Four of the nine Victoria crosses won that day went to the Ulster Division. On 12 July 1916, Belfast held five minutes silence for the

victims. The sacrifice contributed to the creation of Ulster in the Home Rule settlement after the war. Today, the Ulster Tower at Thiepval marks the spot.

WORLD WAR II (1939–45)

Worldwide conflict involving Britain and all her dominions, including Northern Ireland. Eire, under the government of Éamon de Valera, followed a policy of neutrality throughout.

The 1937 Constitution created by de Valera made Eire effectively a republic. It reversed many of the points demanded by Britain in the peace of 1921, including rights to the use of naval and military bases in the south. This was to have serious consequences for Britain's maritime security during the war, especially during the early part of the Battle of the Atlantic, when large quantities of merchant ships were sunk off the south and west coasts of Ireland by German submarines.

Neutrality was popular in Eire, although Northern Ireland played a full and active role in Britain's war effort, including provision of troops, bases and manufacturing. This only served to emphasizse the divergent traditions and meant British plans to reinvade Eire could be shelved. In 1945 de Valera offered his condolences to the German people on the death of Hitler.

)))➡ *Éamon de Valera*

FAR LEFT: *Henry II.*
ABOVE LEFT: *Recruitment poster from World War I.*
ABOVE: *Adolf Hitler at a rally.*

WYNDHAM LAND ACT (1903)

British prime minister William Gladstone wanted to pacify Ireland and quell unrest. He introduced his first Land Act in 1870, forwarding money for land purchases in 1885 with the Ashbourne Land Act. This was followed on 14 August 1903 by the Wyndham Land Act, which assisted tenants in buying out their landlords for £12 per acre. A year later £12 million of purchases had been underwritten and by 1908 seven million acres had been sold to tenants. The 1909 Land Act was the final stage in the transformation of land ownership and tenant ownership had become a reality, but did not make an immediate improvement.

)))➤ *Land Acts*

YEATS, WILLIAM BUTLER (1865–1939)

Poet and dramatist. Yeats was awarded the Nobel Prize for Literature in 1923. Although born in Dublin he was raised partly in England and only began to appreciate his Irishness in his early twenties. He met many of the leading cultural activists of the day and began to collaborate with Lady Gregory on the development of an Irish national theatre, later the Abbey Theatre, of which they were both directors and for which he wrote a number of one-act plays. He shared Lady Gregory's interest in folklore and in the myths preserved in the Irish language tradition, although he never mastered the language to the extent of Gregory or J. M. Synge. In the cultural melting pot that was Ireland at the start of the twentieth century he was an influential figure, and his poems in response to the Easter Rising are particularly significant. He served as a senator in the government of the Irish Free State. He died near Monaco and his remains were later buried at Drumcliff in County Sligo, where his grandfather had been rector. Even after his death his remained the dominant poetic voice in Ireland until Seamus Heaney's work began to appear in the 1960s.

)))➤ *Abbey Theatre, Easter Rising, Lady Augusta Gregory, Seamus Heaney, J. M. Synge*

YELLOW BOOK OF LECAN (14TH CENTURY)

This book, which is to be found in the library of Trinity College Dublin, consists of a number of different manuscripts which were bound together in the seventeenth century, although many are of a much earlier date. Part of it was written in what is now Lackan, County Sligo, in 1392 and it includes a version of the *Cattle Raid of Cooley*, religious and genealogical material.

)))➤ **Cattle Raid of Cooley,** *Trinity College Dublin*

YEOMANRY

 Irish volunteer militia. In 1796, to counter the increasingly well-organized groups like the United Irishmen a part-time, volunteer, civilian militia called the Irish Yeomanry was founded. In practice a Protestant force, it built on a tradition of Protestant self-defence, and numbered around 80,000 at its height. The oath increasingly became a symbolic statement of loyalty to the Protestant Ascendancy, while the Yeomanry's brutal repression of the 1798 risings through house and chapel burnings helped polarize Irish sectarianism.

YOUNG IRELAND (1840S)

The most influential group in the growth of Irish political and cultural nationalism. Disenchanted with Daniel O'Connell's faltering political strategies, a group of younger radicals, including Thomas Davis, John Blake Dillon and Charles Gavan Duffy, came together to form a new group. Their weekly newspaper *The Nation* was very influential, but their movement, which culminated in a botched uprising in 1848 was defeated primarily by the disastrous impact of the Great Famine.

)))➡ ***Thomas Davies, John Blake Dillon, Charles Gavan Duffy*, The Nation**

LEFT: William Butler Yeats.
ABOVE: Trinity College Dublin, which holds the Yellow Book of Lecan.

CHRONOLOGIES

CULTURE

AD 650	Book of Durrow begun
AD 807	Book of Armagh compiled
AD 880	Death of philosopher Johannes Scottus Eriugena
1123	Maollosa O'Conchubhair receives the Cross of Cong
1172	Kilkenny Castle built
1177	Work begins on construction of Dundrum Castle
1180	Construction begins of Carrickfergus Castle
1189	Gerald of Wales writes expugnato Hibernica about Henry IIs invasion of Ireland
1431	Annals of Ulster begun
1446	Construction begins on Blarney Castle
1592	University of Dublin is founded
1612	Death of poet Eochaidh Ó hEodhasa
1632	Compilation of the Annals of the Four Masters begins
1643	Death of chronicler Micheal Ó Cléirigh
1644	Death of the writer Seathrún Céitinn
1653	Kerry chieftain and poet Piaras Feiritéar is hanged
1671	Death of historian and scribe Dualtach Mac Firbhisigh
1701	Custom House is built in Dublin
1722	Work begins on Castletown House
1726	Jonathan Swift publishes Gulliver's Travels
1729	Death of poet Aodhagán Ó Rathaille
1738	Death of harpist Turlough O'Carolan
1745	Construction begins on Leinster House
1780	Poet Brian Merriman publishes Cúirt an Mheán Oíche ('The Midnight Court')
1786	Work begins on the Four Courts in Dublin, designed by James Gandon
1789	Charlotte Brooke publishes Reliques of Irish Poetry
1792	Belfast Harp Festival
1795	St Patrick's College, Maynooth built
1796	Edward Bunting publishes General Collection of Irish Music
1798	Death of Betsy Gray

1808	Nelson's Pillar erected
1823	Death of the architect James Gandon
1824	Celtic Iron Age civilization discovered at Halstatt in Austria
1826	Death of the opera singer Michael Kelly
1836	Death of the scholar Simon Macken
1837	Death of pianist and composer John Field
1842	Davis, Gavan Duffy and Blake Dillion found The Nation
1845	Death of radical thinker and writer Thomas Davis
1852	Death of nationalist poet Thomas Moore; John O'Donovan appointed professor of Celtic at Queen's University, Belfast
1854	John Mitchel publishes Jail Journal
1862	Death of scholar Eugene O'Curry
1865	Death of astronomer and mathematician William Hamilton
1866	Death of antiquarian George Petrie
1868	Ardagh Chalice discovered

1873	Nationalist writer Charles J. Kickham publishes Knocknagow
1884	Michael Cusack founds the Gaelic Athletic Association
1891	Gundestupp Cauldron discovered in Denmark
1893	Gaelic League formed
1895	Oscar Wilde's The Importance of Being Ernest first performed
1897	Bram Stoker publishes Dracula
1903	Erskine Childers publishes The Riddle of the Sands
1904	Abbey Theatre opens
1907	Death of the writer John O'Leary; John Millington Synge publishes The Aran Islands
1908	National University of Ireland is founded
1910	Padraig O Conaire writes Deora'ocht
1923	W. B. Yeats wins the Nobel Prize for Literature
1925	George Bernard Shaw wins the Nobel Prize for Literature
1926	Writer Sean O'Casey produces The Plough and the Stars
1932	The Four Courts in Dublin are restored; death of the writer and translator Lady Augusta Gregory
1936	Peig Sayers publishes her autobiography Peig
1938	Poet Patrick Kavanagh publishes his autobiographical The Green Fool
1941	Death of the novelist James Joyce
1945	Death of opera singer John McCormack
1948	Máirtín Ó Cadhain publishes Cre na Cille
1951	Ernest Walton wins the Nobel Prize for Physics
1953	First performance of Samuel Beckett's Waiting for Godot; death of the actress Maude Gonne MacBride
1954	First performance of Brendan Behan's The Quare Fellow
1964	Death of playwright Brendan Behan
1966	Death of writer Brian Ó Nualláin
1969	Samuel Beckett receives the Nobel Prize for Literature
1971	Death of the composer Séan O Riada
1977	Rock band U2 formed
1979	Seamus Heaney publishes North
1988	Death of poet Máirtín Ó Díreáin
1990	Death of the writer Seosamh Mac Grianna
1995	Seamus Heaney receives the Nobel Prize for Literature

POLITICS

1175	Treaty of Windsor signed
1200	Irish exchequer created
1210	King John sets up a civil government in Ireland
1232	Chancery set up in Ireland
1366	Statutes of Kilkenny
1460	Ireland's legislative independence declared
1494	Sir Edward Poynings becomes lord deputy of Ireland; Poynings' Law introduced
1604	Sir Arthur Chichester becomes lord deputy of Ireland
1663	Captain Thomas Blood and his followers attempt to take Dublin Castle
1690	Flight of the Wild Geese
1760	Catholic Committee formed
1769	Steelboys formed
1782	Grattan's Parliament established
1791	Society of United Irishmen formed
1792	Back Lane Parliament convened
1795	Start of the Armagh Outrages; Peep o'Day Boys founded; Battle of the Diamond; the Fitzwilliam Episode; Orange Order established

1851	Irish Parliamentary Party formed
1856	Jeremiah O'Donovan Rossa founds the Phoenix Society
1858	Fenian Brotherhood is formed
1866	Fenian John Devoy imprisoned
1867	Fenian Rising; Irish Republican Brotherhood formed; Manchester Martyrs are hanged
1868	Thomas McGee is assassinated
1870	Michael Davitt is imprisoned for gun-running; Home Rule Association founded
1879	Death of Home Rule campaigner Isaac Butt; Land League formed
1881	Formation of the Invicibles, splinter group of the Fenians; Charles Stewart Parnell imprisoned
1882	Phoenix Park Murders; Kilmainham Treaty agreed
1886	First Home Rule Bill introduced in parliament
1896	Irish Socialist Republican Party formed
1905	Arthur Griffith founds Sinn Fein
1910	Unionist Party formed
1913	Irish Volunteers created; Eamon Ceannt joins the Irish Republican Brotherhood; Irish Citizen Army established
1914	Cumann na mBan founded; Curragh mutiny
1915	Funeral of Jeremiah O'Donovan Rossa
1916	Irish Republican Army formed; Easter Rising; David Lloyd George becomes prime minister of England
1917	Thomas Ashe dies in the Hunger Strike
1918	Countess Constance Markievicz becomes the British parliament's first female MP
1919	Creation of the Dáil Éireann; Cathal Brugha becomes its first defence minister
1920	Bloody Sunday; Kevin Barry hanged; Thomas MacCurtain assassinated
1921	Anglo-Irish Treaty signed; Boundary Commission set up
1922	Irish Free State comes into being; Arthur Griffith is elected president of the Dáil, but dies the same year
1923	Cumann na nGaedheal founded
1926	Fianna Fáil founded
1927	Death of nationalist statesman John Dillon
1932	Formation of the Blushirts; Economic War between the Irish Free State and the United Kingdom breaks out; opening of Stormont
1933	Fine Gael Party formed

1798	United Irishmen leader Edward Fitzgerald dies after a wound received while resisting arrest; Henry Joy McCracken is executed; death of revolutionary Theobald Wolfe Tone
1800	Act of Union passed creating the United Kingdom of Great Britain and Ireland
1803	Robert Emmett launches his unsuccessful uprising in Dublin; death of revolutionary James Napper Tandy
1812	Lord Castlereagh becomes foreign secretary
1814	Apprentice Boys formed
1820	Death of the Patriot politician Henry Grattan
1824	Catholic Association established
1828	Daniel O'Connell wins County Clare election
1829	Catholic Relief Act passed
1842	Young Ireland movement established
1847	Irish Confederation formed; death of Daniel O'Connell, 'the Liberator'
1849	Dolly's Brae fracas

1935 Death of Unionist politician Edward Carson; William Cosgrave becomes leader of the Fine Gael

1936 Sean MacBride becomes IRA chief of staff

1937 Bunreacht na Éireann Constitution implemented; Éamon de Valera becomes Taoiseach

1938 Douglas Hyde becomes first president of Ireland

1943 Sir Basil Brooke becomes prime minister of Northern Ireland

1944 Richard Mulcahy becomes Fine Gael leader

1945 Nationalist Eoin MacNeill dies; Sean O'Kelly becomes president of Ireland

1946 Founding of the Clann na Poblachta

1948 Republic of Ireland Act passed; John Costello becomes prime minister

1951 Éamon de Valera becomes Taoiseach again

1952 Sean O'Kelly re-elected as president of Ireland

1957 Éamon de Valera becomes Taoiseach again

1959 Sean Lemass becomes Taoiseach

1963 Terence O'Neill becomes prime minister of Ireland

1966 Jack Lynch becomes Taoiseach

1969 James Chichester Clarke becomes prime minister; Provisional IRA formed

1970 Social Democratic and Labour Party formed

1971 Gerry Adams interned; Democratic Unionist Party formed; Brian Faulkner becomes prime minister; Ulster Defence Union formed

1972 Bloody Sunday II; Westminster Direct Rule introduced

1973 Erskine Childers Jnr becomes president of the Irish Republic; Ireland joins the European Union; Sunningdale Agreement signed

1974 Irish National Liberation Army formed; Sean MacBride is awarded the Nobel Peace Prize; Dublin and Monaghan bombings

1975 Death of Éamon de Valera

1977 Jack Lynch begins his second term as Taoiseach

1979 Charles Haughey becomes Taoiseach for the first time

1981 Hunger strikes begin in Northern Ireland prisons; Garrett Fitzgerald becomes Taoiseach

1982 Charles Haughey becomes Taoiseach for the second time

1983 Gerry Adams becomes president of Sinn Féin; New Ireland forum convened

1984 The IRA bombs the Grand Hotel in Brighton

1985 Anglo-Irish Agreement reached

1987 Charles Haughey becomes Taoiseach for the third time

1990 Mary Robinson becomes president of the Irish Republic

1992 Albert Reynolds becomes Taoiseach

1993 Downing Street Declaration

1994 John Bruton becomes prime minister

1997 Bertie Ahern becomes prime minister; Mary MacAleese becomes president of the Irish Republic; IRA declare another ceasefire

1998 Good Friday Agreement reached

RELIGION

AD 432 St Patrick lands in Ireland to begin his Christian mission

AD 441 St Patrick climbs the holy mountain to pray during Lent

AD 540 Death of St Jarlath

AD 493 Death of St Patrick

AD 545 Monastery founded at Clonmacnoise

AD 556 Death of St Ciaran

AD 570 Death of St Molaise

AD 577 Death of St Brendan

AD 597 Death of St Colm Cille

AD 615 Death of St Columbanus

AD 618 Death of St Kevin of Glendalough

1038 First cathedral church built in Dublin

1101 Synod of Cashel

1142 St Malachy brings the Cistercian Order to Ireland

1148 Death of St Malachy

1152 Synod of Kells

1155 Pope Adrian IV grants Henry II of England the right to rule Ireland

1160 Jerpoint Abbey founded in County Kilkenny

1180 Death of St Laurence O'Toole; St Mary's Cathedral built in Limerick

1192 St Patrick's Cathedral built in Dublin

1193 Founding of the Grey Abbey in County Down

1224 Dominican Order set up in Ireland

1230 First records of the Franciscan Order of monks in Ireland

1251 St Canice's Cathedral built in County Kilkenny

1308 Death of Johannes Duns Scotus

1622 Death of the cleric Miler Magrath

1625 Death of Catholic cleric Peter Lombard

1644 Catholics expelled from County Cork

1650 Death of cleric Heber McMahon

1657 Death of Franciscan priest Luke Wadding

1681 St Oliver Plunkett executed after the Popish Plot

1791 Theobald Wolfe Tone publishes Argument on Behalf of Catholics in Ireland

1798 Death of Father John Murphy

1802 Edmund Rice founds the Christian Brothers

1829 Synod of Ulster

1834 John McHale becomes archbishop of Tuam

1845 Maynooth Grant for St Patrick's College

1859 Religious revival begins in Ulster

1869 Church Disestablishment Act passed

1879 Marian vision scene at Knock

1912 Ulster Protestants sign the Solemn League and Covenant

1925 Death of ascetic Matt Talbot

1932 Eucharistic congress held in Dublin

1951 Ian Paisley establishes the Free Presbyterian Church

1979 Cardinal Tomás Ó Fiaich made head of the Roman Catholic Church in Ireland; Pope John Paul II visits Ireland

ROYALTY

AD 218 Cormac mac Airt becomes king of Ireland

AD 254 Cormac mac Airt abdicates

AD 260 Death of Cormac mac Airt

AD 383	Niall of the Nine Hostages becomes first High King of Ireland
AD 842	Mael Sechnaill I becomes king of Ireland
AD 863	Death of Mael Seachaill I
AD 876	Flann Sinna becomes king of Ireland
AD 916	Niall Glundubh becomes king of Ireland
AD 980	Mael Seachnaill II becomes kings of Ireland
1002	Brian Boroimhe becomes High King of Ireland
1014	Death of Brian Boroimhe and Mael Morda
1042	Death of Sitric Silkenbeard, king of the Vikings of Dublin
1126	Diarmaid mac Murchadha becomes king of Munster
1154	Henry II becomes King of England
1166	Death of Muirheartach mac Lochlainn
1171	Richard de Clare becomes king of Leinster
1172	Death of Breifne king Tiernan O'Rourke
1175	Rory O'Connor becomes the last High King of Ireland
1176	Death of Richard de Clare
1316	Edward Bruce crowned king of Ireland
1318	Death of Edward Bruce
1377	Richard II becomes king of England
1415	Death of Art mac Murchadha
1461	Edward IV becomes king of England
1487	Pretender Lambert Simnel is crowned Edward V of England in Dublin
1509	Henry VIII becomes king of England
1558	Elizabeth I becomes queen of England
1685	James II becomes king of England
1688	William III becomes king of England

SOCIETY

700 BC	Eamhain Macha becomes the capital of Ulster
300 BC	The Celts arrive in Ireland
AD 575	Convention of Druim Ceat
AD 795	First Viking raids on Ireland
AD 841	Vikings establish a settlement at Dubh-linn

1152	Diarmaid mac Murchadha elopes with Devorgill
1166	O'Rourke's Revolt
1186	Hugh de Lacy the Elder, 1st Lord of Meath is assassinated
1318	Beginning of the Kildare Supremacy
1348	Black Death reaches Ireland
1366	Statutes of Kilkenny
1468	James fitzThomas Fitzgerald becomes 8th Earl of Desmond
1478	Gerald Fitzgerald becomes 8th Earl of Kildare
1513	Gerald Fitzgerald becomes 9th Earl of Kildare
1520	Conn O'Neill becomes 1st Earl of Tyrone
1522	Red Piers Butler becomes lord lieutenant of Ireland
1534	Pardon of Maynooth
1537	Execution of Silken Thomas, 10th Earl of Kildare
1567	Death of Shane O'Neill, 'the Proud'
1569	First Desmond Revolt
1578	Pirate Grace O'Malley imprisoned

1579	Second Desmond Revolt
1580	Baltinglass Rebellion begins
1590	Death of the Gaelic chieftain Sorley Boy MacDonnell
1593	Hugh O'Neill, the Great Earl becomes chief of the O'Neill clan
1597	'Black' Thomas Butler created lieutenant governor of Munster
1598	Plantation of Ulster
1601	First Poor Laws introduced
1602	Death of Red Hugh O'Donnell
1603	Rory O'Donnell created 1st Earl of Tyrconnell
1607	The Flight of the Earls
1610	Plantation of Ulster
1618	Derry's Walls completed
1620	Richard Boyle created Earl of Cork
1626	Charles I grant the priveleges known as The Graces
1642	Murrough O'Brien becomes governor of Munster

1652	Cromwellian Plantations begin
1693	Williamite Plantation
1702	The first Hedge Schools set up
1761	Whiteboy society formed
1763	The Oakboys, or Hearts of Oak society formed
1780	First Irish convicts transported to Australia
1795	Society of Defenders formed
1799	The Guinness Company is established
1800	Despard plot hatched against George III of England
1803	Death of Commodore John Barry
1815	D'Esterre duel
1818	General Post Office (GPO) is opened in Dublin
1825	Ordnance Survey begun
1830	Beginning of the Tithe Wars
1832	Cholera epidemic breaks out in Ireland
1834	Poor Law Amendment Act
1836	Royal Irish Constabulary founded
1837	Feargus O'Connor founds the Chartist newspaper Northern Star
1838	Ancient Order of Hibernians founded
1839	Night of the Big Wind
1845	Great Famine sweeps through Ireland
1846	Repeal of the Corn Laws
1856	Death of railway engineer James Beatty; death of Temperance campaigner Father Mathew
1861	Derryveagh evictions begin
1870	First Land Act Passed
1880	Land War begins; Charles Boycott leaves Ireland after a run-in with the Land League
1890	Radical politician Charles Stewart Parnell is found to be having an affair with married woman Kitty O'Shea
1894	Irish Trade Union Congress
1903	Wyndham Land Act passed
1907	Ernest Shackleton leads the British Antarctic Expedition
1911	Irish patriot Roger Casement is knighted
1912	Sinking of the Titanic
1913	Dublin lockout; beginning of the Great Transport Strike

1920	Attacks begin on Catholics in the Belfast Pogroms; Black and Tans established; politician Terence MacSwiney dies after a hunger strike
1922	Royal Ulster Constabulary formed
1947	Death of trade unionist James Larkin
1948	Dr Noel Browne instigates a hospital-building programme
1967	Northern Ireland Civil Rights Association founded
1969	Burntollet Bridge ambush
1970	Arms Crisis and Trial
1974	Conviction and incarceration of the Birmingham Six; Ulster Workers' council and strike
1998	Omagh bombing

WAR

AD 919	Battle of Dublin
AD 968	Battle of Sulcoit; Brian Boroimhe recaptures Cashel from the Vikings
AD 980	Battle of Tara
AD 999	Battle of Glen Mama
1014	Battle of Clontarf
1172	Henry II of England lands in Ireland to exert his authority over Richard de Clare
1177	John de Courcy seizes Downpatrick
1204	John de Courcy is captured by Hugh de Lacy
1261	Battle of Callann
1270	Battle of Ath an Kip
1316	Battle of Athenry
1318	Battle of Faughart; Battle of Dysert O'Dea
1535	Battle of Maynooth
1575	Rathlin Island Massacre
1577	Mullaghmast Massacre
1580	Battle of Glenmalure
1588	Spanish Armada
1598	Battle of Yellow Ford
1601	Battle of Kinsale
1603	Treaty of Mellifont
1641	Confederate War breaks out after the Catholic Rebellion

1642	English Civil War breaks out
1646	Battle of Benburb
1649	Oliver Cromwell becomes lord lieutenant of Ireland; Siege of Drogheda
1689	Siege of Derry
1690	Battle of the Boyne
1691	Battle of Aughrim; Treaty of Limerick
1693	Death of Patrick Sarsfield
1789	Year of the French Revolution
1798	Battle of Ballinamuck; General Joseph Humbert sent to command the French troops in Ireland; Battle of Vinegar Hill
1815	Battle of Waterloo
1914	World War I breaks out; Howth and Larne gun-running episodes
1915	Sinking of the Lusitania
1916	War of Independence breaks out; Roger Casement captured at Banna Strand, Easter Rising
1919	Daniel Breen leads the Soloheadbeg ambush
1920	Kilmichael ambushes
1922	Irish Civil War breaks out
1939	World War II breaks out

GLOSSARY

Ard Ri
Gaelic term meaning High King of Ireland.

Absentee
Usually applied to a landlord who owned property in Ireland but lived elsewhere and left his estates to be run by his agents. Such a landlord often had little interest in the welfare of his tenants and wished only to reap maximum financial return from his holding.

Abstentionist Policy
Political policy of refusing to actually take up any seats won in the Dáil Éireann or the parliament at Westminster. The Abstentionist policy is frequently used by members of Sinn Féin and other republican parties.

IRELAND
just before
THE ENGLISH INVASION

Scale of English Miles

Act of Settlement (1662)
Act by which the restored English monarch Charles II returned lands to those to who they had belonged before the English Civil War. The Act naturally caused much resentment amongst Cromwell's beneficiaries.

American Revolution
Also known as the American War of Independence. Eighteenth-century revolution in which members of the 13 British-owned colonies in North America rebelled against British rule. The colonists eventually gained independence.

B-Specials
Part-time auxiliary force connected to the Royal Ulster Constabulary.

Beaker People
Among the earliest settlers in Ireland. Evidence of this Bronze-Age civilization has been found across Ireland, mainly in the form of tombs and pottery, for which the Beaker folk are best-known.

Belgae
Tribe of ancient peoples from the continent. It is possible that the Belgae were some of the first peoples to invade and settle in Ireland, although there is little archeological evidence to support this.

Blackmen
Name given to members of the Royal Black Institution, one of the best-known loyal orders, along with the Orange Order and the Apprentice Boys.

Blarney Stone
Stone situated just under the battlements at Blarney Castle near Cork. The stone is believed to hold mystical powers and it is thought that kissing the stone bestows the gift of eloquence.

Bogside
Area of Derry made up largely of working-class Catholics, many of whom support the Republican

movement. The name originally applied to one street but now includes a large section of the city.

Bronze Age
Period from around 3000 to 2000 BC, when ancient peoples started using metals, in particular bronze, for making tools and weapons.

Camogie
Women's version of the traditional Irish game hurling. Played in teams of 15 people; normally the women wear protective helmets.

Celtic Tiger
Term used to describe the economic boom experienced by Ireland in the 1990s.

Celtic Twilight
Term used to describe the literature and culture at the end of the nineteenth and beginning of the twentieth centuries – from the title of a book by W. B. Yeats (1893).

Cessation
Peace agreed by Charles I during the Confederate War in Ireland. The Cessation confirmed Protestant fears of the king's Catholicism and backing for the rebellion that had sparked the war in the first place.

Chieftains
Leaders of Irish clans or tribes in early Ireland.

Crannóg
Artificial island, constructed as a fortified lake dwelling.

Dáil
The lower house of the Irish parliament.

Decommissioning
The disposal or handing over of weapons used by the various paramilitary organizations in Northern Ireland. This laying down of arms has been the major issue in the Peace Process.

Devolution
The passing of authority from a central government, i.e. in London, to a regional one.

Dissolution of the Monasteries
Widespread closure of religious institutions initiated by Henry VIII of England after his break with Rome in 1536; the beginning of Protestantism across England and Ireland.

Duanaire
Family poem book, the collection of poems written for a particular family over the years.

Fascism
Form of government that places emphasis on the nation or state before the individual, advocating rule by an authoritarian leader (often leading to a dictatorship), opposes democratic and socialist movements, and embraces racism, such as anti-semitism, and military aggression.

Fianna Éireann
In Irish mythology, the band of warriors led by Fion mac Cumhaill, tales of whom are recorded in the Fenian myth cycle.

Fiefdom
In the Middle Ages and medieval times, land granted to a subject by his lord as payment for military services.

Flying Column
Active service unit during the guerilla campaigns of the War of Independence.

French Revolution
Popular uprising in France towards the end of the eighteenth century. The monarchy was overthrown and the country's aristocracy deprived of their lands and titles, and often executed. The century of revolution had a great influence on Irish feeling at this time.

Gallowglass
Group of mercenaries formed in the thirteenth century and employed by the Irish chieftains. The name comes from the word gallóglach, meaning 'foreign warrior'.

Galltacht
Term used to describe the English-speaking area of Ireland, as opposed to the Irish-speaking Gaeltacht.

Garda Síochána
Unarmed police force of the Irish republic (lit. 'Guardian of the peace').

Gerrymandering
The practice of dividing up a voting area in such a way as to give a particular political party an unfair advantage.

Glorious Revolution
Name given to the overthrow of the Catholic James II of England and the arrival of the Protestant William of Orange and his wife Mary II to the English throne. James II used Ireland as a launching pad for his retaliatory campaign.

Hill Forts
Celtic settlements of which many remains have been found across Ireland. These settlements often incorporated farmsteads, graves and sometimes even palaces and reveal much about the lives and culture of early Irish inhabitants.

Huguenots
Strict Protestants, usually Calvinists, of French origin, who were driven out of France by persecution during the French Wars of Religion in the sixteenth century and came to settle in England and Ireland.

Hurling
Traditional Irish game, played since ancient times. The teams are 15 players strong. The ball is known as a sliother and the stick is called a hurley or camán.

Internal Settlement
A political settlement in which control of Northern Ireland would remain exclusively in the hands of the British government, with no contribution by the Irish Republic.

Irish People
Newspaper founded by the Fenian James Stephens in an effort to raise funds for the movement; the establishment of the paper actually blew the organization's cover but was the first step towards Fenianism becoming a mass political movement.

Laudabiliter
Papal bull believed to have been granted to Henry II of England by Pope Adrian IV in which he granted the king ownership of Ireland. Scholars still debate the truth of this.

Long Barrows
Also known as Court tombs. Neolithic burial places, evidence of which have been all over Ireland, but mainly in the northern half of the island.

Loyalism
Term used to describe those who are loyal to the British Crown. In the context of Northern Ireland it is used to denote those who support the use of force by paramilitary groups to maintain the union.

Loyalist Paramilitaries
Paramilitary groups which use violence as a means of ensuring the union with Britain. Loyalist paramilitary groups include the Ulster Defence Association (UDA), the Ulster Freedom Fighters (UFF), the Ulster Volunteer Force (UVF) and the Loyalist Volunteer Force (LVF).

Manx
Language of ancient Ireland; one of the Q-Celtic languages, along with Irish and Scots Gaelic.

Mendicant Friars
Members of religious orders who relied solely on alms and other charity for their living.

Mesolithic
Period from around 5000 BC, during the Stone Age; a small population of Mesolithic peoples is believed to have inhabited Ireland at this time.

Monster Meetings
Term used to describe the huge protest meetings organized by Daniel O'Connell in his campaign for Repeal.

Nationalism
Political belief in and campaign for a sovereign nation state.

Neolithic Era
Period from around 3000 BC until around 2400 BC. Much evidence has been uncovered of Neolithic peoples in Ireland, including long barrows and megalithic tombs.

Nobel Prize
Established by Albert Nobel, a prize awarded to people who made outstanding contributions to different fields, such as Physics, Medicine, Literature or efforts towards world peace.

Oireachtas
The Irish parliament.

Paganism
Religious practices and beliefs in Ireland before the arrival of Christianity. Little is known for certain about pagan traditions in Ireland as it appears to have forbidden the use of written script.

Paramilitaries
Groups of people which form military organizations to fulfil political aims. During the Troubles in Northern Ireland a number of paramilitary groups have arisen, most of which are deemed to be illegal.

Partition
A long-held desire by some that Ireland should be divided into two parts: the north belonging to Britain and the south as an independent state. The Anglo-Irish Treaty of 1921 contentiously made this idea a reality.

Passage Graves
Type of Neolithic tombs found in Ireland. They were made up a long entrance passage with a stone roof, which led to a stone tomb.

Patriotism
Strong devotion to one's own nation or country, often manifesting itself in a desire to defend it, by force if necessary.

Peace Process
General term used to describe efforts by all parties to resolve the conflict between the many factions in Northern Ireland.

Pogrom
From the Russian word meaning 'riot' or 'devastation'. Name given to the organized persecution and attack on Catholics in Belfast in the early 1920s.

Poor Law Extension Act
Act of parliament passed in 1847 during the Great Famine. The Act increased the basic Poor Rate and the extra money raised was used to fund the workhouses during a time of great social and economic hardship.

Privy Council
Governing body in England, from the sixteenth century. Although largely ceremonial, today it still holds powers used to administer legal disputes from Britain's overseas dependencies, including capital punishment cases.

Reformation
Name given to the sixteenth-century movement that swept across Europe aimed at reforming the Catholic Church. Followers of the Reformation became known as Protestants as they were 'protesting' against corruption in the Established Church.

Republicanism
Political ideology in which the head of a state or nation is not a monarch but an elected representative.

Seanad
Senate, or upper house of the Irish parliament.

Sectarianism
In Northern Ireland, actions motivated by religious disagreement or even hatred. These actions are often violent, for example Loyalist or Republican paramilitary murders are frequently referred to as sectarian. 'Sectarian violence' is used to differentiate between this type of action and that with other motives (non-sectarian).

Suffrage
Term used to identify which citizens are eligible to vote in elections. The UK has universal adult suffrage (over 18 years old) with a few exceptions. Universal suffrage is a key tenet of modern democracy.

Synod
Ecclesiastical council formed to discuss affairs of the Church in Ireland.

Tanáiste
Official title of deputy prime minister in the Irish parliament.

Taoiseach
Prime minister of the Irish Republic. The term was first used in 1937 after the Bunreacht na Éireann Constitution.

Shankill Road
The main road through the Protestant area of west Belfast, in an area with a strong Loyalist contingent.

Smallholding
A piece of land, usually for cultivation, which is smaller than a farm. The number of people owning smallholdings dropped dramatically during the Great Famine in Ireland.

Stuart Dynasty
Scottish and English royal dynasty from the beginning of the seventeenth century and spanning the period of the English Civil War and the Glorious Revolution in which William III replaced James II on the English throne.

Teachta Dála
Elected representatives of the Dáil Éireann, the lower house of the Republic of Ireland's parliament. Known as TDs, they are responsible for electing the Irish government.

Temperance Movement
Popular movement begun in the nineteenth century by Father Mathews, in an effort to solve what he saw as the widespread problem of alcohol abuse in Ireland.

Tenant Farmers
The majority of Catholic farmers up until the nineteenth century, as few as five per cent of Catholics actually owned the land on which they worked; this belonged to Protestant landowners.

Terrorism
Term used to describe the actions of a paramilitary group. It is mainly used by Unionists and the British government to refer to the often extreme measures taken by the Republicans.

Tithe
Literally 'one tenth' – a tax that was payable by all, no matter what their religion to the Established Church (Church of Ireland) based on one-tenth of their annual agricultural production.

Townland
Smallest individually named division of land within a parish, it can be anything from a few acres to many hundreds.

Treaty of Rome
Treaty signed in 1958 establishing the European Economic Community, which later became the European Union. Ireland joined the Union in 1973, the same year as Great Britain.

Tudor Dynasty
English royal dynasty established in 1485 by Henry VII after the Wars of the Roses and ending with the death of Elizabeth I in 1603. Elizabeth I in particular tried to extend English influence and colonization in Ireland to areas beyond the area then known as The English Pale, or simply The Pale.

Uachtarán
Official title of the President of Ireland.

Unionist
Those who seek to maintain the union with Britain. Unionists are largely from the Protestant community in Northern Ireland.

Workers' Party
Republican political party, originating from the Sinn Féin and with a strong socialist and anti-sectarian thrust.

AUTHOR BIOGRAPHIES

GUY DE LA BEDOYERE
Royalty and War

Guy de la Bédoyère is an archeologist and historian with numerous books to his credit on the Roman world, seventeenth-century literature and World War II aviation amongst others. He has also written numerous travel articles on a variety of historical sites for *The Independent* and has made a number of appearances on television and radio history programmes.

Michael Kerrigan
Geography, Politics and Religion

A contributor to the Time–Life *History of the World* series, Michael Kerrigan has written extensively on aspects of life and culture from the earliest times to the present day. His books cover everything from world literature to the history of torture; he writes regularly for *The Scotsman* and *The Times Literary Supplement*. He lives in Edinburgh.

Séamas Mac Annaidh
General Editor and Culture

Séamas Mac Annaidh is one of the world's leading authorities on Irish History. He has written numerous historical works, novels, short stories and contributed to many books, magazines and television programmes. He is Arts Editor with the Belfast newspaper *Lá*. Previously he was a presenter/producer with BBC Northern Ireland and Writer-in-Residence at Queen's University, Belfast.

Jon Sutherland
Culture and Society

Jon Sutherland is an experienced writer and lecturer in business studies. He has written and contributed to over 100 books and encyclopedias on a wide range of subjects. His specialist area is military history.

Ciarán Ó Pronntaigh
Culture, Politics, Religion and Society

Ciarán Ó Pronntaigh is the editor of the Irish language newspaper *Lá*. Previously he was the editor of the magazine *An tUltach* and worked with the CCEA (Council for Curriculum and Educational Assessment) in Belfast. Ciaran often contributes to BLAS on BBC Online.

BIBLIOGRAPHY

Arnold, Bruce, *A Concise History of Irish Art*, Thames & Hudson, 1977

Blacker, William and Wallace, Robert.H, *Formation of the Orange Order, 1795-98*, Grand Orange Lodge of Ireland Education Committee, 1994

Boylan, Clare, *Home Rule*, Abacus, 1997

Bradley, Ian, *Celtic Christianity*, Edinburgh University Press, 1999

Brennan, Helen, *The Story of Irish Dance*, Mount Eagle Publications, 1999

Bryan, Dominic, *Orange Parades: The Politics of Ritual, Tradition and Control (Anthropology, Culture and Society Series)* Pluto Press, 2000

Burgess, John, *Dublin and Irish History*, J Burgess Publications, 2000

Bury, John B., *The Life of St Patrick and his place in History*, Dover Publications, 1998

Byrne, F.J., *Irish Kings and High Kings*, London, 1973

Campbell, Flann, *The Dissenting Voice: Protestant Democracy in Ulster from Plantation to Partition*, Blackstaff, Belfast, 1991

Charles-Edwards, T.M., *Early Christian Ireland*, Cambridge University Press, 2000

Connolly, James, *Sinn Fein and Socialism*, C.W.C Publications, 1997

Connolly, S.J., *The Oxford Companion to Irish History*, Oxford University Press, 1999

Coogan, Tim Pat, *De Valera*, Arrow, 1995

Coogan, Tim Pat, *Michael Collins*, Arrow, 1991

Coogan, Tim Pat, *The 1916 Easter Rising*, Ebury Press, 2001

Cooney, John, *John Charles MacQuaid: Ruler of Catholic Ireland*, O'Brien, Dublin, 1999

Costello, Peter, *Dublin Castle*, Wolfhand Press Ltd, 1998

Davis, Courtney and Gill, Elaine, *Saint Patrick*, Blandford, 1998

Dickson, R.J., *Ulster Emigration to Colonial America, 1718-1775*, UHF, Belfast, 1998

Doerries, Richard, R., *Prelude to the Easter Rising*, Irish Academic Press, 2000

Donnelly, James S. Jr, *The Great Irish Potato Famine*, Sutton Publishing, 2001

Douglas, Roy, Harte, Liam and O'Hara, Jim, *Ireland since 1690: A Concise History*, Blackstaff, 1999

Farr, Carol, A., *The Book of Kells; Its Function and Audience*, British Library Publishing, 1997

Foster, R.F., *Modern Ireland, 1600-1972*, Allen Lane, 1988

Foy, Michael and Barton, Brian, *The Easter Rising*, Sutton Publishing, 2000

Garland, Roy, *Gusty Spence*, Blackstaff, Belfast, 2001

Geraghty, Siobhan, *Viking Dublin*, Royal Irish Academy, 1996

Hamilton, Arthur, *The Sinn Fein rebellion as they saw it*, Irish Academic Press, 1999

Graham, Brian (ed.), *In Search of Ireland: A Cultural Geography*, Routledge, 1997

Hart, Peter, *The IRA and its enemies*, Oxford University Press, 1999

Harvie, Christopher and Jones, Peter, *The Road to Home Rule*, Polygon, 2000

Henderson, Frank and Hopkinson, Michael (Editor), *Frank Henderson's Easter Rising: Recollections of a Dublin Volunteer*, Cork University Press, 1998

Hodge, Tim, *Parnell and the Irish question*, Longman, 1998

Kee, Robert, *Ireland, A History*, Abacus, 1995

Kelly, Vivien and Cooke, Stephen, *Home Rule*, Northern Ireland Centre for Learning Resources, 1991

Kerrigan, Gene and Brennan, Mary, *This Great Little Nation: The A-Z of Irish Scandals and Controversies*, Gill & Macmillan, Dublin, 1999

Kostick, Conor and Collins, Lorcan, *The Easter Rising*, The O'Brien Press, 2000

Law, Gary, *The Cultural Traditions Dictionary*, Blackstaff, Belfast, 1998

Liam, Cathal, *Consumed in Freedom's Flame: A Novel of Ireland's Struggle for Freedom 1916-1921*, St.Padraic Press, 2000

Loughlin, James, *Gladstone, Home Rule and the Ulster question, 1882-93*, Gill and Macmillan, 1986

Lyons, F.S.L., *Culture and Anarchy in Ireland, 1890-1939*, Oxford University Press, Oxford, 1982

Malton, *Georgian Dublin*, Colin Smythe Ltd, 1964

McMahon, Sean, *Charles Stewart Parnell*, Mercier Press, 2000

MacKillop, James, *Dictionary of Celtic Mythology*, Oxford University Press, Oxford, 1998

MacMahon, Sean (ed.), *A Book of Irish Quotations*, O'Brien, Dublin, 1984

Meehan, Bernard, *The Book of Kells*, Thames & Hudson, 1995

O'Croinin, Daibhi, *Early Medieval Ireland*, Longman, 1995

O'Day, Alan, *Irish Home Rule: 1867-1921*, Manchester University Press, 1998

O'Duibhir, Ciran, *Sinn Fein: the first election 1908*, Dromlin Publications, 1991

O'Hegarty, P.S. and Garvin, Tom (Introduction) *The victory of Sinn Fein*, University College Dublin Press, 1998

Parry, Melanie (ed), *Chambers Biographical Dictionary, Sixth Edition*, Chambers Harrap, Edinburgh, 1997

Reynolds, James A., *Catholic Emancipation Crisis in Ireland, 1823-29*, Greenwood Press

Thornley, David, *Isaac Butt and Home Rule*, Greenwood Press, London, 1976

Strout, Joseph, *The Parnell Influence*, Writer's Club Press, 2000

Sturgis, Mark, *The Last days of Dublin Castle*, Irish Academic Press, 1999

Walsh, Dermot, *Bloody Sunday*, Gill & Macmillan, 2000

Walsh, Dermot, *Bloody Sunday and the rule of Law in Northern Ireland*, Palgrave, 2000

Ward, Alan J., *The Easter Rising: Revolution and Irish Nationalism*, Harlan Davidson, 1980

Warwick-Haller, Sally and Adrian, *Letters from Dublin, Easter 1916*, Irish Academic press, 1995

Weir, A., *Early Ireland: A Field Guide*, Belfast, 1980

Wilson, Thomas, *Ulster under Home Rule*, Greenwood Press, 1986

Ziff, Trisha, *Hidden Truths, Bloody Sunday 1972*, Smart Art, 1997

PICTURE CREDITS

The Art Archive: 20 The Art Archive/Dagli Orti, 21 The Art Archive/Cava dei Tirreni Abbey Salerno/Dagli Orti, 25 The Art Archive/Tate Gallery London, 26 The Art Archive/British Library, 27(t) The Art Archive/Dagli Orti, 35 The Art Archive/ Musee des Beaux Arts Lyon/ Dagli Orti, 38 The Art Archive/British Museum, 38-39 The Art Archive/Dagli Orti, 39 The Art Archive/Jarrold Publishing, 48(r) The Art Archive/Jarrold Publishing, 50 The Art Archive/Eileen Tweedy, 52 The Art Archive/Pitti Palace Florence/Dagli Orti, 64(t)The Art Archive/Album/ Joseph Martin, 68(b) The Art Archive/ St Benedictine Sacro Speco Subiaco Italy/ Dagli Orti, 72(bl) The Art Archive/Pinacoteca di Siena/Dagli Orti, (tr) The Art Archive, 73 The Art Archive/Burnley Art Gallery, 75(br) The Art Archive, 93(b) The Art Archive/Dagli Orti, 95 The Art Archive / Palazzo Barberini Rome/Dagli Orti (A), 96 The Art Archive/Jarrold Publishing, 97(t)The Art Archive (b) The Art Archive, 107 The Art Archive/Trinity College, Dublin, 115(b)The Art Archive/J.A Brooks/ Jarrold/Jarrold Publishing, 125 The Art Archive/Eileen Tweedy, 141(t) The Art Archive/Eileen Tweedy, 142(t) The Art Archive, 168 The Art Archive/Musee Carnavalet Paris/Jean Loup Charmet, 170 The Art Archive, 173(t) The Art Archive/ Jarrold Publishing, 176(bl),The Art Archive/ National Maritime Museum London/Eileen Tweedy, 188(bl) The Art Archive/Eileen Tweedy, (tr) The Art Archive/ British Museum, 189 The Art Archive/ Pinacoteca di Siena, 191(b) The Art Archive/ Victoria and Albert Museum London/ Eileen Tweedy, 195 The Art Archive, 200 The Art Archive, 201(tl) The Art Archive/ Imperial War Museum/Eileen Tweedy

Bill Doyle: 8(t), 24(t), 34(t), 42(t), 46(b), 56(t), 67(h), 80, 83, 88(t), 126, 129, 137(t), 148(t), 194(bl)

Foundry Arts: 156(bl), 186(r)

Image Select: 130(b)

Impact: 9 Geray Sweeney/Impact, 19 Jeremy Nicholl/Impact, 23 Christophe Bluntzer/Impact, 49 Geray Sweeney/Impact, 51 Christophe Bluntzer/Impact, 57 Jeremy Nicholl/Impact, 63 John Arthur/Impact, 64(b) Bruce Stephens/Impact, 65 Geray Sweeney/Impact, 68 (t) Alan Blair/Impact, 82(t) Geray Sweeney/Impact, (r) David Slimings/Impact, 85(b) Christophe Bluntzer/ Impact, 86 Mark Henley/Impact, 87(t) David Reed/Impact, 113(b) Geray Sweeney/Impact, 121 Bob Hobby/Impact, 132(l) Geray Sweeney/ Impact, 134(b) Michael George/Impact, 135 Bob Hobby/Impact, 151 Lesley Smith/ Impact, 156(tr) Geray Sweeney/Impact, 158(t) Geray Sweeney/Impact, 184(t) Homer Sykes/Impact, 190,Petteri Kokkonen/Impact

Mary Evans: 12, 14(t), 16(all), 18(t) Mary Evans/National Portrait Gallery London, 27(b), 29(t), 31(t), 36(t), 37(b), 42(b), 46(t), 51(c), 53(l), 55(l), 58, 59(t), 60, 61(r), 69, 70, 74, 77(t), 78(l), 79, 87(b), 89, 90-91, 93(l), 99(t), 100, 101(tl) Mary Evans/Jeffrey Morgan, 106(r) Mary Evans/Jeffrey Morgan, 109(bl), 110, 111, 112, 116(b), 123, 128(tl), 131, 133, 136, 140(b), 141(b), 152(b), 153, 155(tr), 159, 160, 161(bl), 163(c), 164, 165(all), 173(b) Mary Evans/Mark Furniss, 174(t), 176(br), 178, 179(t), 181, 193, 194(r) Mary Evans/ Edwin Wallace, 197(all), 199, 202

Photo Images Picture Agency, Dublin: 47, 103, 127(r), 128(r), 132(t), 134(t), 137(b), 145, 146(t), 158(b), 175, 179(b)

Graham Stride: 13(t)

Topham Picturepoint: 8(b), 10, 11(all), 13(b), 14(b), 15, 17, 18(b), 21(b), 22(all), 24(b), 28, 29(b), 30, 31(b), 32(all), 33, 34(b), 37(t), 40, 41, 43, 44(all), 45, 48(tl), 53(r), 54, 55(r), 56(br), 59(b), 61(b), 62(all), 66, 67(r), 71(all), 75(bl), 76, 77(b), 78(t), 81(all), 84, 85(t), 88(b), 90, 91(t), 92, 94(all), 98, 99(b), 101(br), 102, 104, 105(all), 106(l), 108, 109(br), 113(t), 114, 115(t), 116(c), 117, 118, 119(all), 120, 122, 124, 127(bl), 129, 130(t), 138, 138-39, 139, 142(b), 143, 144, 146(b), 147, 149, 150(all), 152(t), 154, 155(bl), 157, 161(tr), 162, 163(tr), 166, 167(all), 169, 171(all), 172, 174(b), 177, 180, 182, 183, 184(l), 185(all), 186(bl), 187, 191(t), 192(all), 196(b), 198, 203

INDEX